Of Chalk and Flint

A Way of Norfolk Magic

—— *of* ——
CHALK & FLINT
A Way of Norfolk Magic

Val Thomas

TROY BOOKS

Published by Troy Books
www.troybooks.co.uk

Troy Books Publishing
BM Box 8003
London WC1N 3XX

Cover design: Gemma Gary

Dedication

This book is dedicated to two elders of Norfolk's Nameless Tradition: Nigel Pennick and Ray Loveday. They have both, in their very different ways, taught us so much over the years and have been more influential and inspirational than they realise.

Acknowledgements

So many people have contributed to the writing of this book and to the many years of magical work and exploration on which it is based. I would like to acknowledge all those humans, animals, ancestors and spiritual beings who have ever honoured us with their presence in the magical garden and everyone who has contributed to the life of Norfolk's magical community. Special thanks are due to Matthew Hannam, who was a driving force behind much of our early work here and still plays an important part in the Nameless Tradition, albeit from thousands of miles away. I also owe a huge debt of gratitude to the Hermits (previously) of Mole End for all their hospitality, plant knowledge and creative ideas, and to Rod and Rue Chapman for so generously sharing their knowledge of the county's history and magic. I am grateful to Michael Clarke and Vicki Dolley for allowing me to use their experiences of meeting the Fair Folk. Thanks also to Denise H. and Andy Gaines who worked with us for so many years and to Helen, Bob and Simon who, amongst other contributions, helped us develop our magical techniques for working with the heroes. I am grateful to Julie Mytton, Mel Burridge, Szara Froud, David Crowe and Sharon Shute for offering so much of themselves and their magic, and of course to Jean for all she did for us in life and all the messages and inspiration she continues to send us. Thanks to Gareth Lloyd for persuading me to take up cycling again and explore Marriott's Way, to Gilberto Lascariz for showing us how to perform the sieve and shears ritual, to Adrian Marsden for his insights about Faunus, to Chris and John Collins for so many entertaining magical discussions, to Mary Martin for the term "fortune basket", to Pammie Couchman for her contribution to the rhyming couplets about the seasonal festivals and for the little glass charm which has hung for over a decade in the pear tree, to Andrea for the story of her kiln god and to Dave and Barbara Gardner for their generosity, hospitality and kindness to so many of us in Norfolk's Nameless Tradition. Thanks also to Paul Jackson for all his wonderful stories, but especially his retelling of Kett's Rebellion in 1999, and for his song at the wreath-laying at the castle. Thanks to Nigel Pearson for inviting me to speak about Norfolk Magic at his own book launch for The Devil's Plantation. I am also grateful to Antonella Parker-Hall and Sadie Huxford of the Norfolk Goddess Temple for their perspective on Andraste, and to Penny Hunter for reading the first draft of the book and for her encouraging comments. A special thank you to all who took part in in the closing ritual for Harvest Moon 2015, including those not mentioned elsewhere: Pete Jennings, Marian Green, Matt Fox, Kevin Ward, Amanda and Andre Henriques, Brenda and Robert Tungatt, and Alix and John Freeman. Thanks also to Inkubus Sukkubus for making that evening such a memorable one and especially to Candia for giving Birch the Ferret his "claim to fame".

This book would never have come into being without the wonderful practical and magical support (and nagging) of Nettles, Alice, Pherlin, and Vicki, and their conviction that the book would turn out well. Most importantly, I am grateful to my husband, Chris Wood, for being part of the story from the very beginning and for setting aside his own writing projects to go through every chapter with a fine-tooth comb, checking facts, references, spellings and commas, and challenging careless expressions and sloppy thinking. I would also like to extend my heartfelt thanks to Gemma and Jane of Troy Books for their friendship since the earliest days of Minor Arcana and for their significant role in our magic. They also continued to believe in this project even though it took me such a long time to complete it and (as they do with all the books they produce) they have transformed a piece of plain text into a work of art.

Contents

Photoplates
between pages 192-193

Photo 5 by Jane Cox, all other photos by Chris Wood

Introduction

Norfolk is a county filled with magic. The search for knowledge of other realms, the desire to communicate with the Eldritch World and to understand the tales of humanity's long relationship with the land, form so much of the warp and weft of this Eastern-most curve of the UK, with the North Sea to the East and to the North, and the Wash in the West. There is something in the soil and in the play of the morning Sun over the waves and waterways which calls to the seeker. The chill East wind and the movement of leaves and branches sing of ancient secrets, while the many ghost-filled Flint churches, which grace the open landscape, stand as a testament to the spiritual aspirations of generations.

Indeed, spiritual quests in all their many and varied forms, from state religion to heresy, from the orthodox to the maverick, have been, and still are, intertwined with the lives and history of the county's inhabitants, although magic and otherworldly matters touch people in different ways, depending on their inclinations and sensitivities. Nowadays there are representatives here of all the world's religions, for the most part thriving side by side in an atmosphere of respect and friendly curiosity.

Witches and magicians flourish here too. There are those who follow Traditional Witchcraft, Wiccans of both Gardnerian and Alexandrian persuasion, and those who use the name Wicca more loosely. There are New Age Hedge Witches and members of old Witchcraft families, whose very secret practitioners still work their ways at the field's

11

edge and in the tangled undergrowth. Some of Norfolk's witches were born here, others drawn in from elsewhere by the subtle, magical pull of the deities and spirits of place. Many now consider themselves to be Pagan, but there are still lots of practitioners who use Christian magic and venerate saints. There are plenty of witches, cunning folk, or otherwise magically-inclined people, who have no particular desire to label themselves or the groups they work with, for the Quest is never static, but forever changing and developing. So many prefer not to be fettered by names and rules, but to enjoy the freedom to explore ideas and to work with other practitioners without necessarily being bound to them. We live under a huge and beautiful sky and, like the many birds who sometimes flock together and sometimes fly alone, so we gather and disperse as we see fit. The threads of connection between groups, or those which link individuals and groups, may be strong in certain cases, light and tenuous in others, but magical influences swirl around, inspiring and informing our spells and our rituals. So there has developed a Nameless Tradition: a loose association of magical people who love this land and the winding ways of its magic.

We embrace outside influences too. We all read books and use the internet, and many of us attend conferences, travel great distances and share ideas with those from far away. Our magical practices are not pure and unadulterated because, as Nigel Pennick has taught us, in his many writings and by example, "centred pluralism" is a way of remaining true to our place and to our roots without becoming insular and backward-looking. We draw into our work things which we learn from a multitude of sources, old and new, and develop them in ways which suit us, our groups, the needs of the land and the requirements of the moment.

There are things which are specific to the county and inform its magic, touching its practitioners knowingly or subconsciously: its place within the geography of the Isles of the Wise, its relationship with sea and land, the rising Sun and the rising Moon and its particular flora and fauna.

Underlying it all is its geology of Chalk and of Flint. These are the things which have powered Norfolk's natural history, its social history, its architecture, as well as the kind of magic it fosters. They create our herbs, our animal totems, our sacred landscape, our saints and heroes, the materials for our spells and the tools of our many crafts. More than that, they become part of the fabric of our flesh and the solidity of our bones, particularly if we eat locally-grown food, which, as far as possible, most witches do. It is the land which nourishes us; it becomes us and we become part of it. As Chris Wood (2015) has said:

In as much as we live in the land, breathe its air, drink its water, eat its food and honour it, then we are all native.

We send down such deep roots that leaving the place, even for a few days, can be difficult. It is always with an enormous sense of relief that we cross the border back into Norfolk on a return trip from elsewhere in the country, or even the world. Some perhaps feel this more strongly than others, but it is there for most of us who work some kind of natural magic. The spirit of place, or "Anima Loci", as Nigel Pennick (1997) calls it, is a powerful force in Norfolk, and our relationship with it develops all the more as we work the county's magic. The more we appreciate it, the more we can draw into ourselves, and use in our magic, that spiritual force which Nigel describes as "spirament" and which Gemma Gary (2008), in far-away Cornwall, refers to as "sprowl" (now a very popular expression in Norfolk too).

So, I have written this book as a magical offering and as a celebration of a quarter of a century of living, gathering sprowl and working magically in a special space, in a jewel of a city, at the heart of a varied and beautiful county. On October 8th, twenty-five years ago, I boarded a train heading for Norwich. It was a place with which I was quite familiar and where I had many friends and acquaintances, although on another level, it was a new adventure for me. My "witch's cottage" awaited: an ordinary terraced house, but one with a magnificent secret garden, hidden in an old stone quarry. As soon as my husband, Chris, and I had seen it, we knew it was the right place for the next step on our magical path. It had been way out of our price range, but magic can truly work wonders when there is the need and the will.

As I sat on the train with our two lovely cats in a basket, I gazed out of the window seeking, as most magical practitioners would in such a situation, signs in the passing landscapes which would provide some clues as to how this new life might unfold, and guidance on how best to approach it. As the sky widened before me, I saw Wood Pigeons and a Fox, a group of Deer grazing peacefully, Rabbits scampering as the train approached. A single Hare stopped for a moment in a patch of honeyed Autumn sunlight, long ears alert before it bounded for cover. Everywhere had an atmosphere of good harvests well-gathered and stored, of richness and diversity. I interpreted these things according to my knowledge and understanding at the time. When we stepped into "our" garden, that too offered a harvest of sweet Bullaces. They had been left for us and had remained fresh on the branches despite the lateness of the season. All would be well. There would be richness and good harvests if we were prepared to work for them according to the seasons and the requirements of the landscape.

This book honours and celebrates the county of Norfolk, its crisp air, its wide beaches, its rich farmlands and forests, its mysterious wetlands, its towns and the city of Norwich, all steeped in centuries of history and magic. If I could, I would sing all this to you with the voice of Norfolk's birds, dance with its insects, leap with the Hares and run with the Deer. I would speak with the deep wisdom of the storytellers of old and weave a fabric of wonder to wrap around you. I would distil the fragrance of all Norfolk's herbs and offer it to you in a precious vial. I have done my best, for the land and its spirits deserve no less. For all the successes and failures, the laughter and the tears of the last two and a half decades, I know I have but scratched the surface of all there is to learn here, so I offer some of the treasure I have now and then I will continue to learn and share if the gods are willing.

In writing this book, I do not presume to speak for anyone but myself, and a little for those with whom I have worked closely over the years, developing a magical style which has suited me well, and other practitioners too, for longer or shorter periods of time. We have taught others and, in a small way, influenced and hopefully inspired some individuals and groups. Indeed, we once tried to list all the people who had ever done magical work with us in our garden. Having reached two hundred, we gave up counting, wishing that we had kept a record, although years ago we had not fully appreciated the desirability of doing so. Nevertheless, despite the numbers of people involved, we have tried to balance openness, hospitality and the welcoming of genuine seekers with a prudent level of caution and secrecy, so as not to lay open the work to ridicule or to undermine its power in any way. So many people have blessed our path in various ways: the givers and the takers, the students and teachers, the challengers, the tricksters and the deadly serious. I remember them with fondness and gratitude for all they have contributed to the Nameless Tradition.

Our way of magic is not the only way, nor would we claim it is the best way. Hence the title of this volume: it is a way of Norfolk Magic. Because what we do is real and practical, not just academic, this we know for sure: it is meaningful, it is powerful and it works.

Throughout the book, I have referred to many historical and folkloric sources. However, what I wish to present is by no means derivative. All the places described are ones which my magical colleagues and I visit regularly; the tools, materials and spells are those we really use and, unless stated otherwise, we have worked with all the deities, Fair Ones, heroes and saints that are mentioned, and communicated with them directly, for this book is about our lived experience within the Nameless Tradition. Although we revere the fact that Norfolk's magic is rooted in its past, we work with it now in ways which suit the needs of our time. Our ancestors have much to teach us but we do not claim to work as they did or to be able to perform some of the magics they had mastered. What we do have in common with them is that we draw inspiration from the land, from the poetry of the natural world, from story and from the crafts of hand, mind and heart.

References

Gary, Gemma (2008) Traditional Wichcraft: A Book of Cornish Ways, Troy Books.
Pennick, Nigel (1997) Earth Harmony: Places of Power, Holiness and Healing, Second Edition, Capall Bann.
Wood, Chris (2015) What are the Gods? Quest 182 (June 2015), pp. 13-22.

The Lord and Lady of Norfolk

The magic of the land rises from beneath the rocks and the soil on which we walk, and into which we allow our roots to grow. It is the basis of everything we do, for it is from this Earth that our trees spring and our herbs draw their nourishment. It provides building materials and governs the kinds of human activity which take place in any given locality, and so informs the culture which develops, in the mundane and the magical spheres. The solidity of granite or the smoothness of slate may suit the magic of some practitioners, who are then born to, or drawn to, such areas and landscapes, and learn to dance their spells to the ancient music which pulses from deep within the ground.

Those who work well in Norfolk are generally people who thrive on the magical twin influences of the white and grey powers of the Lady of the Chalk and the Lord of the Flint. If one peels back the geological layers of the county, there are other soils and rocks to be found here too. There is the Kimmeridge Clay from the Jurassic, which forms a fine, bluish-grey mud, the Lower Greensand of the Cretaceous, which forms the beautiful carstone, used for the distinctive buildings of parts of West Norfolk, or the Gault Clay, clearly visible as the red rock band in the wonderfully striped cliffs at Hunstanton. These have their practical and magical uses, often specific to the areas of the county in which they are found. The Chalk and the Flint, however, have a county-wide appeal, a greater visibility and much clearer mundane, practical and magical uses.

Of course, Chalk and the Flint are not exclusive to Norfolk. They are to be found in Yorkshire to the North, where the Iron Age Parisi tribe carved the Chalk warrior figures (Stead, 1988). They are present on the slopes of the Gog Magog Hills in Cambridgeshire, on the Downs of the South, the slopes of the Chilterns and all along that magical trackway, known as The Ridgeway. In Wiltshire, the Chalk is honoured with the magnificent Horse carvings in the hills, while Wilmington, in Sussex, has its Long Man and Dorset its Cerne Abbas Giant. However, such forces have a different feel, depending on other features of the locality, best understood by the practitioners of those areas. Their manifestation here in Norfolk takes on a special form, of far greater complexity than that of "mere" geology. That is why, when we call upon them, which we do in every ritual (for it would be rude not to), we refer to them by the titles of Lord and Lady of Norfolk, although they go by many names, some of which are known to us and others which remain a mystery. These beings are the most ancient ones, the Earth beneath our feet, our firm foundation; they profoundly influence what grows and flourishes on the land and what might just wither and die.

The Chalk and the Flint predate humanity by such an unfathomable length of time. When we pick up a piece of either from the ground, we feel that human beings are just children in the context of such ancient beings, and that our individual lives are miniscule in such a vast context. Yet these forces are also so much part of our everyday lives that they are, on one level, comprehensible and approachable. After all, since our arrival in these lands, they have shaped the development of our culture, what we grow, the tools we have used, how we build and express our spirituality, as well as the form and shape of our magic. We see and touch them every day, whether we choose to notice them or not; they are ordinary and yet hold the keys to the greatest of mysteries.

Lord of Norfolk, Grey Lord of the Flint

In our magical work, we often visualise the Lord of Norfolk in human form, because that is the way we are best able to approach and comprehend his being. He appears as a huge and ancient grey-clad figure, a hunter with bow and arrows, a strong and powerful builder, a protector and defender of the land, striding along the coastline, beside the meres, across ploughed fields or though the woodlands. Sometimes he seems to emerge so clearly, from the mists of the veil, that it is almost possible to glimpse his features, to make that step towards a richer understanding, a greater knowing; and then the moment passes. Nevertheless, the physical signs of the extraordinary remain with us, for the Lord of Norfolk is there in the stones, in our gardens and fields, as they work their way to the surface, blunting tools or needing to be removed to allow delicate plants to thrive. At other times, we hear his voice as the waves endlessly shift the shingle, back and forth upon the beach, creating smooth and sea-tumbled pebbles, or we catch a sharp reminder of his presence on bare feet or careless fingers.

The Lord of Norfolk is embodied by a magical stone indeed. Flint is composed almost entirely of silica, and only diamonds are harder and more durable. Yet because it flakes so easily it can be worked into different shapes (Russell, 2000) and has a multitude of different uses. Although we see the Lord of Norfolk as a Grey Lord, his stone varies in colour, and may be yellow, brown or amber, if iron oxides or other pigments have seeped in through the pores of the stone and left their own special magic. The core of a piece of Flint is usually smooth, dark and lustrous, while its outer surface, known as the cortex, is less dense and much more porous, and can be seen as a clear white line when a stone is broken open. Once Flint is cut and exposed, the process of cortication often transforms the colour from black to pale bluey grey, although the rate of the change is delightfully unpredictable. On some Medieval buildings, the shiny core is as little changed as on some Victorian buildings. Another process, patination, gives the Flint a yellow or white waxy look, somewhat reminiscent of ivory (Hart, 2000). Such a rich assortment is useful when selecting stones for magical work, as is the range of shapes and textures. Pieces found in Thetford Forest are often angular and rather waxy looking, with blue patterns on them, sometimes surprisingly like broken pieces of Willow Pattern crockery, but also containing runes or other forms of written messages.

The Lord of the Flint's domain extends far beyond Norfolk, and the buildings of the whole region of East Anglia are expressions of centuries of interaction between this magnificent being of the Earth and the ingenuity and skill of human craftspeople, at one with their materials, which come directly from the Source. The Lord of the Flint provides the raw materials for the simple hearth and home of ordinary folk, grand abodes for the rich, the protection of Norwich's city walls, the spiritual aspiration of the great wool churches.

Some of the constructions use "as-found" Flints, sometimes set into mortar, in an apparently random patterning, sometimes in coursed arrangements, where clear horizontal lines are visible. Herringbone patterns are often seen, as is galletting, when small flakes of flint are added to the mortar before it dries, to provide extra packing between irregular shaped stones, or for purely decorative purposes. A rich vocabulary has developed to describe the different kinds of Flint work, which have become part of the Flint Lord's poetry. Knapped work may be "select", "squared" or "rough squared"; it may use "ovals", "scales" or "blocks". In combination with other stone or brick, the patterns formed may be "chequer", "Flemish chequer", "banding", "morse" or "diaper". The names can be read as spells, and indeed used as such, with their "diamonds", "lozenges", "trellises" and "lattices". Flushwork uses the contrasting characteristics of Flint and ashlared freestone, mostly brought to East Anglia, by water, from Lincolnshire limestone quarries, to produce distinctive designs, which are full of symbolism, meaning and magic. The earliest example of this technique is thought to be St. Ethelbert's Gate, in Norwich, built in 1316, although restored in 1815 by William Wilkins (Hart, 2000). Flushwork on other buildings shows seasonal patterns, merchant's marks, the tools of many trades, wheels, foliage, intricate interlaced patterns, heraldic designs and protective or religious or spiritual symbols and even the Glastonbury Thorn. Just like the foliate heads, seen in so many Medieval churches, a wealth of Pagan and magical imagery can be seen in these flushwork designs (Talbot, 2004).

Not only does this Grey Lord represent protection from the weather and from attack, He also provided our ancestors with the means to hunt and grow their food. Arrowheads, sickles, polished axe heads and grinding stones were all made from mined Flint, at that liminal point in our history when we made the gradual transition from being hunter gathers to domesticating animals and cultivating crops (Russell, 2000). In honour of this, we attach Flint heads to the arrows we use on the garlands in some of our rituals.

Probably the most dramatic and focused way to experience the power of the Flint Lord, as he manifests in His Norfolk form, is to visit Grimes Graves, in Thetford Forest, where our Neolithic forebears risked their lives to bring out, from the depths, the most prized, unweathered, black Flint floorstone, which was to be found ten to thirteen metres below the surface, in seams just 20-30cm thick. Although there were lesser Flint workings, Grimes Graves was the largest and most complex in Britain (Forrest, 1983), with 433 shafts, many with galleries radiating out from them.

None of this is easily discernible from ground level though. Approaching the site (now owned by English Heritage) along a straight, single-track forest road, one is just aware of an open grassy area of mounds and dips, a car park and a small building, which is the visitors' centre. In the

Summer, there are Skylarks all around. The flora of this once industrial area, but now a Site of Special Scientific Interest, is rich and diverse, and there is a discernible crackle of ancient magic all around. Reciting just a few of the wonderful plant names associated with this place is one simple way of alerting the spirits to your desire to be fully present in the enchantment of both the past and the now. Heather, Harebell, Knapweed, Mouse-ear, Stonecrop, Hawk's-beard, Eyebright, Squinancywort, Gentian and Mignionette can all be words of power, which skim the surface and initiate a little quivering, which allows the eye to see more as you attune to what is really all around you.

Once you know what is in the ground beneath you, it is not difficult to picture an underground constellation of deep shafts and star patterns joining them all, in a fantastic, invisible network. The presence of another of the powerful gods of this land, the Norse/Anglo-Saxon deity, Odin or Woden, can also be felt to wander across the strangely-textured surface of the place, as it is by one of his many names that this site is known. There are no representatives of Odin's Ravens, Hugin and Munin, here, but we are reminded of them in the constant cawing of the Rooks, in the distance trees, and the many black feathers lying in the grass amongst the shards of Flint. Besides, both Thought and Memory are important aspects of any visit here.

Fortunately, at the time of writing, it is still relatively inexpensive to buy a ticket, which allows you to go down into the one pit which is open to the public. Visitors are required to wear a yellow hard hat (which would not be my first choice of headgear when going to meet a major deity), but they are permitted to go down unsupervised. The thin metal rungs of the alarmingly narrow, but very stable, ladder are chilly to the touch, and grow colder as you make the descent, passing the various layers of Flint – the topstone and the wallstone – and watching the circle of the sky above diminish, the deeper you travel into this underworld of the ancestors. The tap of antler picks on stone can still be heard by those who are prepared to listen, and the power and presence of the Lord of Norfolk is all around. There is an indescribable tingling when you step off the last rung of the ladder, place both feet on the floor of the chamber, breathe in, and reach out for that magical understanding of ancient power and wisdom. Low arches lead off into tunnels, but these are now barred against physical entry, although it is possible to glimpse into that network of passages which join one pit to another.

Standing there, we think of the many antlers which were used to mine the Flint. These were most often Red Deer antlers, with the crown and first two tines either burned or cut away. When the tools broke, or became blunted, they were discarded, and in just two of the pits, a total of 244 such antlers were discovered, many of which had been worked smooth by the hands of the miners. On some there were even finger prints in the Chalk which covered them (Clarke and Clarke, 1937). So, the Lord of Norfolk is most definitely a horned god, and the magic of the Deer is woven deeply into the fabric of the county. Naturalistic depictions of Red Deer, engraved into floorstone, were found during the early excavations of the site, although many commentators now consider these to have been part of a hoax designed to convince people that this was a Palaeolithic site (Russell, 2000). Nevertheless, this does not undermine the depth of the connections between the Grey Lord, the Deer and the landscape of the county.

It is not difficult to imagine the miners making offerings of antlers, carvings and drawings, as well as the exquisitely worked axe heads. Craftspeople of great skill worked the Flint, inspired or guided by the Lord of Norfolk who, millennia later, can still be called upon to give assistance to the county's makers and artists. I think this is one of the reasons why all of the practitioners of Norfolk's Nameless Tradition do some form of art or craft work, drawing on thousands of years of inspiration and magical help, in the development of the skills of hand and eye.

Of course, the process of going down into the pit at Grimes Graves can be done purely in the mind, in meditation or pathworking. Those who are especially skilled at knowing and visualising what they have not experienced with their mundane senses, can even do this without having been to the place in person. For most of us, though, the physical experience is important, and the effort of a regular visit becomes an act of pilgrimage.

On re-emerging from the shaft, a visit to Thetford's Ancient House Museum can provide a moving insight into the skills of the 20th-century Flint knappers. The Museum is home to an exquisite Flint alphabet, knapped by Bill Basham, in his spare time, over a period of two years. He also made a delicate necklace of seventeen circlets and a heart, which he sold, in 1927, for just £10. Sadly, like many of the Flint knappers, Basham died of silicosis, in 1932, at the age of 38 (Forrest, 1983). But the art of Flint knapping is far from lost. Will Lord, the son of earlier custodians of Grimes Graves, is an expert Flint knapper, and continues to teach the skill, as well as running prehistoric experience courses (www.will-lord.co.uk).

The Lord of Norfolk is a being of Fire as well as of Earth, for this everyday, common, yet intensely magical stone also carries within it the stuff of stars, which can light the hearth fire or ignite the divine spark within. The Flint as a strike-a-light is of enduring significance.

However, like so many things, the power of the Flint can be used for good or for ill and has not always been adapted for purely peaceful purposes. Flint arrowheads come in various shapes and styles, ranging from the chunky to the slender and elegant. The sheer numbers which have been found are thought to suggest that people may have used them in warfare, not just for hunting (Wymer, 1994). Indeed, Flint weapons have been said to be Britain's oldest industry, from Neolithic arrowheads from 2000 BCE, to the gunflints made in Brandon, and much prized for use during the Napoleonic Wars.

The Lady of Norfolk: Our Lady of the Chalk

Twice in any twenty-four-hour period, it is possible to watch the Lady of Norfolk stepping from the sea. As the tide recedes, just to the East of Sheringham, She begins to appear, in the form of an outcrop of rocks, sometimes white and gleaming in the sunshine, but sometimes more subtle, and draped in seaweed. This small sliver of rock provides us with a little glimpse of Norfolk's Chalk reef, which is a rich and diverse marine habitat, our Lady's submerged treasury, from which she offers many magical gifts, and tells her wordless story of the ancient history of the landscape. For the physical aspect of this great being, technically and unromantically given the chemical name of calcium carbonate, is made up of the solid remains of millions of creatures, whose lives and dramas unfolded long before the Ice Age, when most of the land was still beneath the sea. So, every piece of Chalk we casually pick up holds within it something of these ancient memories.

Of course, the concept of a White Goddess of love, beauty, caring and nurturing, stepping from the sea, is found in other traditions worldwide. I have been fortunate enough to visit the birthplace of Aphrodite, in Cyprus, and to see the brilliant white rock which represents her emerging from the blue green of the Mediterranean, lapped all around with perfect white sea foam. She is indeed grand and dramatic, and tourists arrive constantly to see her and pay their respects. Our Lady of Norfolk is much quieter, less theatrical, and only ever whispers her secrets. However, there is nothing more lovely than watching her appear from a cold, grey North Sea, when only a few dog walkers or beachcombers are around, and far too distant to disturb our musings.

The Lady of the Chalk, our White Lady, is Mother of the Flint, although precisely how the Flint forms within the Chalk remains a mystery, as so it should. It has been suggested that burrows within the Chalk become filled with dissolved silica, which is derived from the skeletons of sponges (Hart, 2000). These form nodules which become freed from their Mother over millions of years of erosion.

We see the Lady of Norfolk as a nurturer of crops and a nourisher of the creatures and the people of the land. This is reflected, in practical terms, in the process known as "marling", which was particularly popular in the 18th and 19th centuries, when Chalk was dug from pits and spread onto the fields to enhance the soil structure and to neutralise acidity (Williamson, 1993). We may not need to spread physical Chalk on our own small areas of land, but we can certainly call on the Lady to bless our gardens and the places we forage for wild fruits, nuts, herbs or craft materials, for on all levels, she can help make the conditions right for things to thrive. She can do this on the inside as well as in our environment, since Chalk tablets are taken by many people as an antacid, and many toothpastes contain finely ground Chalk.

The Lady of Norfolk is also associated with the white milk of fostering, for just as she is Mother of the Flint, she is also a Mother to us all. It is interesting that, at the Christian shrine at Walsingham, there was a vial of "Our Lady's Milk", brought to Norfolk from the Holy House at Bethlehem, where Jesus was born. This "milk" was long regarded as a precious relic, full of miraculous potential. Yet, what it appears to have been (and even modern Christian scholars agree on this point) is scrapings of Chalk from the walls of the place of the Nativity (Spencer, 1980). So, powdered Chalk, from a distant Holy Land, representing another White Lady, has been brought to a hallowed place within our own sacred, Chalk landscape (Wood, 2017). From a magical point of view, this adds many more layers of meaning and interest, and merits much thought and meditation.

Like a good Mother, the Lady of Norfolk is one who can hold together her magical family, just as the mortar, of which her physical being is a part, holds in place the Flints or the bricks of the buildings which shelter us. We might barely notice her in this aspect, but she is there, informing the subtle patterns which we create together, as she fosters cooperation and community.

The Lady may also be called upon to protect our communities and our own hearths and homes. This is enhanced by chalking protective symbols onto fenceposts, doorsteps and pathways. Various runes may be used for this purpose. Particularly popular is the bindrune known as the Helm of Awe, although "running eights" work especially well on doorsteps. Although it is sometimes tempting to create the more elaborate patterns from colourful, commercial chalk (which is usually made out of gypsum or talc), to invoke the Lady's protection to its full extent, it really needs to be worked with Chalk found locally.

Because it is physically possible to write with Chalk, the Lady can also be called upon to assist magically those of us who work with the craft of writing, while the practical uses of her gifts in numerous other crafts (for example, tailor's chalk for those who sew, checking the fit of joints in woodwork) provide a route to summoning her assistance in all the skills of the hand and the imagination. Thus, both the Lord and Lady of Norfolk have very strong associations with the practical crafts, which are so embedded in the magical work of the county.

Chalk carving is a craft which can certainly be said to have been associated with the Goddess in ancient times, and one controversial depiction of her was "discovered" in 1939, in Pit 15 of Grimes Graves, by the archaeologist A. Leslie Armstrong. She was sitting on a Flint plinth, with antler picks, and a Chalk vessel beneath it. There was a carved Chalk phallus on the floor and Flint nodules arranged, in a phallus shape, in a gallery not far away. This "Venus of Grimes Graves", or "Chalk Goddess", became an iconic figure, appearing on the official site guidebooks and attracting much academic speculation about her role as an Earth Goddess, reminiscent of other European, Palaeolithic "Venus" figures. She is indeed very well rounded, with large, pendulous breasts, and appears to be pregnant. It was also suggested that she might have been placed in the pit, to petition for a more abundant seam of unweathered floorstone in the next excavation. However, there have been many questions raised about the authenticity of the figurine. Armstrong, who had been implicated in other fraudulent finds, had been alone in the pit, prior to the discovery, having forbidden other colleagues from joining him. Then, when he brought his finds to the surface, his friend, Ethel Rudkin, angered him by making a copy of the figure from a discarded piece of Chalk, using a Flint knife, thus proving how easy it was to make a "goddess" of this kind (Russell, 2000).

For historians and archaeologists, the matter of whether or not the Chalk Goddess is real is obviously of great importance. However, for magical practitioners, this need not necessarily be the case. Even if the figure was made by Armstrong or any other hoaxer, it has already developed a considerable aura of power and presence. This was evident from her appearance at the Unearthed exhibition at the Sainsbury Centre, in Norwich, when this Chalk Lady returned to the county, from the British Museum, where she currently resides, to take her place amongst a wealth of Japanese figures, known as dogu, and a collection of South East European figurines. She was placed in a large glass display cabinet, some distance from the other exhibits, in an area of dim lighting. Rounding the corner, and coming face to face with her, was a breath-taking experience. She exudes enchantment and significance, small and simple as she is in mundane terms. Of course, she could well have the ability to embody the Lady, however recently she was made. Magical practitioners are well aware of how quickly depictions of deities can become ensouled, and it must have delighted her to return to Norfolk, if only on a temporary visit.

The face of the Grimes Graves Goddess is very simple and plain, with no adornments. However, the Lady of Norfolk most definitely has an aspect as a horned goddess. Sometimes these are the antlers of a Deer, unusual in Does, of course, but an apt crown for a one of such quiet power.

At other times, she appears to bear upon her head the points of the crescent Moon, reflecting the soft whiteness of her stone.

Although the Lady of Norfolk is a gentle and approachable deity, abuse of what she offers us may be met with retribution. Her gifts have been quarried and mined for centuries, and the city of Norwich still has many places where it is obvious that quantities of stone have been removed, leaving strange, scooped out forms in the hillside. Chalk mining was at its height during the industrial revolution when large quantities were required for quicklime, and an unmapped labyrinth of old mining tunnels extends for miles underneath the city. Occasionally, one of these tunnels collapses, opening up a vast chasm in someone's garden, bringing down part of a building, or stopping traffic, as famously happened in 1988, when a bus fell into a hole which opened up on Earlham Road, not far from the city centre.

Revelations

Sometimes the Lord and Lady of Norfolk choose to reveal their presence in a moment of drama or of great beauty. In the late afternoon, on a late Autumn day of blustering storms and spectacular bursts of sunshine, they may appear as a rainbow, or even a double rainbow, against grey and white clouds. On a warm morning of sunlight, sand and gentle waves, they may show themselves in the dark and light sheen of a sea-washed Oyster shell. There is a clear and discernible distinction between the ordinary loveliness of the natural world and an announcement of the proximity of these deities, which can take the breath away, inspire an outpouring of creative work, or provide confirmation that we are heading in the correct direction, magically.

On one occasion, we had just completed a Maytime ritual with a large group of people, when one of our number glanced up and noticed a pair of Woodpigeons on a Sycamore branch, cooing and pecking each other's beaks.

31

"Look," she said, "It's the Lord and Lady of Norfolk", and we all gazed up into the fresh green foliage and knew that she was right.

Such revelations can take many forms. At Thompson Water, one Spring, three of us stood on one of the fishing jetties, watching a Heron in the Reeds, Egrets in the trees across the lake and Terns performing their aerial acrobatics above our heads. We had planned a musical offering for the spirit of this place. One of us sang and I played a wooden flute I had brought with me, especially for this purpose. As the last notes faded away, an enormous Grass Snake appeared, swimming right towards us, paused by the jetty, and seemed to acknowledge us before disappearing under the murky water. This was a blessing indeed. We have sought this magnificent creature on subsequent visits, but have never seen it again, not that we really expected to, as this was obviously a manifestation of the presence of deity.

The Lord and Lady may appear in any form, at any season. One dark, moonless night in Winter, we were driving along a remote country lane in North Norfolk, having just completed a piece of protection work, when a magnificent Stag stepped onto the road right in front of the car. We stopped. He inclined his head just slightly and gave us haughty look before continuing on his way, in a slow and stately fashion, closely followed by the rest of his herd. We knew this to be a blessing on the work we had completed. Then, to add to our delight, rounding the next corner, we were greeted by the sight of a mother Cat playing, in the middle of the road, with a large litter of kittens. We stopped again and enjoyed watching their antics, in the beam of the car headlights. They continued their game for some time, until the mother decided that was enough and carried her kittens, one at a time, into the safety of the hedge. These are not small, forgettable incidents, but real treasures, which we store in our memories as the rewards for our magical work.

References

Clarke, W.G., and Clarke, R. Rainbird (1937) *In Breckland Wilds*, Second Edition, Heffer.

Forrest, A.J. (1983) *Masters of Flint*, Terence Dalton.

Hart, Stephen (2000) *Flint Architecture of East Anglia*, Giles de la Mare

Russell, Miles (2000) *Flint Mines in Neolithic Britain*, Tempus.

Spencer, Brian (1980) *Medieval Pilgrim Badges from Norfolk*, Norfolk Museums Service.

Stead, I.M. (1998) Chalk figurines of the Parisi, *The Antiquaries Journal* LXVIII Part 1, pp. 9-29.

Talbot, Margaret (2004) *Medieval Flushwork of East Anglia*, Poppyland.

Williamson, Tom (1993) *The Origins of Norfolk*, Manchester University Press.

Wood, Chris (2017) A Walsingham Pilgrimage, *Quest* 191.

Wymer, John (1994). The Neolithic Period, in Wade-Martins, Peter (ed.) *An Historical Atlas of Norfolk*, Norfolk Museums Service.

the Stockton Stone

Sacred Places: Stories within the Landscape

The magic of Norfolk's Chalk and Flint landscape is quiet, unobtrusive and a little secretive, for the Lord and Lady of Norfolk do not need to flaunt their power. There are none of the glamorous stone circles or other clearly recognisable signs of ancient mysteries to which so many magical folk are drawn in other parts of the country. Our magic is not so easily noticed by the casual observer, yet none the less significant for all that. It is necessary to look more closely, pay attention and wait patiently for the land to give some clues. Much is hidden, and it takes time to find what we later realise has been in plain sight the whole time. For indeed, there is no part of this magical county which is not, in some way, sacred. Every field and tree, every beach, every town and village is in the care of the Lord and Lady of Norfolk. Every garden can be somebody's temple. Even in those areas where humanity has abused the land and rendered it "gast", to use Nigel Pennick's (2015) expression, there may still be a beautiful view across the North Sea, a tiny plant struggling through, a creature making the most of what is available, an attractive stone lying on a path or vigorous Brambles and Ivy covering the mess that people have made and, albeit slowly, restoring the soul of the place.

Each working group may favour a particular spot whose energies are well-suited to the kind of magic they perform. Some are attracted to the better-known sites, whereas others prefer the secret, hidden places, known only to themselves. There are those who like to vary where they work, drawing on different streams of energy, depending on the season or the type of work in hand, and those who find it more congenial to be consistent and to work in the same Circle year after year, building a deep reservoir of power and a kind of magical security, inasmuch as that is ever possible.

For my own work, I fall into the latter category, having worked for a quarter of a century, honouring the Lord and Lady of Norfolk at every seasonal festival, in the same ritual manner and the same sacred Circle. Many other spells and blessings have been carried out in this spot, as well as magical experiments, but always acknowledging this stream of the Nameless Tradition in which we are honoured to play our part. Very few people know of the existence of our ancient quarry garden, even amongst those who live on the same street as us, and a sense of awe and wonder is often experienced on seeing it for the first time. This is typical of Norfolk magic: it is very close and yet can be difficult to find, until the veil is lifted, and the seeker is admitted.

Our work involves teaching others, so the relative safety of the place is conducive to helping students take their first steps within this Tradition, and it is a great delight to see them gain in confidence, to the point at which they can take what they have learned and continue the work in their own way, in another sacred spot of their own choosing. So, the Tradition develops and continues, each practitioner just a berry on one of the Bryony necklaces which deck the autumn hedgerows and woodlands of the county.

Our dedication to this particular spot does not preclude us from travelling around the county and working at other sites when appropriate. We have our favourite places to visit, to honour, and from which we gather their "spirament" or "sprowl". It is hard to make a list of them, for everyone wishing to work in this Tradition will find their own, and somebody is sure to say "Why didn't you mention...", or perhaps they will be pleased that it has been left out, if they wish it to remain behind the veil. The places I have mentioned are relatively easily accessible and fairly well-known to the magical community in general.

Sacred Waters

The Element of Water is a powerful magical force in Norfolk, a county surrounded by sea to the North and to the East, with the mysterious Wash in the West. It is crossed by slow, dark rivers, with such evocative names as the Wensum, the Yare, the Ant, the Bure and the Ouse, and graced by the waterways of the Broads which attract so many visitors.

The county thrives on the gifts these waters bring, and yet, as is so often the case with the natural and the magical, it is also threatened by these waters' deadly power. Over the centuries, many Norfolk folk have lost their lives, drowned beneath the turbulent North Sea, and many have been the tales of brave rescues by heroic lifeboat crews. Most famous among the many heroes was Coxswain Henry Blogg (1876-1954), who served for 53 years on the Cromer Lifeboat, holding the position of coxswain for 37 years and saving 873 lives (Jolly, 1958) becoming the RNLI's most decorated lifeboatman (RNLI, 2015). Nor should it be forgotten that the RNLI's motto, "Never turn back", originated from the Caister Lifeboat disaster during the Great Storm of 13th November 1901, in which 9 lifeboatmen lost their lives. After the tragedy, it was reported that, "Caister men never turn back" (based on an inquest statement by lifeboatman James Haylett, see http://www.caisterlifeboat.org.uk/about.html). Such heroism becomes woven into the magical fabric of the county, as well as its mundane history, and its energy can be respectfully drawn upon if needed.

The balance of sea and land is a delicate one. The soft, boulder-clay cliffs are crumbling away in places all along the coastline. Many settlements have already disappeared, including Shipden, Clare, Keswick and Wimpell. One eerie image is that of the church tower of St. Mary's, Eccles, which stood alone on the beach after the rest of the church had been washed away. It finally succumbed in 1895 and was buried beneath the sand (Hill, 2012).

Walking on the beach at Happisburgh, it is possible to see the ruins of homes, lost not so long ago, to find pebbles the waves have already worn smooth from their soft, Norfolk brick. To hold them is to remember recent sadness in the place where, in May 2013, the oldest human footprints outside Africa were discovered, being some 850,000 years old (Ashton et al., 2014). So, layer upon layer of history are mixed by the melancholy tides, which are gradually shaping and reshaping the landscape. At any time, a tidal surge could change everything, as it did in the Great Flood of 1953 and as it could so easily have done in 2013, when good preparation and sea defences saved lives and land.

Allowing the poignancy of such a vulnerable landscape to stir the imagination draws us both forward and backwards through the years, giving us a glimpse of how tiny, yet how exquisite our own lives are in the context of millennia of striving, love and loss.

Further inland, the rich waters of Broadland tell their own complex story of humanity's relationship with Earth and Water, for these are not natural freshwater lakes, but inundations of Medieval peat diggings (Lambert et al., 1960; Williamson, 1997). Yet this is a sprowl-filled landscape, where we seek a glimpse of the rare Swallowtail butterfly, admire the stately Heron, and listen, in the hope of hearing the boom of a Bittern in the reeds. A little water from the Broads can be bottled to bring into the home something of their special magic, and for use in ritual. There is also a number of holy wells in Norfolk, whose stories are brimming with magic and whose waters are much prized.

St. Walstan's Well, Bawburgh

This site is just three miles outside Norwich, near the village church of St. Mary and St. Walstan, in Bawburgh. The well itself is down a track beyond the church, just behind some farmhouses. It is encircled by a brick wall and has a slightly dilapidated, wishing-well style roof over it. The water level can be quite low, so anyone requiring some of the water needs to take a mini bucket (the grill over the water prevents the use of a large one) and a good length of string.

Although the historical Walstan was Christian, magical elements of his story shine out to inform all who are open to his message, regardless of any particular religious or spiritual affiliation. He was born in 975 CE in Bawburgh, to a wealthy Anglo-Saxon family with royal connections. Called by a vision to renounce his comfortable life, He gave everything away and walked to Taverham, where he became a humble farm labourer.

The farmer's wife, Nalga, felt sorry for him because he always walked barefoot, and she gave him a pair of shoes. When he gave these away to a beggar, Nalga, incensed by his ingratitude, told him to collect a pile of Brambles, then walk on them as a punishment. In true magical fashion, as he stepped onto the thorny branches, they transformed into a fragrant bed of roses. The symbolism of this tale is rich indeed. There is the magic of transformation, of anger and bitterness turned to love, the magician saved from harm, as well as all the meaning of the plants themselves. It is worth noting that in the context of East Anglian magic, the Bramble, although often associated with the Fair Folk, with making connections and tying things together, is also used to make a sprite flail to banish unwanted spirits. The Rose has numerous associations with love, deities and alchemy, and is important in many traditions worldwide.

Nalga and her husband developed such a love for Walstan that they wanted to make him their heir. He refused and would accept only two white calves, again magical creatures, associated with Druidry, divination and sacrifice.

During his years as a "simple" farm labourer, he healed many of his fellow workers of sickness and injury, and likewise cured many animals of their ills, something which he has continued to do to this day. Walstan felt his death approaching on 30th May 1016, in a field where there was no water for purification before taking the final sacrament. He knelt in prayer, and a well sprang up. Then, at the moment of his death, a white dove was seen to fly from his mouth and up to Heaven. In accordance with his instructions, his body was placed on a cart pulled by the two white Oxen. Followed by a crowd of people, the Oxen made their way to Costessey, where they rested. Here, a second spring began to flow, in a place which is still known as The Roundwell. In an intensely magical spanning of the landscape, the procession's route took them across the two river valleys of the Wensum and the Yare. As the procession approached the rivers, the water became solid, allowing the Oxen, cart and all the people to cross easily. The final resting place of Walstan's body was back in Bawburgh, where he had been born and where, now, the most famous of his three wells appeared (Twinch, 1995; 2004; 2015). Looking across the valleys at the right moment, it is possible to imagine the long line of people, making their way across the landscape on their magical journey.

Many miracles of healing occurred at the well in Bawburgh and, in 1047, Bishop Aethelmar of Elmham had the church rededicated to St. Mary and St. Walstan. The site remained a very popular pilgrimage destination throughout the Middle Ages and the village of Bawburgh thrived as a result. After Thomas Cromwell's "visitors" had done their worst in 1538, during the Reformation, there were no more pilgrimages and the village fell into poverty, as sometimes happens when an ancient sacred site no longer receives the reverence due to it. Pilgrims are returning though. On a recent visit, I noticed a scallop shell (a symbol of pilgrimage) and a red ribbon beautifully placed against the grey and white of the old flint wall of the church. This simple token's magic lifted my spirits and reinforced the subtle power of the saint and his holy place.

Such powerful spiritual forces as those embodied by St. Walstan cannot just be erased from the landscape, and may remerge when they are most needed. A tumble-down forge in nearby Bowthorpe was dedicated as St. Walstan's prayer cell in 1989. There is now a candle where the blacksmith's fire once burned, fresh flowers and, at times, there has been an icon of the saint by Anna Dimascia. This was stolen in 1992, returned in 2000, then stolen again in May 2015. No doubt it will reappear in due course. Local people of all spiritual persuasions make use of the place for prayer and meditation, for it has such a peaceful yet inspiring atmosphere, and an appeal which far transcends the restrictions of organised religion. Children leave little scribbled "spells" for things they want; there are always requests for healing pinned onto a board or left on cards beside the brick chimney, notes of thanks for wishes granted and tributes to people who have died. Some of the notes are desperate indeed, for this is an area where many inhabitants do not have easy lives.

30th May 2016 was the thousandth anniversary of St. Walstan's death. There was a pilgrimage walk, a magnificent flower festival was held in the church, and a special play was written and performed. I even gave a talk about him to Norwich InterFaith Link, stressing that this patron of agriculture has resonances in many traditions, but is rooted in the landscape and the lives of humble folk who work with the soil and the seasons.

Within the Nameless Tradition, St. Walstan represents a more recent aspect of the Lord of Norfolk. While the Grey Lord wields the Flint axe and the arrow, St. Walstan blesses those more modern tools which are born of the fiery forge. He empowers rituals of increase, of protection for garden or field, of consecration of tools, of sowing, planting or harvesting, or for the care and healing of animals. The water from the well, although it may not be safe to drink untreated, is magically beneficial, and can be sprinkled in spells to bless fields, gardens, stables or the pens of small creatures. A little left out in a bowl for the Fair Folk will be much appreciated too.

St. Withburga's Well

Just as St. Walstan is an Anglo-Saxon avatar of the Lord of Norfolk, St. Withburga is an emanation of the Lady. St. Withburga's Well stands within the graveyard of the parish church of St. Nicholas, a short walk from the main shopping street of East Dereham. The area of the well itself is Victorian and probably replaced a 14th-century grotto. It is surrounded by iron railings, within which a flat, paved area leads to an arch with a plaque explaining that this was the original burial site of St. Withburga. There are some flowers there, but the well itself has a wealth of Harts Tongue Ferns growing out of the damp walls, extending even to its darker depths.

The full story is fascinating indeed, and one which is still very much alive in the imaginations of people locally and of great relevance to our magical practice. I wrote of it in my first book (Thomas, 2002), but have no hesitation in revisiting the story, as it is of such importance to our magic. Besides, in the intervening years, I have had many more insights into the meaning of the story and the power of St. Withburga herself.

St. Withburga was the youngest and poorest daughter of the Anglo-Saxon King Anna of East Anglia. When he was killed in battle in 654 CE, she moved from Holkham on the North Coast to East Dereham in Mid-Norfolk and decided to build a nunnery. However, her funds ran dry and she had no way of feeding the workmen. She prayed for assistance and was visited by a vision of the Virgin Mary, who instructed her to send two serving women down to the river, where two Does would stand and allow themselves to be milked. This she did, and the Deer gave the community enough milk to provide for their needs.

All was well until the evil Reeve, jealous of Withburga's success, set out with a hunting party to kill the Deer. However, in an exquisite example of divine or magical protection, before any harm could be done, the Reeve was thrown from his Horse, broke his neck and died. This scene is dramatically depicted on a frieze-like sign which spans the High Street in the centre of the town.

After Withburga's death (the date of which is unclear) and humble burial, many people visited her grave, and there are numerous tales of healing and other miracles. Some fifty-five years later, her uncorrupt body was translated into the church in Dereham (Ridyard, 1988), where the miracles continued. Despite having plenty of holy relics of their own, the monks of Ely were jealous of East Dereham's possession of the remains of such a remarkable saint, and in 974 CE (interestingly, just a year before the birth of St. Walstan), Abbot Brythnoth ordered her body to be translated to Ely. Subterfuge was required as it was clear that the people of Dereham would never willingly give up their saint, so the monks of Ely, on a visit, offered to provide a feast for the Dereham community. They were generous with the alcohol, but remained sober themselves and, while the good folk of Dereham were sleeping off the effects of the party, they made off with Withburga, still in her tomb, put her on a cart and stole her away. The men of Dereham gave chase, as soon as they realised what had befallen, but were unable to catch the thieves. Returning home in despair at their loss, they went to the church to discover that a spring had miraculously risen from the original grave. More miracles occurred at the spring and pilgrims flocked to the site in greater numbers than ever before. The water still retains a reputation for curative properties, although it is not currently advisable to drink it due to the proximity of so many, more recent graves. Meanwhile the bones of St. Withburga and the other Saints of Ely were mostly scattered and lost during Viking attacks on the Abbey, according to the people of Dereham.

Magically, St. Withburga is a gentle provider who will assist in times of genuine need and can be called upon to support various spiritual endeavours. She is both a saint and a goddess, and we work with her accordingly, meditating on her story and ever acknowledging her place within the sacred landscape. Her quiet persistence and the flow of her healing love, in the face of so much jealousy, are much needed qualities in the modern world.

St. Withburga also has significant connections with the Fair Folk. It is said that, during their journey back to Ely, the thieving monks rested at Brandon, before placing St. Withburga on a boat for the remainder of the journey. Nuns from the convent at Thetford made their way down to the river and covered the saint's body with magical Cuckoo Pint flowers (Arum maculatum). This is an interesting floral choice, hardly in keeping with standard notions of Christian purity. The plant's other names include such evocative phrases as Lords and Ladies, Willy Lily, Snake's Meat, and Devils and Angels, so it is certainly a symbol of potency. As the river journey proceeded along the Little Ouse, some of the flowers fell into the water and took root in the banks. Within an hour, the river banks from Brandon to Ely were covered in these delightful flowers, which glowed at night and thus became known by the Fenland lightermen as Fairy Lamps or Shiners (Mabey, 1996).

To call upon St. Withburga, the classic image of her with her two Does may be used. A Deersfoot bell can be rung, and a Deer's skull, some Cuckoo Pint flowers and some Harts Tongue Ferns, placed upon either a white or a red and blue altar cloth. Water from her well is useful too, but is not easy to obtain. However lovely a full Withburga ritual can be, she will also respond to simple requests if the situation is appropriate.

It should be remembered, when working with St. Withburga, that, as a Wuffing princess, she is descended from Odin, via a long line of powerful men and women, many of whom were wonder-workers and magicians and so seen as saints from a Christian perspective, because they had "sanctity in their blood" (Newton, 2018). Even from her earlier years, Withburga was performing acts of magic. A 12th-century Life of St. Withburga tells a tale from her childhood when she was living on the coast, at Holkham. She persuaded her playmates to collect pebbles from the beach and gather them together in a heap, ready for building work, as if a church were to be constructed. Those few stones Withburga collected multiplied, much to the envy of the other children, who tried to scatter her pile of stones. However, when she made the sign of the Cross, the stones clumped back together again "as if rooted and grounded" (Love, 2004) . A church dedicated to St. Withburga still stands on this site today, on a strangely raised mound, surrounded by Deer. No one can say for sure whether this odd landscape feature is natural or man-made. Some say it is an ancient barrow, but many accept that it is the result of Withburga's magic. This fascinating incident in the saint's life, perhaps poorly understood by Goscelin of Saint-Bertin, who recorded it, resonates well with our local magic. Withburga collects the gifts of the Flint Lord, thrown up at a liminal place of meeting between the Elements, and uses his power of building to create something of spiritual value that will endure for centuries. Withburga may well have been weaving connections with the past since, very near to this site, in the heart of Boudica's territory, was an Iron Age fort, and perhaps some of the stone for the new project was being recycled from a much older structure.

Another recurring theme in stories about St. Withburga is that her magic frequently arouses the envy of other people who then try to sabotage what she is doing. Yet St. Withburga is divinely protected, whether by Odin or by the Christian God, and apart from the children, all her opponents come to a violent end.

St. Helen's Well

This is a strangely beautiful spot, which forms a point of connection between the Earth and the leaves and the water of the land itself, the scars of quarrying, echoes of ancient Pagan veneration, faint traces of Anglo-Saxon Christianity, the brutal power of Victorian industrialisation and a new, Pagan appreciation of sacredness. It is in Thetford Forest, not far from the village of Santon Downham, and can be found from the path leading from that village to the car park at Six Mile Bottom. If you are quick, you can also see it from the train between Thetford and Ely, as the line passes right over the top of the sacred waters. Either way, it is easy to miss it.

The Anglo-Saxon church of St. Helen once stood on the verge of heathland, forty feet above the river and some twenty yards from the spring itself, although the holy well, which was probably a place of pilgrimage in both Christian and pre-Christian times, was destroyed long ago, by quarrying for Chalk. It is possible that the coming of the railway may even have saved the sacred pool by putting an end to the quarrying. In the 18th century, it was also known as Tenant's Well and later as Tanner's Well (Clarke and Clarke, 1937). The current pool lies far below where the original church and well must have stood. It is surrounded by Hazels, which at times dip their branches into the water, just as they do in the Irish tales of the Salmon of Wisdom, although in our version no Salmon are visible, for the wisdom is to be sought by other means.

To reach the pool from the path, there is a gentle grassy walkway to the left, or a precipitous clamber down the side of the quarry to the right. Once there, you are likely to lose all sense of time and to emerge several hours later, thinking that only minutes have passed, much in the nature of a visit to Fairyland. You may just gaze into the clear water, examine the flora, chat to the many birds which live there or listen to the large Hazel, which in recent years has been used as a clootie tree by some visitors. (This practice, of tying rags and other offerings to trees at sacred spots, has found its way to us from our more westerly colleagues and is not one which I personally feel particularly comfortable with, mainly because so many people use items made of synthetic materials, which do not rot away like wool or linen, and end up just looking like a lot of litter desecrating the place. It is very rare in Norfolk, though and, even at St. Helen's, there are only ever a few of them.)

Although I have never met anyone else down there, it is obvious from the energy and from some of the items one occasionally finds, that various groups and individuals do a lot of magical work there. Wands can sometimes be respectfully cut from one of the Hazels and the water itself is, of course, very powerful and useful in a variety of magical contexts. St. Helen, or Helen of the Roads (also known as Elen of the Ways) is considered by John and Caitlín Matthews (1985) to be one of Britain's oldest native deities. Since she is associated with travel, water from her well can be used for magic relating to physical journeys, but also to help with pathworkings and with quests to seek ancient knowledge and wisdom. This is a spot which should be visited, if possible, over the Yuletide period, as well as in warmer times of the year, when the vegetation is at its lushest. This chilly visit, armed with festive food and flasks of mulled wine, usually involves a meditation on the imminent new Quest of the Year, and the blessing of the Lady Elen on the path ahead.

Stones of Power

The Flints which find their way to the surface of the land are beautiful and varied but nevertheless quite small. The few larger stones which are found around Norfolk are mostly glacial erratics. Due to their relative rarity, such stones are considered remarkable and are rich in history, often having been meeting places where significant decisions were taken. Unsurprisingly, they have much magical lore associated with them and retain considerable power, which can be drawn upon for magical purposes. This sometimes involves spells but is more often a means of developing our understanding of unwritten history. After all, the memory of stones is deeper and denser than the Mercurial gifts of pen and ink or of the whispered word. The sonorous voices of these stones have a language of their own, unfettered by grammar and vocabulary. They "speak" to one another across the landscape, maintaining, not only their ancient kinship, but also an intricate pattern of silent power lines. The following examples represent just a small selection. There are more which can be sought out.

The Cowell Stone

This stone is to be found on Swaffham Heath, about 150 yards from the B1122 road to Downham Market. It stands at a truly liminal spot, marking a hundred boundary, as well as those of the parishes of Swaffham, Marham and Narborough. Part of the Icknield Way, marked as Peddersty or Saltersty, and the East-West Fincham Drove, which is a Roman road, pass very close to it (Clarke and Clarke, 1937). Its magic draws together the footsteps of the many who have trodden these paths and lived and died in the surrounding parishes.

The origin of the stone's name has a number of possibilities. Ben Ripper (1979) suggests it is named after Cow Hill, or a corruption of coal, since the stone once guided pilgrims to a beacon hill near Colkirk (Coalchurch). The stone used to be situated in a field nearby, where workers sat on it to eat their dinner. However, in the 1980s, it was moved by two local historians, Ben Ripper and Peter Howling, as it was considered to be at risk of damage from ploughing. The move seems not to have disrupted its energy in any way, perhaps because it was conducted with respect and honourable intentions. It has a warm, welcoming energy, one which encourages the seeker to both broaden and deepen their quest for knowledge, not just of stones, but of all aspect of the magic of the land.

The Merton Stone

The Merton Stone, nestled in a shallow marl pit, just off the Peddars Way near the boundary of the parishes of Merton and Threxton, is thought to weigh between twenty and thirty tons and to be the largest glacial erratic in the United Kingdom.

Some people say that to stand on it is a chilling experience, where the presence of malevolent spirits can be felt. However, on a warm, sunny day it is more likely to be a very pleasant, and indeed healing experience. It is well known that, continuing a centuries-old tradition, young ladies wishing to fall pregnant still sit on the stone and find its magic effective. The plants around it, especially the Mugwort, seem to derive extra energy from their proximity to such a powerful character.

There is a long-held local belief that, if the stone is removed, the waters will rise and cover the entire Earth (Clarke and Clarke, 1937). Moving the stone was apparently attempted by the 5th Lord of Walsingham, one of the ancient de Grey family. He assembled all the local men and women, together with much beer and many ropes, but the failed attempt ended in an "erotic debauch". Another attempt to move it, in the 1930s or 40s, this time using a large rotary plough, was equally unsuccessful (Burgess, 2005b), although I have been unable to find out whether this ended the same way as the previous escapade.

The Stockton Stone

The Stockton Stone currently stands on the raised grass verge of a lay-by on the A146, between Beccles and Norwich, just outside the village of Stockton itself. This lichen-covered, sandstone glacial erratic weighs several tons and is said by some to have been an ancient track marker. According to Michael Clarke, it marks the old meeting place of the Clavering hundred, possibly the place where the 10th century Danegeld was paid, although Geldeston, near Beccles, might be a more likely candidate, given its name.

Like the Merton Stone, the Stockton Stone has a curse upon it that anyone who moves it will fall victim to terrible misfortune or death. Much to the consternation of many local people, it was indeed moved, in the 1930s, to accommodate the widening of the road. Not surprisingly, one of the workmen involved collapsed and died.

In spite of its unfortunate location, so close to a very busy road, this stone retains an amazingly powerful energy and people still leave small offerings there. While paying our respects recently, a group of us found a rather attractive blue stone egg, which looked as if it had not been there for very long. Moved by the moment and by the atmosphere, one of our party suggested that we should hold hands and dance around the stone three times, which we duly did, much to the amusement of passing motorists!

The Great Stone of Lyng

This is another erratic brought to us by the glaciers of the Ice Age. There are many local tales surrounding this mysterious Stone, which is said to bleed if pricked with a pin. Some claim the blood is that of victims from a time when the stone was used as a sacrificial altar, while others are of the opinion that it is the blood of those who fell during a ferocious battle between King Edmund and the Danes. Others tell of treasure hidden beneath it and how the landowner has never been able to move the stone to unearth the spoils (Burgess, 2005a).

The grove in which the stone stands, almost hidden beside the path, does have a rather unnerving feel to it. One can "see" all too easily soldiers struggling up the steep escarpment and the bodies of the slain sprawled on the bank to the other side of the path. Rod Chapman informs me that, not so very many years ago, some of the children of the village had to walk through the grove, past the stone, in order to get to school and, in the winter, these children were allowed to leave school early so that they could walk through before it was dark. This is completely understandable. On climbing out of the hollow to the fields above, the atmosphere suddenly changes completely. There is almost a sense of relief and a feeling that one no longer needs to speak in hushed whispers.

There is a recent tale of a brave, tough, yet inexperienced witch who was determined to camp out for a night by the stone, in order to become better acquainted with the ghosts and spirits of the place. He pitched his tent right near the stone and was confident that he would have an interesting and informative night's vigil. However, he became so frightened by the eerie sounds and the terrifying atmosphere that he was forced to run from the place and ring a fellow practitioner to come with their car and rescue him!

The stone does look something like a Dragon and has a hole in it just where the eye would be, which is deep enough for an adult to insert their entire arm. Quite a few people I know have done this and come to no harm, although it is not a pleasant experience.

Not far from the grove, in the middle of a field, are the ruins of a nunnery known as St. Edmund's Chapel, which was said to have been built to honour those who died in the battle.

It has been suggested that Blood's Dale, between Drayton and Hellesdon, on the slopes leading down to the River Wensum, where the Danes are also said to have fought the Anglo-Saxons, may have been the site of King Edmund's death in 896 CE. Abbo of Fleury (870 CE) tells us that King Edmund died at Hellesdon, and Joe Mason (2018) argues convincingly, that the unusual number of churches dedicated to St. Edmund along this stretch of the River Wensum is significant. The survivors, having found the King's severed head with the help of the Wolf, could have taken his body upstream to Lyng, to the aforementioned chapel. Although not fully excavated, some pottery dating from the time of King Edmund, has been found there. Furthermore, an old tithe map refers to the Grove as King's Grove and a map published in the Eastern Daily Press in 1939, names the Great Stone as King Edmund's Stone. Perhaps this would have been a suitable burial place for the miracle-working king? (Mason, 2018) Some of us would like to think so. Certainly, the Ash keys collected from a tree growing on the ruins of the nunnery are particularly effective in assisting those who wish to speak with spirits of the dead.

The Aldeby Rune Stones

Not all our standing stones are ancient, and just as exciting are those being erected now for the benefit of ourselves and of future generations. Aldeby, in South East Norfolk, is a wonderful such example. Here, seven standing stones have been carved with runes and with Christian symbols, and placed around the parish boundary as part of a Millennium project, known as "Pathways in Stone". The runes spell out the name of the village but are also related to the powers of the stones themselves. The Stone of Dawn, for example, features the Day Rune (dagaz) and a Medieval symbol of the World and the four Elements, while the Stone of Wisdom has the God Rune (ansuz) and the square and circle symbol for the material and spiritual worlds. One stone, the Stone of Destiny, combines all the symbols found on the outlying stones, with the addition of the othel rune, symbolizing ancestral land and heritage. The stones are carboniferous limestone, so had to be brought in especially for the project, but in spite of having been in place for a relatively short time, some of them are already giving off some very interesting energy.

These stones form a pilgrimage walk around the village and are best seen in the Winter when they are not obscured by vegetation.

The Druid Stone of St. Andrew's

When Ray Loveday pointed out to me his "Druid Stone", at the North-east corner of St. Andrew's Church, in the centre of Norwich, I was astounded that I had walked down St. Andrew's Hill so many times, admiring the cleverly-knapped Flint of the church wall, without noticing this stone. It is another of those magical items which are hiding in plain sight, but once the attention is drawn to it, the remarkable ancient power it holds becomes apparent. This stone, at least what can be seen of it above ground, is not large, and has a fairly flat top with a number of circular indentations which are often filled with water, and work well as scrying pools. Ray is unsure whether they are a natural feature, were deliberately carved out or have developed over centuries as a result of water dripping from the church roof. There are several smaller, less well-rounded dips too, which tend to get rather muddy. The stone, which has a very feminine feel to it, welcomes small, discrete offerings, such as a ring of twisted Periwinkle stems or a little Daisy chain; nothing too elaborate or containing any artificial materials. It certainly deserves respect and attention, as it appears to form part of the magical foundation of the city.

Dwellings of the Ancestors
As Chris Wood (2019) has written:

> *Humans are nostalgic animals. In general, we have an urge to seek a contact with our ancestors, whether genetic or those who have lived in a place before us.*

It is therefore not surprising that we find ourselves drawn to those places which speak to us of the past and of the lives of our ancestors in the landscape, of their great deeds and their day-to-day concerns.

Warham Camp
One such place, which is thronging with layers of ancestral memoires, is Warham Camp, an Iron Age fort in North West Norfolk, not far from Wells-next-the-Sea. It is on the flood plain of the beautiful River Stiffkey, which now draws an elegant curve around its South and West sides, through the marshy areas which must have provided a useful aid to the fortress' defence. There is a deep moat and a wonderfully chalky, circular earthwork enclosing a 1.5-hectare area, which is full of wild flowers and a single Holm Oak tree near the South Eastern side.

It is not that easy to find as it is hidden down a lane, which leads off a winding, single track road, with high hedges on either side. The lane itself is intensely magical, forming a processional path which aids the transition from the more mundane parts of the journey into the world of the fortress. Ancient Ivy, Bramble and Hawthorn line this path and a sea of gnarled faces watch everything which happens there. On the other side of the vegetation, beings of various kinds move through the arable fields, some flitting, some marching and some apparently riding on horseback. It is often possible to hear them, sometimes quite clearly, to feel their presence and, where the Ivy grows less thickly, to glimpse them out of the corner of the eye, so long as you do not try to look at them directly. Not surprisingly, the Mugwort (Artemesia vulgaris), which grows on the sunnier side of the lane, is some of the best I have ever used, both medicinally and magically, and there have been times when I have made the hour-long journey from the city specially to pick a couple of stems of it for very important purposes.

Climbing over the stile into the field, where the camp has stood for so many centuries, is to forge a tangible link between our own lives and those of Boudica's time, and yet this place is usually so calm and tranquil, speaking to us much more of peaceful natural magic of war.

Walking the path around the top of the inner wall, one is surrounded by the botanical treasures of Chalk upland: there is Scabious, Lady's Bedstraw, Campions, Self Heal, Harebells, Wild Thyme, Daisies, Fairy Flax and much, much more, depending on the time of year. In late September, it is even possible to see Autumn Gentians. The Lady of the Chalk has a strong presence here. The white of her robe shines through the grass and the flowers which are her cloak and her jewels. The Sheep in the next field are at one with her, especially when, at twilight, with a view of both sunset and moonrise, it is hard to distinguish their woolly forms from chalky outcrops.

Then the Barn Owls turn their pale faces towards us and they glide along the line of the river, where the best hunting grounds must be.

For those who love Butterflies, a sunny day here at Lammastide is a treat indeed. There are clouds of them, making a second circle above the ring of the earthworks. They are all wonderful, especially the now declining Chalk Hill Blues (Lysandra coridon), whose Latin name refers to the Arcadian shepherd, Coridon, in Virgil's Eclogues. It is a magical feeling indeed to stand on this ancient earthwork surrounded by such delicate, short-lived creatures. At Lammas in 2013, I lay down on the chalky ground amongst the Harebells and the feeding butterflies while the rest swirled above me. Looking into the sky, which is always magnificent from the vantage point offered by the wall, I saw a Sun halo form: a completely circular rainbow with the Sun at its centre, with two Sun dogs on either side. I was within three circles, between Earth and Sky. They represented at once so many different ideas and possibilities: the Three Crowns of East Anglia, the Three Worlds, the Three Fates and much more besides. It was a breath-taking moment, one of intense blessing and one which I can still picture in my mind as clearly as if I were back there.

Warham is one of those places which are perfect for "sitting out" for hours at a time, just watching the flora and fauna and whatever spirits happen to be passing. There is also a very powerful Ash tree, which is hollow in places and is clearly used for spells, though I have never worked one there. A few of us have just occasionally done some simple ritual work at Warham, each person standing far from the others on top of the wall, working wordlessly through movement and gesture alone. At other times, it is just not appropriate to do anything more than sit quietly and observe and, once or twice, it has been made clear that it is time to go. The atmosphere just changes and we walk immediately back to the gate, turn, bow reverently and proceed back down the lane to the road.

Castle Rising

Equally atmospheric, although in a completely different way, is Castle Rising. The whole sandy area around Castle Rising and North Wootton, just outside King's Lynn, is a place which nurtures and attracts witches, and has done so over the many centuries of its colourful history. Most striking now is the Norman Castle, built in 1176, still standing proud on its mound, above a deep, dry moat. It is possible to walk around most of the castle, to climb the old stone steps and to look out across the countryside as Isabella, "the She-Wolf of France", must have done during her 27-year imprisonment there. Isabella, said to have been the most beautiful woman in Europe, took the throne after she conspired with her lover, Mortimer, in the gruesome murder of her husband, Edward II. However, her own son eventually overthrew her, had Mortimer executed and his mother confined, in not inconsiderable luxury, in Castle Rising (Dutt ,1904). The atmosphere is intense during the daytime, eldritch but unthreatening. Nights however are another matter. There is much pain and anger, and memories you would not wish to make your own.

Not least of the tales of fear and wonder are those related to a mysterious tunnel, claimed by some to have been built on Isabella's orders between the castle and the Red Mount Chapel in King's Lynn. The tunnel is haunted by a beautiful white Wolf, whose eyes are ablaze and whose mouth drips blood. One day a drunken fiddler, by the name of Curtis, boasted that he could walk the 10-mile length of the tunnel, with his dog, playing music as he went. A crowd of people followed the sound of his music coming up through the earth. They traced his tuneful journey to Gaywood, then South Wootton and on to Ling Common, where the music disappeared. Neither Curtis nor his dog were ever seen again, but strange music is still sometimes heard on the Common (Lupton, 2013).

Between 1609 and 1615, Henry Howard, Duke of Northumberland, built the "Rising Hospitall", an almshouse for 12 needy women, who were to be over 56 years of age, literate, honest, single and religious. Their clothing included cloaks and black conical hats! Perhaps counter to the Duke's intention, the women may well have practised their magical arts (Dence, 1980) and, as Nigel Pearson (2015) has suggested, spread their influence to the villages beyond Castle Rising. The building, known as the Trinity Hospital, still stands in the village and houses a number of ladies who, on special occasions, still wear red cloaks with the Howard family crest on them. While their hats are still black, though, they are no longer conical, and I have heard no suggestion that anyone living there now has magical interests.

In September 1963, this area once again achieved notoriety when bricklayer, Conrad Gore, discovered two nude plasticine figures, one man and one woman, nailed to the oak door of Castle Rising Castle. The female figure's heart had been pierced with a Hawthorn, and a Sheep's heart, stuck with 13 thorns, was also nailed to the door. On the floor, there was a circle of soot and fragments of animal bone. A detailed and fanciful interpretation of this, made by "witchcraft and black magic expert", Frank Buckley, was published, and people in King's Lynn began to suspect their friends and neighbours of being either witches or practical jokers. Gossip was further fuelled when similar ritual material was found at the ruins of St. James' church Bawsey the following January, and again at Babbingley church in the February of 1964 (Jones, 1965). The latter episode caused particular consternation, as it was on the royal estate at Sandringham and it was feared that the royal family might be under threat.

Personally, I do not know who was behind any of these incidents, although I have heard rumours. Practitioners of the Nameless Tradition generally prefer to be discrete about spells and rituals and to leave no physical evidence of them.

Caistor St. Edmund / Venta Icenorum

Not far from the present village of Caistor St. Edmund, lies the site of the old town of Venta Icenorum, built under Roman rule as the civitas capital (equivalent to a county town). There have been settlements in this ancient, sacred landscape, near the confluence of the rivers Yare and Tas, since at least the Neolithic. The area has a large concentration of Bronze Age barrows, is only a short distance from the Arminghall henge site and is only 800 metres form the multi-period Harford Farm site, where many significant archaeological finds have been made, including a fabulous Anglo-Saxon brooch, which can be seen in the Castle Museum in Norwich. A walk around the raised wall of what was once the town is a delight at any season. The view is beautiful; there is a wealth of flora to enjoy and the eldritch calls of the Rooks can transport the mind back to the time when the apparently empty square was once a thriving settlement. Time slips easily here.

Once, on a Spring outing with others from the magical community, we stopped beside a Hawthorn on the South wall, initially to listen to the archaeologist who was leading the event. We became aware of a strange rushing and cracking noise. It took us several minutes to realise and to accept that we were hearing the sound of the tree growing, with all the enthusiasm of the time of rising sap. The full details of the lecture I have long since forgotten, but that magical sound has remained in my memory all these years and I will remember it with awe for the rest of my present lifetime.

For those who love the darker side of the plant kingdom, there are some Hemlock plants to be found outside the East wall, not far from the stone crucifix belonging to the nearby church. The tall stems which bear the flowers make excellent stangs for the careful practitioner of dark Moon magic and other such rites, so long as it is remembered that the dry plant material retains its poison. Care should be taking in cutting and transporting it too, as the plant has a powerful spirit. A magical colleague and I once collected a stang each. It was a beautiful Summer's day, sunny and bright, and we were full of life, laughter and a childlike delight at finding such perfect Hemlock stems. We joked, as we cut them, about remembering to wash the knives well afterwards or the next picnic might not go quite as intended. On the way home, the car was filled with a strange and heady scent, not the mousey smell normally associated with this plant. It lifted our spirits all the more, in a manner not entirely conducive to road safety! In retrospect, we wondered whether we should perhaps have been a little more reverential in our approach to such a powerfully poisonous plant, and yet it was the plant spirit itself which encouraged our light-hearted behaviour. As a cold poison, which paralyses the nervous system (it is reputedly the herb used to execute the Greek Philosopher, Socrates), it is ruled by the planet Saturn, but on this occasion and specifically from this sacred spot, there was definitely a Mercurial aspect to it.

A rather darker entity, which can be seen to the West of the town, and must be approached with utmost caution, is the spirit of the Tas, a winding river which rises near New Buckenham and joins the Yare just South of Norwich. Standing at the bend of the river, beside a large Willow tree, it is possible to sense and sometimes even glimpse, a gnarled, ancient, feminine figure, with long, wild hair, draped in river weeds. She is awe-inspiring and terrifying. To her, our little lives are but the blinking of an eye and the rise and decline of the town of Venta Icenorum must seem a recent, but not terribly significant, occurrence in her landscape. She may impart a little of her wisdom, but one must be wary of coming too close or asking too much for she might well demand a greater sacrifice than any of us would willingly give. An awareness of her presence and the opportunity to acknowledge her from a safe distance should be enough.

Arminghall Henge

It would be a serious omission not to mention Arminghall Henge, which, as a site of such great antiquity and probable ceremonial use, is popular with the local Pagan community. It was discovered in 1929, through the aerial photography of Wing Commander Insall. There are two concentric rings, the inner one of which is actually horseshoe shape and, as excavation revealed, had eight massive oak posts dating back four or five thousand years. The posts must have been mature trees, as the holes are 0.90m across and go down to a depth of 2m (Edwards and Wade-Martins, 1987; Taylor, 2015).

A footpath leading to the site is just a short walk from the village of Trowse, going South West, along the aptly named White Horse Lane, and under the Trowse Bypass, which carves its way through the countryside and joins the Southern Bypass which covers the Harford Farm site, mentioned above. There is a pylon in the same field as the henge, overhead power lines and an electricity sub-station close by. I know that there are those who are able to ignore such unfortunate on-lays and tap into the old magic of the place. Indeed, Norwich Pagan Moot regularly held its Winter Solstice ritual there over a number of years. I must admit that it has never appealed to me as a working space, although I am certainly not of the opinion (as some people are) that there is evil emanating from it or that some destructive energy needs to be pinned down. I prefer to just visit occasionally and pay my respects to those ancestors who created what must once have been a site of great power and beauty.

Seahenge

Wooden henges are so much more ephemeral than their stone counterparts, but there is a special magic which remains, even once the physical evidence of their existence has disappeared. This was certainly the case with Seahenge. It mysteriously "appeared" from the sea near the village of Holme-next-the-Sea in North West Norfolk in 1998, and caught the attention of many Norfolk people, of archaeologists, the media, Pagans, locally and nationally, New-Agers and many others. This Bronze-Age structure was not, strictly speaking, a henge (as it had no bank and ditch), but a wooden palisade consisting of fifty-five oak posts, set in a 15-foot-wide, 18-foot-long ellipse surrounding an up-turned oak bole. Many theories emerged as to its purpose, but almost everyone involved recognised the fact that it was special. Not everyone agreed about what should happen to it, however, and the ensuing, bitter battle over its fate saw archaeologists, English Heritage and the Norfolk Wildlife Trust set against the wishes of local people and many within the Pagan community (Wood, 2002).

Few of us were ever able to see it because we heeded the requests of the Wildlife Trust to stay away while the wintering birds were feeding on the mudflats. Before long, in an appalling act of vandalism, a huge chunk of the central bole had been hacked out with a chainsaw for tree-ring analysis. In spite of the fact that the majority of local people wanted it left where it was, even if this did risk it being washed away by the sea, it was dug up and taken to the Bronze-Age centre at Flag Fen, near Peterborough, as a few rootless lumps of preserved timber. More than half of the timbers are now also on display at the museum in King's Lynn.

Terrible as the destruction of Seahenge was, the mudflats and salt marshes still have a wonderfully sacred feel to them, as they are truly liminal spaces between Earth and Sea and Air. Fire too must be acknowledged there when the Sun shines in the wide sky and the flame spirits dance across the water. There is a vast amount of magical energy at all seasons of the year and berries and leaves foraged here are often more delicious and more potent than those gathered from other spots. There is a vast expanse of Sea Buckthorn bushes in the dunes and their delicious, tangy, orange berries are one of the very last of the fruit harvests. Few people pick them, and they scent the air with sticky sweetness as they ripen. Collecting them is a challenge, though, as their spines are plentiful and vicious, but the deliciousness and nutritional benefits of the preserves made from them make all the lacerations worthwhile. At Holme itself, it is possible to find some of the largest shells of anywhere in Norfolk and there is never any shortage of them along the strandline. They make lovely offering bowls for Fairy magic and some of the Oyster shells have been transformed by the sea into little moons.

Along the Coastline

There are not distinct, separate beaches to visit here, rather a wide sweep of coastline, where the energy of one place blends into another, although each has its own, special characteristics. Heacham, for example, has many Cockle shells, along with some other precious beauties, while Old Hunstanton has its sand dunes, beach huts and Rabbits. Titchwell beach is covered in Razor Shells and Holkham is a good place to pick Samphire. Further East, all the way from Sheringham to Cromer is excellent hunting ground for hag stones and elf bolts, while West Runton has its fascinating rock pools. There are places to "sit out" for hours on end, suitable ritual areas and to create sand sculptures as offerings to the sea. We visit them often, to honour the spirits of place, to gather materia magica and to re-energise with the sprowl which abounds there.

St. Benet's Abbey

St. Benet's Abbey is a strange and mysterious place, set in Broadland's special inland watery landscape, which is so rich in history and wildlife. It provides such a curious insight into human interaction with the spiritual forces and energies of the land. The ruin stands beside the River Bure, not far from Ludham, and can be seen from miles away. An especially good view of it, in the context of the surrounding countryside, can be had from the top of the tower of the beautiful and magical church at Ranworth.

St. Benet's was a religious house, thought to have been founded in 800 CE, destroyed by Danish invaders some seventy years later, but revived under King Cnut, who, in 1020, endowed it with such generous gifts of land that it became one of the most important monasteries in East

Anglia. It survived a serious flood in 1287, an attack during the Peasants' Revolt in 1381, and was the only religious house in England to be spared dissolution by Henry VIII. Although only a little of the gatehouse, a few walls and evidence of the fishponds remain, the Bishop of Norwich is still Abbot of St. Benet's and an annual outdoor service is still held there (Snelling, 1974; Pestell, 2008).

It is unclear when the monks abandoned the abbey, but much of the stone was taken for use in other buildings. Sometime during the 18th century, a brick mill was built right into the gatehouse. Its purpose was not drainage, as is so often the case with the mills seen around Broadland, but the crushing of Colza seed to produce lamp oil, a fiery activity indeed, one designed to bring light into darkness. Although the top of the mill, along with its sails, was blown away in a gale in 1863, it is this brick cone which dominates the surrounding area (Snelling, 1974). We have speculated as to the reasons for incorporating the mill into the gatehouse in such a bizarre fashion. Perhaps it was simply to make thrifty use of the existing stone structure, but sometimes it feels as if somebody wanted to restrain or subdue a difficult or unwanted energy of some kind. Were the monks indulging in other than straightforward and virtuous Christian studies? In the 15th century, a complaint was made to the bishop that the monks were kept so busy singing canticles that they had no time for study. Were they being deliberately kept busy to keep them from doing some really interesting magical work? By the 16th century, there were complaints about the number of dogs being kept there, eating food which should have been given to the poor, about the prior not getting up for matins and wearing boots instead of sandals! A suspicion appears to have arisen that the place was obnoxious and that there was a conspiracy of silence (Snelling, 1974; Pestell, 2008).

To appreciate the strangeness of the place, a magical practitioner needs only to stand within the gatehouse mill, looking up at the small circle of sky framed by the top of the cone. Everyone experiences it in their own way, but it does seem to make people want to perform ritual or to invoke or evoke something, whilst at the same time the energy is uncomfortable and problematic.

There may be some link between this and the story of the Ludham Dragon. According to the early-20th-century local historian, William Henry Cook, a Dragon was terrorising the villagers of Ludham, coming out of its lair during the hours of darkness. It was 12-15 feet long, covered in scales and had monstrous teeth. On one occasion, to the horror of the parishioners, it emerged in daylight to bask in the sunshine. One brave soul blocked the entrance to the lair with a large, round rock (not easy to find in Norfolk). The infuriated Dragon bellowed and lashed its tail before making its way along the causeway to the ruined abbey gatehouse. Having beaten the walls with its tail, it then circled round and round, sending mud and stones high into the air before disappearing beneath the gateway, never again to trouble the Ludham villagers (Meeres, 2010). W.H. Cooke's (c. 1912) account of the story, along with his delightful illustration of the Dragon itself, can now be found in the Norfolk Records Office.

I was once fortunate enough to take part in a Ludham Dragon Festival. A large craft fair was held in St. Catherine's church, where I demonstrated spinning and sold some of my own work. The highlight of the day was the appearance of a magnificent green Dragon, created by the parents of a number of children, who walked along inside it. They danced and capered and took obvious delight in chasing a man dressed as a monk. The religious authorities were happy to allow commerce within the church but were insistent that the children must remove their Dragon costume before entering: an interesting example of the uncomfortable relationship between Christianity and primordial energies of the land.

There is a less well-known legend that the Devil, having dug out a barrow-full of gravel at Neatishead, howled with fury when he dropped some of it, thus forming How Hill and dumping the rest at St. Benet's Abbey.

Whatever the power of this place, and however humanity may have twisted and attempted to contain it over time, it retains a kind of enchantment which draws us back time and again, through the village, seeking the broken wooden sign pointing down an inauspicious-looking farm track, which must have been the route taken by the Dragon itself. We have stood by the Cross marking the position of the high altar, and watched the Albion, a black-sailed trading wherry, pass silently along the Bure. We have sought the Dragon at twilight beneath the gate; we have visited in the wind and rain of Winter and basked, Dragon-like on the grass in summer. We have also sought for understanding of this matter in books and records, in stories passed on to us by others and through seeking the memory of the Earth and the stones themselves.

A Field of Bones: East Wretham Heath

The dry, sandy landscape of the Brecks, just over an hour's drive from St. Benet's, offers a very different, yet complementary kind of magic to other areas of the county. One place where this magic is particularly intense is East Wretham Heath, just off the A1075 between Watton and Thetford, a place we often refer to as "The Field of Bones" or "The Bone Place". Walking across the grass, which is cropped short by the nibbling of Rabbits, it is possible to collect basketfuls of the bones of these magical creatures. Rabbits have been an important part of the Breckland economy for centuries, providing fur and meat, with warrens being fiercely protected and poaching severely punished. Rabbits are generally considered to be lucky, magically, and the Rabbit's foot good luck charm is common throughout Britain. However, in both Thetford and Bodney, places which had very large warrens, tales are told of a huge, menacing rabbit, sometimes described in a manner not dissimilar to the more common phantom dog, often known as Black Shuck. Nevertheless, we consider Rabbits to be very lucky and often make little "Lucky Breckland Rabbit" charms, and keep any bones we find. Picked clean and scoured white by wind and Sun, they encapsulate the harsh beauty and magic of the landscape, which holds traces of our ancestors from the receding of the glaciers to the present day (Clarke and Clarke, 1937). In the midst of so many reminders of the passing of generations, human, animal and plant, we feel the intensity of our own existence and a simple handful of Rabbit bones, which carry the memory of the heathland wind, can form a simple charm to enhance our love of life. After all, when Jasper Petulengro, one of the Romany characters in George Borrow's Lavengro (1851), includes the wind on the heath as one of the sweet things of nature, along with the Sun, stars Moon, night and day, he adds, "Who would want to die, brother?"

East Wretham Heath is very much part of Odin/Woden's territory, and it is not difficult to see his solitary, cloaked figure, gliding across the wide grassy expanses or standing motionless beneath the great trees, listening to the constant calling from the vast Rookeries. He wanders too beside the enchanted, mere-folk-inhabited pools of Langmere, Ringmere and Fenmere.

The area is now in the care of the Norfolk Wildlife Trust and has been since 1939, although it was requisitioned for military training during World War II and was part of East Wretham airfield until 1970. How quickly Nature recovers, though. What was once a bunker beside the runway is now home to five different species of bat. Other natural treasures of the site include Woodlarks, Stone Curlews, Dark Mullein, Wall Pepper, Lady's Bedstraw and Viper's Bugloss, not to mention the most magnificent gnarly Scots Pines, which were planted at the time of the Battle of Waterloo (Norfolk Wildlife Trust, n.d.).

Just a mile West of the reserve, on either side of the Harling Drove, lie the largest of the heathland meres,

Fowlmere, noted for its fish and its ice-skating, and the smallest, the Devil's Punchbowl (Clarke and Clarke, 1937). The latter is a completely circular mere, surrounded by Scots Pines and Elder. It is quite a steep climb down to the water, but worth the effort. I am sure the Devil in the name is not the Christian Devil at all, but refers to Odin/Woden, the Allfather of Norse and Anglo-Saxon pantheons, for he certainly walks here too, and the Autumn mists which sometimes hang over the pool are known as "The Devil's Nightcap".

Should any confirmation be needed of the enduring magic of this area, one only has to look at the village sign of East Wretham, erected in 1977. Along with a Ram's head, a kind of Beetle known locally as a "Chovie" or "Chovy", a Norfolk name for a Cockchafer (Marren and Mabey, 2010), and three Partridges, the sign depicts a witch and her Cat on a broomstick, flying over some grassland towards a stand of Conifers.

Magical Trees

Norfolk has a wealth of magical trees adorning the landscape with their gnarly mystery or their stately splendour. One could mention the Bayfield Oak, the Beeches at Felbrigg, the Witches' Tree on Mousehold Heath, and many more, as well as the Breckland Pine rows, the Broadland rows of pollarded Willow and the many magical and ancient woodlands.

The Hethel Thorn

All the great trees and woodlands of the county deserve a visit, but none more so than the Hethel Thorn, which grows in South Norfolk, in a field outside the churchyard on an unexplained earthwork. She is one of the oldest Hawthorns in England and is claimed by some to have grown from the staff of Joseph of Arimathea. She is said to have been the place where peasants met in an uprising during the reign of King John and, fascinatingly, she was referred to as The Witch of Hethel in the 19th century (Barnes and

Williamson, 2011). We still use that title for her today. Whilst one would never take any part of her for magical use, wands or stangs made from other Hawthorn trees can be blessed and empowered by touching the Witch. Thorns for making Albion Knots, which are protective brooches made from Hawthorn adorned with a twist of red wool, are also best if consecrated in the presence of this magnificent being. Sadly, she is currently looking rather sorry for herself. The girth of her trunk was measured at over twelve foot when it was described by Grigor, in 1841, but she is now considerable diminished, and the span of her branches is much less than it was in her prime. She is also weighed down by a huge amount of Ivy, twining thickly around her trunk and smothering her once-magnificent crown. She remains a powerful force of ancient wisdom and protection, though, and is a good place to begin any working involving the rune Thorn or thurisaz, and with the god Thor.

The Witch's Leg
At East Somerton, in the grounds of Burnley Hall, almost hidden amongst the trees and other tall vegetation, the ruins of the Medieval church of St. Mary contain a dark and forceful magic. The Flint walls are covered in Ivy, which drapes in curtains across the remains of archways and windows. To stand inside the roofless building, where the plant life is claiming back its territory, is like stepping into a gothic romance. The place has that special smell of dampness, leaves, moss and forgotten stone, and very little sunlight warms this strange and secret location.

In the middle of the nave is a tall Oak tree, leaning at a strange angle. Legend has it that a witch with a wooden leg was buried alive under the floor. In retaliation, her leg sprouted the Oak tree which destroyed the church. She, of course, is said to haunt the place, along with a number of monks who will poke and prod unwanted visitors. The energy here is not peaceful or easy to work with, and it is important to think twice before taking home any tokens from this place where vengeance is the key motif of the story. However, should one be determined to take revenge for something, with or without regard for the consequences, this is an excellent place to come for counsel on the matter.

Dancing around the tree three times is a way of releasing the witch's spirit, and this I have tried with some magical colleagues, muttering, "Round and round this magic tree, set the witch's spirit free". Having done this, on one occasion, with a group of people (not, I hasten to add, in order to exact revenge on anyone), we noticed a baby Crow sitting in a corner, squawking at us. We listened for a while, noted the message we had been given, then went discretely on our way.

Wayland Wood

In complete contrast to the gloomy mystery of the woodland surrounding the Witch's Leg, Wayland Wood is light and colourful, despite the tragic associations of some of its stories. This piece of ancient woodland is a Site of Special Scientific Interest, currently in the care of the Norfolk Wildlife Trust. The name suggests a connection to the Divine Smith, and Wayland is the name given to the old Anglo-Saxon hundred, the area in which it lies, just to the south of Watton, on the A1075.

It is thought to be some 20,000 years old, dating back to the last Ice Age. It is a small remaining area of the Great Forest which once covered so much of our land, and which still lives in our memories as that powerful magical force, the Enchanted Forest. Wayland is known for its rich flora, including Bluebells, Yellow Archangel, Early Purple Orchids, Wood Anemones, Bugle and Water Avens, and is the only place in Norfolk where the Yellow Star of Bethlehem is known to flower (Norfolk Wildlife Trust, n.d.c). It is home too, to the Golden Pheasant, and seeing that flash of gold amongst the long, wet grass is a sure omen of wealth to come.

Wayland Wood is also known for its Bird Cherry trees. Some of them are tall and stately, while others have bent over with higher branches rooting their tips into the earth and forming exquisite green arbours, in which it is possible to sit and meditate or to make oracular pronouncements. As a species, the Bird Cherry is extremely frost hardy. It covers a vast geographical area and thrives in the chilly climes of Scandinavia, Finland and Russia, where the black Cherries are used to make liqueurs, the wood for carving, and their flowers and bark for various medicinal preparations. The powdered flowers have disinfectant properties and a decoction of the bark can be used to treat coughs and bronchitis and as a mouthwash (Uusitalo 2004). In Britain it is found in woods and by streams in Scotland and Northern England, extending as far South West as the Derbyshire Dales and the gorges of the Welsh Marches (Mabey, 1996). In North Yorkshire it is sometimes called "White Lilac". In Wayland Wood, though, the Bird Cherry is extra special, particularly as this is one of the southernmost places in which it grows naturally.

The Bird Cherry is a fascinating and beautiful deciduous tree, sadly under-appreciated by many in Britain. The blooms remind us of those lands to the North and the magical current which has flowed to us across the North Sea, and a stang or wand made from Bird Cherry wood can help us to enhance that connection. In Sweden, the expression "mellan hägg och syren" (between Bird Cherry and Lilac) denotes the short time that many Swedes consider to be the loveliest of the entire year. Indeed, stately, full-grown Bird Cherries in bloom in the sunshine across a May-time landscape, against the intense blue of a Swedish sky, is a breath-taking sight. They have such an uplifting effect and a powder made from the flowers can help those upon whose shoulders the cares of life weigh heavily. Bird Cherry blooms will also help heal an unrequited love and the wood can be used to detect and remove curses. In Wayland Wood, these lovely trees usually bloom just after Beltane, and fill the place with enchantment. If you catch them at exactly the right moment, you can take home with you a boost of magical energy which can last a good long while. But they bloom only for a very short time and one day's hot sunshine can easily wither them.

There are many Bird Cherries, Oaks, Ashes, Sallows, Field Maples, Hornbeams and Hazels in Wayland Wood, with branches which have been embraced by Honeysuckle or Wild Clematis for so long that they have grown in a spiral shape. These are much prized for wand or stang making.

A more sinister aspect of this sacred place is its association with the Babes in the Wood legend, from which the area derives its alternative name, Wailing Wood. The ballad, Babes in the Wood, was first published by Thomas Millington in 1595, in Norwich. The tale tells that an orphaned girl and boy were placed in their uncle's care. On reaching their majority, they were to inherit their father's estate but, in order to gain that for himself, the unscrupulous uncle hired two murderers to take the children to the wood and do away with them. Although the men were too soft-hearted to carry out the actual killing, they left the children in the wood, where they died of starvation. The well-known tale is supposed to be connected to nearby Griston Hall, and the sign for the town of Watton depicts the babes under the Oak tree where they died, a tree which was said to have been struck by lightning after this sad event.

Some people have seen the shadowy forms of the children flitting amongst the trees, but I cannot claim to have seen any such thing. I have never felt anything but positive energy here, although the entrance may appear a little forbidding at times, and I do know people who sense something uncomfortable in certain areas of the wood. The Fair Folk can be mischievous, though, and may purloin items from unwary picnickers. We always leave them an offering: a little food, some specially made herbal mixture or Fairy perfume, a song or a tune played on a wooden flute, any of which they usually find acceptable.

There are some appealing ritual spaces in Wayland Wood but, as is often the case in Norfolk, we usually find that it is better just to experience the place rather than to impose anything formal upon it.

Foxley Wood

Like Wayland, Foxley Wood is full of Fair Ones, flitting along the paths and darting between the tangled branches, always ready to lead astray the unwary visitor. In this, the largest piece of ancient woodland in the county, dating back 6000 years, it is easy to become "piskie led", as our Cornish cousins would say. Various groups and individuals favour this spot for ritual work, as well as for the gathering of herbs or wood for wands and stangs.

Although the place is well known to all those locally who enjoy country walks (not just magical practitioners), it is rare to see many other people there and it is serene and tranquil most of the time. It may have been considerably busier in the past, when it was of great economic importance, producing good-quality poles, fuel, timber and grazing, as well as bark for the tanning industry. It is even mentioned in the Domesday Book. It went into decline in the 20th Century and sadly, in the 1960s, some of the ancient Oaks were felled to make way for Conifer planting. Fortunately, it has been under the care of the Norfolk Wildlife Trust (n.d.b) since 1988, and is now managed through coppicing, the gradual removal of Conifers and the reinstatement of grazing glades.

Some of the rare treasures which can be seen there are Wild Service Trees, Small Leafed Limes, Midland Hawthorn, the mysterious and magical Herb Paris, as well as White Admiral and Purple Hairstreak butterflies. I am especially fond of the Guelder Rose trees, also known as Cramp Bark, as an excellent medicine can be made from them to relieve pain and help lower blood pressure. The berries are an amazing translucent red and somewhat poisonous if eaten raw. However, they make a very tasty and nutritious jam which glows in the jars with all the richness of rubies.

Magical Gardens

Gardens are liminal spaces, poised between the world of human control and the wildness of Nature. We shape them with our physical effort and with our magical will, to a greater or lesser extent, depending on our skill, time and taste. They are our most convenient places for "sitting out" to commune with deities, spirits, the Fair Folk and wildlife of all kinds. Our gardens are havens of solace and beauty, as well as treasure troves of magical materials and even firewood. Each garden within the Nameless Tradition has its own character and we try to adapt our wishes to the particular requirements of the space, moulding it only in accordance with what is appropriate to its nature. Some willingly produce herbs, fruits and flowers or vegetables, while others are determinedly wild.

Some, like the garden at Mole End, originally created by two practitioners of Traditional Craft, known as the Hermits, welcome rare exotics which flourish happily alongside native plants. There, narrow woodland paths wind between Elder, Laburnum, Show Currant and Hazel, which grow beside amazing Tree Ferns and Chinese Windmills. The ground cover includes unusual Ivies and Lamiums, and the paths lead to a number of arbours and to a greenhouse filled with the fragrance of Tea Roses and Myrtle. There is a magical Circle there, but it is tiny, set at a crossroads of pathways, with discrete stone markers hidden behind Ferns or French Cranesbills. Although the Hermits moved away and now live "over the water", I believe that the new guardians of this place have retained the spirit of what the Hermits had achieved, so its magic continues, although its creators are gone. I think very fondly of the magical times I have spent there. It was a place of crafting and inspiration on so many levels. From an upstairs window, this garden looked like a rain forest, but everything about it was muted and tasteful, like the plumage of the many birds who enjoyed this place of sanctuary when the Hermits lived there. No Cats were allowed, and the familiars were Rabbits and Guinea Pigs. Few people, even within the Nameless Tradition, saw this place, yet the effect of its gentle power cannot be overestimated.

Our gardens are our Green Chapels, our first point of connection with the soil and the changing seasons. Between each of these Green Chapels, which are, or have ever been, a part of the Nameless Tradition, are shimmering, silvery paths which connect them, maintaining a powerful network of magical centres within the county and beyond. We enhance this web by sharing on many different levels. Plants with special connections or stories are given and received. Their spirits remember and reach out to one another across the miles and the years. My garden has Roses from Mole End, Rhubarb from the magical sock-maker down the road, as well as Japanese Anemones and Michaelmas Daisies from the gardens of my childhood. Gifts from further afield include Apple trees from a Green Chapel in Solihull, White Currants from one in Bristol and Bluebells from the Tamar Valley. Likewise, the flow moves in other directions too. I have sent Balsam Poplar trees to many other places, as well as Woad seed, herbs of all kinds and Holly, Yew and Rowan seedlings. Of course, most gardeners love to exchange plants, many without realising that they are performing acts of magic, but when this is done with intent, it can be powerful indeed.

However, it is more than physical seeds and cuttings which spread the magic. Astral seeds from our meditations, spells and rituals are swept up by the smoke of the bonfire or the perfumed curls of incense. They are caught on the breeze and carried like thistledown, swirling and dancing along their airy path. Sometimes we see the results of such seeds reaching their destinations and become aware of new growth and a new flowering. At other times we just trust that what leaves our Green Chapels will flourish beyond the borders of our conscious awareness.

Pathwalking

Most practitioners of the Nameless Tradition love walking. The simple act of putting one foot in front of the other creates a rhythm which enhances our contact with the earth, with the ancestors who have trodden these paths before us and with those who will walk here long after we have gone to the Mole Country. We walk along beaches or city streets; we wander on soft forest tracks which smell rich with leafmould or cross the heathlands and cover our shoes with a fine layer of Breckland sand. As we walk, we observe, we collect, we loosen the edges of our being and let our minds flow out across the land and across the centuries.

There is a number of long-distance pathways which criss-cross the county and sometimes extend much further afield. Some of these may be ancient trackways, while others are more recent paths, but each, in its own way is gathering footsteps and offering its special insights.

The Peddars Way

The Peddars Way is an old Roman road which may well have upgraded pre-existing paths. It begins in Chelmsford, in Essex, and heads towards Norfolk via Ixworth, in Suffolk. The path has a powerful magical resonance, which is exquisitely captured in A Norfolk Songline: Walking the Peddars Way, in which storyteller, Hugh Lupton and artist and sculptor, Liz McGowan, tell, in words and pictures, of a nine-stage journey along the Norfolk section of the Peddars Way. The traveller begins at Knettishall Heath, in the South, and makes their way through Stonebridge, Little Cressingham, Great Palgrave, Castle Acre and Little Massingham, then on to the coast beyond Ringstead. At each point, the traveller has a vision of a tiny moment from the lives of the ancestors, from the Stone Age to the present day.

The Icknield Way

At Knettishall Heath, on the Norfolk-Suffolk border, the Peddars Way National trail, meets the Icknield Way long-distance path, which is based on what T.C. Lethbridge (1957), amongst others, considered to be a prehistoric trackway running along the Chalk from Dorset, along the Ridgeway, along the Chiltern Hills and through Norfolk to the mouth of the Wash. Commentators from Guest (1857) onwards have made a connection between the "Ick" part of the name and the Iceni (the ancient British people of what is now Norfolk and North Suffolk). Romantic as the idea sounds, the path's antiquity is a matter of dispute (Harrison, 2003). However, although he is unconvinced that the Icknield Way is literally ancient, Chris Wood (2019) describes it as "sanctified by tradition", and a place where the presence of ancient peoples can be felt.

It is also a pathway which is lined by the presence of spirit beings. A number of us were walking on Knettishall Heath one Beltanetide. The open stretch of the track had fabulous views in all directions across Breckland forest and farmland. We could see the Exmoor ponies, which are kept to maintain the wildlife area, grazing peacefully in the distance at the woodland edge. We were chatting and laughing, but as the path narrowed and the scent of Hawthorn flowers became more intense, we were required to still our voices and lighten our steps. One of our number had just bought a Deersfoot bell from an antique shop and could not resist occasionally ringing a gentle note upon it, attracting the attention of spirit beings on either side of the path. We could see them flitting beside us, just at the edge of our vision, coming ever closer as twilight approached. They were clearly curious about us, but did not step onto the path, just as we did not step off it.

Marriott's Way

Marriott's Way is a lovely foot, bridle and cycle way, which transports the traveller rapidly from the centre of Norwich to the delights of the surrounding countryside. It is unashamedly recent, returning this corridor of land to peace, tranquillity and a more natural rhythm, after a period of industrial use. It runs along the route of a disused railway lines between Norwich and Aylsham and is named after William Marriott, who was the chief engineer and manager of the Midland and Great Northern Railway.

For much of its length, this path follows the magical Wensum Valley, which has a wealth of wildlife, powerful magical places and so much foraging potential. So, depending upon the time of year, it is possible to return, not only filled with spirament, but with baskets of herbs, Blackberries, feathers, Crab Apples, Sloes and even Oak galls for ink making. It is a very popular place with all kinds of people, from dog walkers to lycra-clad cyclists, commuting to the city, and there is something about this path which lifts the spirits of almost everyone who steps onto it. People always exchange a friendly greeting, and many will stop to chat and sometimes even share their life stories.

While cycling may not have the ancient resonance of walking, it is still simple and magical in its own way. The Marlpit Cunning Man and I often choose to cycle along Marriott's Way because it enables us to cover such a distance in a short time. It offers a different way of appreciating the landscape too, as we pass rapidly, yet still at a human pace, through leafy tunnels, where the track is often muddy, to open fields and a gravely path, through the sandy section which smells of vinegar and under the huge, generous Sweet Chestnuts, where the air is always cool. We often stop on the bridge at Lenwade, eating our sandwiches while we watch all sorts of fish, which the Cunning Man, being something of an expert, can identify with ease. Once we even saw a Pike and, on another occasion, an Otter. In the Spring, we usually try to get as far as the old station at Whitwell because the stretch of track approaching it is lined with the most exquisite Primroses in many shades of yellow, pink and dusky mauve.

Riverside Walk

The city of Norwich is itself a jewel within the landscape. In the 17th century, Thomas Fuller described it as, "either a City in an Orchard or an orchard in a City, so equally are Houses and Trees blended in it". It is a magical place full of magical places, many of which are linked by the Riverside Walk. The River Wensum winds through the city's heart, rich and dark, linking the old and the new. Sometimes, treading the path along the Riverside Walk from Pull's Ferry, past Cow Tower and over the wooden footbridge by the old swan pen, you may hear a number of church bells ring and slip effortlessly into another century. There is so much to see from this path: monks and friars gliding prayerfully to their places of worship, boats on the river bringing merchandise and building materials, the poor and the wealthy going about their business, sometimes legitimately, sometimes furtively.

There is an abundance of plant life, making this an ideal place for a city herb walk. There are stately Horse Chestnut trees, producing an Autumn bounty of shiny conkers, excellent for spells, games and medicine. There are Poplars which, in Summer, cover the ground in a downy fluff, suitable for making Fairy beds or for other spells requiring airy softness and an ability to ride the breeze. There is Alder, Hawthorn, Elder and Weeping Willows which trail their long tresses into the water, as well as enough smaller plants to fill an entire medicine chest. Ducks, Swans and Geese, including the glamorous and exotic Egyptian Geese, glide by or sit on the bank, hopeful of titbits from pedestrians and picnickers. Cormorants often fly over, following the curves of the river, and sometimes one may sit on a small moored boat at Quayside, the old Medieval landing stage. On a really auspicious day, one might be lucky enough to see the electric blue flash of a Kingfisher skimming across the water.

Old and new bridges span the dark waters, providing excellent vantage points for scrying and spell casting. The oldest is the 14th-century Bishop Bridge, the only surviving Medieval bridge in the city, which provides a home for the Dalbenton's Bats, who relish the twilight insect life which throngs above the waters in the Summer, while citizens and tourists alike enjoy their spooky history lessons on the ghost walk. Two semi-circular projections in the parapet mark the position of the two angle turrets of the gate which once stood there (Meeres, 1998). People often stand by the wall of the bridge, lean over, and try to throw a coin into a dip in the top end of one of the wooden posts projecting upwards from the water. It is not easy, but succeeding will bring good luck for the next twenty-four hours at least. It is just a piece of simple, everyday magic, but many people cannot resist the lure of trying it, even if they do not "believe" in such things. I recently pointed out the post to two ladies who were visiting the city from Newmarket. Although they did not succeed in throwing the coin into the right place, they were thrilled to have discovered what they referred to as a "wishing post".

Not far from Bishop Bridge, at a sharp bend in the river, is the Flint and brick Cow Tower, built in the 14th century. It once had three floors, with a large fireplace on the ground floor, and was used as part of the city's defences (Ayers et al. 1998), although it has also been used as a tollhouse and a dungeon (Meeres, 1998). Now it is a home to Pigeons and a source of fascination to many who wander past and long to hear the tales the stones can tell.

There is a popular little beach beside the Cow Tower, where Dogs and children love to play, and where watery spells can easily be sent on their way. On the other side of the path is another example of modern-day magic. In 2014 a memorial "sky watch" seat, of the kind developed for visitors at Minsmere RSPB reserve to lean back and watch the birds, was placed there, in memory of Thomas Leo Keenan Richardson, who loved this riverside spot. He died in 2013 falling from his top floor flat, which had caught fire. The inscription on the seat includes lyrics from Fat Freddy's Drop, "Pull the catch as one", and from Jimi Hendrix' Purple Haze, "Excuse me while I kiss the Sky". There is a Japanese Cherry Tree too, whose protective framework is always covered with Buddhist prayer flags and other offerings left in memory of Thomas. It is a magical shrine to someone who was clearly much loved, and many pause as they pass, to offer their respects.

Energy Lines and Leys

An intricate network of less visible pathways embraces the land, creating a gossamer-fine web linking places of power and significance, and teasing the mind with whispers of ancient magic. The seeking out of leys, lines of power or interesting alignments (and inevitably disputing their nature) is a discipline some within the Nameless Tradition have added to their treasury of skills, poring over old maps, reading old books, perfecting their use of the pendulum and the dowsing rods, walking the ways and drawing on the knowledge in their magical work.

Both Norfolk and Suffolk enjoy a wealth of leys, according to W.A. Dutt who, in a letter to Alfred Watkins, gave the example of fourteen leys connecting the Tasburgh Hill fort with ancient earthworks at Attleborough, Ovington, Wormegay, Wymondham, Mileham, North Elmham, South Creake, Smallburgh, Ilketshall St. John, Bungay, Denton, Rumburgh, Eye, Kenninghall, Garboldisham, Lidgate, Bunwell, New Buckenham, Burwell and possibly Ringland. Watkins also connects place names which include "hole" and "lane" with leys, citing a number of examples in the city of Norwich (Watkins, 1925). It is also not without significance that Watkins identifies the word "dodman" (the Norfolk word for a snail) as meaning an early surveyor, using a pair of staves. He says of the snail:

> *He carries on his head the dodman's implements, the two sighting staves.*

For some, the line which most stirs the imagination is the Michael and Mary Line, which begins at Hopton in the far South East of the county and snakes its way West, all the way to Cornwall. What a wealth of magical places this dual serpent path strings together (Miller and Broadhurst,

1989), following the Sun's journey from dawn to dusk. In the other direction, warm air from the Gulf Stream is carried on the West wind to nurture the plants and creatures of the East. These lines vary in significance, depending on the focus of the individual practitioner, but they form an undeniably powerful East-West flow, nourishing the magical connections between the lands of the rising Sun with those of the setting Sun in distant Cornwall. Although our landscapes are so unlike one another, there is most definitely a strong magical link between the two, and the bonds of kinship between ourselves and our Cornish cousins are a matter for celebration.

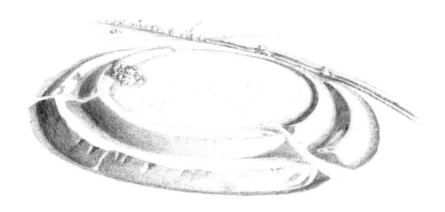

Warham Camp

References

Abbo of Fleury (870) *The Martyrdom of St. Edmund: King of East Anglia* (reproduced in Sweet, Henry (ed.) (1961) *Anglo-Saxon Primer*, Oxford University Press).

Ashton, Nick, Lewis, Simon G., De Groote, Isabelle, Duffy, Sarah M., Bates, Martin, Bates, Richard, Hoare, Peter, Lewis, Mark, Parfitt, Simon A., Peglar, Sylvia, Williams, Craig, and Stringer, Chris (2014) *Hominin Footprints from Early Pleistocene Deposits at Happisburgh*, UK, PLoS ONE 9(2) (available at: https://doi.org/10.1371/journal.pone.0088329, accessed 3rd December 2018).

Ayers, Brian S., Smith, Robert, Tillyard, Margot, and Smith, T. P. (1988). The Cow Tower, Norwich: A Detailed Survey and Partial Reinterpretation, *Medieval Archaeology* 32 pp. 184–207.

Barnes, Gerry and Williamson, Tom (2011) *Ancient Trees in the Landscape: Norfolk's Arboreal Heritage*, Windgather.

Borrow, George Henry (1851) *Lavengro: The Scholar, the Gypsy, the Priest*, John Murray.

Burgess, Mike (2005a) Lyng: The Great Stone of Lyng, *Hidden East Anglia: Landscape Legends of Eastern England* (www.hiddenea.com/norfolkm.htm; accessed 3rd December 2018).

Burgess, Mike (2005b) Merton: The Merton Stone, *Hidden East Anglia: Landscape Legends of Eastern England* (www.hiddenea.com/norfolkm.htm); see also the Merton Green page at www.merton.ukgo.com/ (both accessed 3rd December 2018).

Caister Lifeboat (n.d.) *Saving Lives Since 1791* (www.caisterlifeboat.org.uk/about.html; accessed 3rd December 2018).

Clarke, W.G., and Clarke, R. Rainbird (1937) *In Breckland Wilds*, Second Edition, Heffer.

Dence, Colin S. (1980) *Portrait of a Village: Castle Rising*, self-published.

Dutt, William A. (1904) *Highways and Byways in East Anglia*, Macmillan.

Edwards, Derek, and Wade-Martins, Peter (ed.) (1987) *Norfolk from the Air*, Norfolk Museums Service.

Fuller, Thomas (1662) *The History of the Worthies of England*, Thomas Williams.

Love, Rosalind C. (ed. & trans.) (2004) *Goscelin of Saint-Bertin: The Hagiography of the Female Saints of Ely*, OUP.

Guest, E. (1857) The Four Roman Ways, *The Archaeological Journal* 14, pp. 99-118.

Harrison, Sarah (2003) The Icknield Way: Some Queries, *The Archaeological Journal* 160, pp. 1-22.

Hill, Chris (2012) Photo Gallery: Exhibition reveals secrets of Norfolk's Lost Villages, *Eastern Daily Press*, 19 August, 2012 (available at: https://www.edp24.co.uk/news/environment/photo-gallery-exhibition-reveals-secrets-of-norfolk-s-lost-villages-1-1485864, accessed 3rd December 2018).

Jolly, Cyril (1958) *Henry Blogg of Cromer: The Greatest of the Lifeboat Men*, Harrap.

Jones, Athalston (1965) Witchcraft in King's Lynn, *Fate* (April 1965), pp. 23-32.

Lambert, J.M., Jennings, J.N., Smith, C.T., Green, Charles, & Hutchinson, J.N. (1960) *the Making of the Broads: A Reconsideration of their Origin in the Light of New Evidence*, The Royal Geographical Society.

Lethbridge, T.C. (1957) *Gogmagog: The Buried Gods*, Routledge & Kegan Paul.

Lupton, Hugh (2013) *Norfolk Tales*, The History Press.

Lupton, Hugh and McGowan, Liz (1999) *A Norfolk Songline: Walking the Peddars Way*, Hickathrift Books.

Matthews, John and Caitlín (1985) *The Western Way: A Practical Guide to the Western Mystery Tradition*, Arkana.

Mabey, Richard (1996) *Flora Britannica: The definitive new guide to wild plants, flowers and trees*, Sinclair-Stevenson.

Marren, Peter, and Mabey, Richard (2010) *Bugs Britannica*, Chatto & Windus.

Mason, Joseph C.W. (2018) *St Edmund and the Vikings 869–1066*, Lasse Press.

Meeres, Frank (1998) *A History of Norwich*, Phillimore.

Meeres, Frank (2010) *Paranormal Norfolk*, Amberley.

Miller, Hamish, and Broadhurst, Paul (1989) *The Sun and the Serpent*, Pendragon.

Newton, Sam (2018) *Wonder Women of Anglo-Saxon England*, presentations on a study-day for Wuffing Education, 23rd June 2018, Sutton Hoo.

Norfolk Wildlife Trust (n.d.a) *East Wretham Heath* (www.norfolkwildlifetrust.org.uk/wildlife-in-norfolk/nature-reserves/reserves/east-wretham-heath; see also: https://www.wildlifetrusts.org/choose-your-adventure/time-capsules; both accessed 3rd December 2018).

Norfolk Wildlife Trust (n.d.b) *Foxley Wood* (www.norfolkwildlifetrust.org.uk/wildlife-in-norfolk/nature-reserves/reserves/foxley-wood; accessed 3rd December 2018).

Norfolk Wildlife Trust (n.d.c) *Wayland Wood* (www.norfolkwildlifetrust.org.uk/wildlife-in-norfolk/nature-reserves/reserves/wayland-wood; accessed 3rd December 2018).

Pearson, Nigel (2015) *The Devil's Plantation*, Troy Books.

Pennick, Nigel (2004) *Secrets of East Anglian Magic*, 2nd Edition, Capall Bann.

Pennick Nigel (2015) *Pagan Magic of the Northern Tradition: Customs, Rites and Ceremonies*, Simon and Schuster, Destiny.

Pestell, Tim (2008) *St Benet's Abbey: A Guide and History*, Norfolk Archaeological Trust.

Ridyard, S.J. (1988) *The Royal Saints of Anglo-Saxon England: A Study of West Saxon and East Anglian Cults*, Cambridge University Press.

Ripper, Ben (1979) *Ribbons from the Pedlar's Pack*, Revised Edition, self-published.

RNLI (2015) Henry Blogg: A lifesaving legend, *RNLI Magazine*, 3 June 2015 (available at: https://rnli.org/magazine/magazine-featured-list/2015/june/henry-blogg-a-lifesaving-legend; accessed 3rd December 2018).

Snelling, Joan (1974) *St. Benet's Abbey, Norfolk*, Second Edition, publisher unknown.

Taylor, Patrick (2015) *Timber Circles in the East*, Polystar.

Thomas, Val (2002) *A Witch's Kitchen*, Capall Bann,

Twinch, Carol (1995) *In Search of St Walstan: East Anglia's Enduring Legend*, Media Associates.

Twinch, Carol (2004) *Saint with the Silver Shoes:* The continuing search for St Walstan. Media Associates.

Twinch, Carol (2015) *Saint Walstan:* The Third Search, Media Associates.

Uusitalo, Marja (2004) *European Bird Cherry (Prunus padus L)- a biodiverse wild plant for horticulture*, Agrifood Research Reports 61, MTT Agrifood Research Finland (available at: http://www.mtt.fi/met/pdf/met61.pdf and http://orgprints.org/14845/1/met61.pdf).

Watkins, Alfred (1925) *The Old Straight Track: Its Mounds, Beacons, Moats, Sits and Mark Stones* (Abacus edition, 1974).

Williamson, Tom (1997) *The Norfolk Broads: A landscape history*, Manchester University Press.

Wood, Chris (2002) The Meaning of Seahenge, *3rd Stone*, 43, pp. 49-54 (2016 updated version available at: www.norwichsphere.org.uk/essays).

Wood, Chris (2019) *The Icknield Way: A Heritage Pilgrimage*, in preparation.

Spiritual Beings

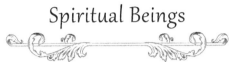

Deities

One of the joys of a Pagan approach to life and to magic is the rich diversity of gods and goddesses who embody ideas and energies, who offer explanations, who inspire artistic, intellectual and magical endeavours, and upon whom we can call for assistance if we wish to. Fortunately, the Lord and Lady of Norfolk are not jealous beings and have welcomed into their lands many deities who have travelled from far-flung realms and found themselves a home in this landscape of Chalk and Flint. These many beings, while retaining much of their original magic, often merge with aspects of the ancient Lady and Lord, who have dwelt here since the land first came into being. Thus, practitioners of the Nameless Tradition may choose to work with any from a vast range of gods and goddesses, from the cold lands to the North and East, the Celtic worlds of the West, from the myth-rich Mediterranean or the Black Land of Egypt. There are even those who find they have an affinity with deities from as far afield as Japan, the Americas or Australasia, perhaps as a result of past life experiences, or something very specific, which is required for now, or will need to be understood for the future. We study those forms of deity to which we find ourselves drawn, which suit our own temperament, or answer questions at any given point upon our magical path.

We seek also to understand the gods and goddesses who offered something to our ancestors, how they were honoured, and whether there are any threads of continuity between ancient spiritual practices and the ways we choose to work today with the Great Ones of Earth and Sky and Sea. The deities of our ancestors can provide a rich source of lore about the land and its relationship with the people who have dwelt upon it over the centuries. Studying these matters can also help us to understand better some of the things we have been inspired to do magically, without necessarily knowing where the connections have come from. Whether or not we decide to work with these remote and sometimes dangerous beings directly, they are nevertheless an essential aspect of the textured magical landscape of the county. They, and their many devotees, have left spiritual resonances which can still guide and inform the work of the modern practitioner. It is therefore beneficial to develop our understanding of them, on all levels, from reading historical and archaeological writings, examining museum artefacts, where possible, and visiting sites associated with them, in addition to engaging our magical senses. Having given due consideration to these deities, practitioners of the Nameless Tradition may then elect to engage magically with them, or may decide that too little is known about them, or that they have not evolved with us sufficiently to ensure that a partnership with them would be either safe or effective. Opinion often differs on this point! This may lead to some interesting discussions but ultimately, each individual craftsperson makes up their own mind and takes responsibility for their own actions, and we all have favourite deities with whom we develop fruitful working relationships.

Romano-British Gods

Not surprisingly, Mercury seems to have been a popular deity in Romano-British Norfolk, with an important temple site at Great Walsingham. Rings from Great Walsingham, North Creake and Saham Toney all have abbreviated inscriptions in his honour (Marsden, 2012). It is indeed still the case that many of Norfolk's magical practitioners are drawn to this versatile, quicksilver being.

So-called TOT rings suggest veneration of the god, Toutatis, and a variety of animal figurines and brooches, including Goats, Cockerels, Ducks, Hares and Leopards are all thought to have had religious significance (Marsden, 2014). There is also a large number of Horse and rider brooches from the vicinity of Hockwold-cum-Wilton and elsewhere, which have been associated with the Celtic goddess, Epona, especially as the Iceni were great Horse breeders (Marsden, 2012), and their coins also depict a Horse, along with what appears to be a wheel and crescent Moons. How like our ancestors we are, in this respect, delighting in creating and wearing jewellery which depicts animals with an affinity to particular gods we favour (or who favour us), or creatures with a special, personal or group totemic significance.

Boudica and Andraste

The Iceni character who most fires the imagination of magical practitioners in Norfolk, is Boudica, whose tale of oppression and ill-treatment, rebellion, and eventual defeat has been told and retold in so many forms. Her courage, her blood and her defiance still nourish the magical soil into which we set our roots; her very name means victory, and her fiery being can still be called upon to protect us or to fill us with the passion and enthusiasm we need for our work. She is there in so much painting and sculpture; her image is passed from person to person on greetings cards; and she is praised in the secret poetry of ritual. We know that she was a physical, historical character, and hence one of the heroes of the land, yet through magic and memory, she now hovers in that misty and mysterious borderland between human hero and deity.

Only the barest bones of the story have come down to us, from the pens of her enemies. The Roman writer, Tacitus, who became Governor of Britain in 78 CE, and Cassius Dio, who was writing nearly two centuries after Boudica's rebellion, are the key literary sources of knowledge about this charismatic heroine. The Iceni tribe, under Boudica's husband, Prasutagus, had a client kingdom arrangement with the Roman Empire, which kept them largely free of imperial interference. However, in 60-61 CE, just as Paulinus was preparing to attack the last stronghold of the Druids in Anglesey, Prasutagus died, leaving half his kingdom to the Roman Emperor and half to his daughters. Dissatisfied, the Roman authorities demanded all the land and the repayment of certain "loans", which the Iceni may well have considered gifts given in exchange for allegiance. When Boudica protested, Procurator Decianus invaded the territory. Boudica was flogged and her daughters raped: not only an appalling act of violence against the women, but also an attack on the royal house, and hence an insult to the entire tribe (Aldhouse-Green, 2006; Wood, 2017).

So, Boudica assembled her 120,000-strong army, and stood before them: a dramatic and inspiring figure, according to Dio:

> *In stature she was very tall, in appearance most terrifying, in the glance of her eye most fierce, and her voice was harsh; a great mass of the tawniest hair fell to her hips; around her neck was a large golden necklace; and she wore a tunic of divers colours over which a thick mantle was fastened with a brooch.*

The speech Dio attributes to her, praises freedom over slavery, and points out the weaknesses of the Romans, who wear armour, and need bread, wine and oil to survive, while the Iceni can live on grass, roots and juice. "Romans", she says are "hares and foxes trying to rule over dogs and wolves". Boudica then released a Hare from under her clothes and interpreted its auspicious path as favouring her enterprise. She then addressed the Goddess Andraste, speaking not in a subservient way but "as a woman speaking to a woman", thanking her and asking for victory.

Following the defeat of Colchester, and later London, Dio claims that the Iceni carried out horrendous atrocities and then made sacrifices to Andate, (he changes the spelling), who was their Goddess of Victory.

However, Boudica's army, which was now 230,000 strong, finally met the army of Paulinus, fresh from its triumph on Anglesey, at a location which is much debated by historians. There was a long battle, but eventually the Britons were defeated. Boudica fell sick and died, was much mourned by her people, and given a costly burial, the site of which remains a mystery. So, successful as Boudica's forces were initially, Andraste did not grant victory in the campaign as a whole. Many Iceni were slaughtered, Boudica was dead, and the Romans tightened their grip on the land. Yet it is Boudica who is remembered now, not Paulinus. It is Boudica and her daughters whose magnificent statue, made by Thornycroft, and unveiled in 1902, stands on the Embankment in London. It is she who is the subject of films, television programmes, novels and songs; it is she whose image overlaps with of Britannia, a female protector of the whole of Britain (Wood, 2017).

But what of Boudica's goddess, Andraste? Most of us within Norfolk's Nameless Tradition consider her too dangerous a goddess to be called upon in anything but the most extreme circumstances. Too little is known of her, other than the price she demands and her apparent relish for blood sacrifice and cruelty. Besides, we are fortunate to live in a time and place of peace, and emphasis on a goddess, whose only known role involves war, may not invoke the right kind of energy for our current circumstances.

Nevertheless, plenty of magical practitioners experience this deity in a very different way. For Norfolk's thriving Goddess Temple, Andraste is a major goddess and those who complete the three-year training programme become Priestesses or Priests of Andraste. Antonella Parker-Hall, Priestess of Andraste of the Norfolk Goddess Temple, kindly provided me with the following information:

Andraste is not just a warrior goddess. There are sacred groves dedicated to her and we look to her also for rites of divination and magic. To see her solely as a destructive force to be used in times of dire need is not our experience. She brings us strength and empowerment in our daily lives and spiritual practice. We experience her as connected to the landscape within which we are living also.

I am grateful to Sadie Huxford, also a Priestess of Andraste of the Norfolk Goddess Temple, for many interesting discussions on this topic. It is very likely that the work of this group is shaping a new approach to, and relationship with, this extremely powerful spiritual force.

Faunus

One named deity, who appears to have been venerated towards the end of the Romano-British period, is Faunus, a Roman god of fields and woodland, of nature, fertility and oracles, who is not unlike the Greek god, Pan. The name Faunus is found on twelve of the thirty-three exquisite, inscribed silver spoons, which form part of the hoard known as the Thetford Treasure, discovered in 1979, at Gallows Hill, just North of Thetford (Johns and Potter, 1983). The site had been a ceremonial complex, dating back to the Bronze Age, but rebuilt at around the time Claudius invaded Britain. The area is near the old Iceni tribal boundary, and the route of the Icknield Way, where many travellers would have passed by (Nash Briggs, 2012).

The spoons, thought to have been made for ritual use of a close-knit group of worshippers of Faunus, include epithets describing him as "Noble" or "Lord", "God of Hoards", "Bringer of Spring Blossom", "Giver of Plenty" and "Shelterer" or "Protector" (Jackson, 1983). These epithets could just as easily be applied to the Lord of Norfolk and have been used in this way in our rituals. Amongst the other objects in the hoard are a ring with a horned face depicted on the bezel, and another with two Woodpeckers, probably a reference to Picus, the Woodpecker God who was father to Faunus. It is possible that the rites of Faunus may have been celebrated in natural places, rather than elaborate temples, with feasting, drinking and ecstatic practices (Johns and Potter, 1983; Marsden, personal communication).

Some archaeologists have suggested that Faunus was the Latin name applied to a more local Earth deity. This might be the character depicted on some Iceni coins, with grain in his hair and beard, and sometimes Ash leaves around him. He is also associated with the Wolf and the Boar (Nash Briggs, 2012). There has even been a suggestion that the practitioners whose magical names are also tantalisingly inscribed on the spoons, may have been part of a witch cult (Johns and Potter, 1983).

Gods from the North

Coins have been used to make connections between the Iron Age gods and the deities from Germany and Scandinavia. One Norfolk coin, struck over 2000 years ago, shows a man with a closed or blinded eye and another, third eye in his mouth, an image which leads Rudd (2011) to suggest that this is a much older counterpart of Odin, who sacrificed an eye in order to gain the wisdom of the runes. Another shows a Wolf chasing the Moon (Nash Briggs, 2012), echoing the Norse story of two Wolves: Hati, who chases the Moon, and Skoll, who pursues the Sun. Such recurrences of pattern are fascinating. While they may not necessarily be evidence of continuity of practice or belief, they do suggest that people notice and honour similar spiritual forces, which are always present within the landscape. Indeed, the Ravens of Brancaster, which have been said to suggest aspects of the Roman Sun God, Apollo, and syncretisation with a more local deity (Marsden, 2014), might also be an older echo of Odin's Hugin and Munin: Thought and Memory. They certainly underline the need to exercise both these faculties.

It is not surprising that many of Norfolk's Traditional Craft practitioners choose to work with the deities whose names and stories came to these lands with the Anglo-Saxons, who began to arrive in the middle of the 5th century. Indeed, the Wuffing Kings of East Anglia traced their ancestry back to Woden, as did many of the Anglo-Saxon royal dynasties. Then, in the late 8th Century, when most of England had been Christianised, the still-Pagan Vikings began their raiding. The first to settle and become "harrowers and ploughers", started to make their homes here in 876 CE, according to The Anglo-Saxon Chronicle (Garmonsway, 1953). So, Woden/Odin, Thor, Frey and Freya and the many other Gods of their pantheon established their presence once again.

The Norse/Anglo-Saxon gods remain a powerful force here. We look up and are reminded of the creation story, in which Odin, Vili and Ve make the sky from Ymir's skull and the clouds from his brains. When we walk through the Cathedral Close in Norwich and hear the eldritch shriek of the Peregrines around the great spire, we think of Freya's magical Falcon-skin cloak, of otherworldly journeying and all the skills of enchantment this goddess has to teach us. It is Freya's blessing we ask for our feline friends, and she we honour with the wearing of jewellery and the collection of beautiful objects. Sif's golden hair is there as the grain ripens in the Lammas fields, and, when we gather the harvest from our fruit trees, we honour Idun and her golden apples of unending youth.

As a god of those who till the soil and care for its creatures, as well as of blacksmiths and all workers of practical crafts, Thor is also a powerful force in our everyday lives. He confers both protection and energy, especially when he drives his Goat-drawn chariot across the sky, hurling his hammer to bring the thunder and lightning. When Thor is raising the storm, we rush out, if we can, and hang our Thor's hammers where they can absorb the magic, and we set out bowls to catch the magical storm water for later use.

Odin's footprints are found on every beach and trackway throughout the county. The swish of his cloak and a glimpse of his wide-brimmed hat are often noted by those who wish to learn from his wisdom and his sacrifice, to look deep into Mimir's Well and to discover the depths of meaning beyond the clear, bright surface of the runes, for those apparently simple forms hold all the mysteries of the universe. The runes are everywhere. It is Nigel Pennick who has taught this generation of Craftspeople to seek them, not only in the bag of runes crafted for divination, but also in the bare twigs of Winter trees. He has shown us the beams of traditionally-constructed homes, where the protection of the algiz rune is embedded in the very structure of the building, and how the inguz rune can be traced in both internal and external brickwork patterning. At any moment, a rune may reveal itself, gleaming and meaningful against the background of the world around us. On one occasion, Nigel had travelled to Norwich to share with us some of his extensive knowledge, for he is one of the greatest of rune masters. Our meeting room had a vertical wooden pillar, crossed by another, at such an angle it formed the nid Rune. Nigel brought this to our attention, as denoting a lack of, or a need for, something. Within minutes, more people arrived unexpectedly, and we could not find enough chairs for them. It was a simple but most instructive example of a kenning.

Craft Deities

There are many spirits or deities who are associated with particular practical craft activities. Weavers may have a god or spirit associated with their loom, blacksmiths might have a special one for their forge, woodcarvers may honour a being who keeps the knives and chisels sharp and shiny. One beautiful example of a local craft deity, whose existence is not secret, is to be found at Andrea Young's Wattlefield Pottery, in South Norfolk. Andrea's bowls, chalices, cups, teapots and other items have a gentle magic to them and exude the love and skill which go into their making, so they grace the kitchens and the altars of many of the practitioners of the Nameless Tradition. The spiritual vibration of her work is noticed by those of other paths too, and she has made chalices and patens for local churches. Her workshop and kiln are in a little brick outbuilding, at the end of a stepping-stone path through her quiet, shady garden. Her kiln god figurine smiles down on all who enter, and this is his story, told in Andrea's own words:

> *Someone once asked me if I had a kiln god. I didn't know what a kiln god was and was told that most potters have a kiln god to protect their firings and to help bring good luck for pleasing results. Glazing and firing can often be unpredictable despite the best of intentions, so it is necessary to have some faith, and to hope and pray that all will be well for when the kiln is finally opened. I was interested to hear about that, but I didn't have a kiln god.*

I went on a two-hour workshop which was a taster session for making figurines. This was something new to me and I enjoyed my session, but ran out of time at the end, and the arms were not in place. Not knowing quite what to do with them, it was almost as if they placed themselves into a thoughtful and meaningful pose, and I was overjoyed by the experience of having tried something new and was very satisfied with my effort.

I took my figurine home and decided that I would put it in one of the kilns at a summer pot camp I go to each year.

During the firing there had been a disaster inside the kiln and a number of kiln shelves had collapsed. Much of the work inside the kiln was either broken, or permanently stuck to other pieces. But my figurine sat there completely unaffected by the calamity surrounding it. I knew it had been looked after and has a special meaning to me. It now sits above my kiln and presides over all of my firings in my workshop.

On the West Wind

There is a strong current which flows into Norfolk from the lands to the West, bringing with it the stories, deities and heroes which make up The Matter of Britain, and which are a unifying force for the diverse landscapes and magics of the Isles of the Wise. Perhaps this is enhanced by the Michael and Mary Lines, which are an open channel of magical East-West communication, drawing our attention to the lands of the setting Sun. Likewise, the magic of the Holy Grail, the goal of the Quest, which is so central to the Arthurian tales, is a compelling concept for all who strive for a deeper understanding of the mysteries of our existence. We are all seekers on the Path, constantly learning and developing our skills, however far we may already have travelled.

So, Arthur, Merlin, the Knights of the Round Table and the Lady of the Lake, be they heroes, gods or some other form of spiritual being which defies categorisation, have all, at times, featured in our magical workings. A particular favourite has always been the well-known story of Sir Gawain and the Green Knight, which has, on several occasions, been the theme of our New Year celebrations. The tale works perfectly as ritual, and encompasses all the magical aspects of the challenge, the harsh journey, glamour, temptation and the strength, not only to fulfil one's promise, but also to return and tell the story. A central image is that of the Green Garter, an emblem of love of life and the protection which is conferred when we are truly ourselves within the physical world of Nature.

From yet further West, across the Irish Sea, the lovely Lady Brigid, or Bride, has also brought blessings to us. Of course, She is a hugely popular saint and goddess, who has spread her blue-sky cloak widely across many lands and spiritual paths. After all, who could not love a Lady who brings wisdom, healing, the fires of inspiration, smithcraft, poetry and good fortune to hearth and home? So, if the wind is westerly at Imbolc, we honour her in our rites, weave a Bride's bed for her of Ivy and sweet herbs, and decorate the house and garden with Bride's crosses. Many are those here who have seen her footprints the next morning or felt the swish of her sky-blue cloak brushing past them.

Exotic

Sometimes deities from a specific landscape and culture make their presence felt in a completely different part of the world, for reasons which we may be able to glimpse, but which are hard to understand completely. Such is certainly the case with the Egyptian goddess, Hathor, who glides through the Field of Reeds of Norfolk's Broadland. Chris Wood (2014) has written at length of the re-enactment of Hathor's myths in the story of the Alan Cozens-Hardy Colman and his sisters, Ethel and Helen. In 1897, Alan, aged only thirty, was dying of tuberculosis. The family took him to Egypt, in the hope that it would benefit him. Sadly, their efforts were to no avail, and Alan died at Luxor, on a Nile cruiser name "Hathor". During the sad trip, Alan's father, Jeremiah, collected many artefacts, which can now be seen in Norwich's Castle Museum. In 1904, Ethel and Helen commissioned, at great expense, a pleasure wherry in Alan's memory, which was to be named "Hathor" and have its internal panelling made from Sycamore wood, not because this is a normal choice for boats, but because the Sycamore Fig is sacred to Hathor. Even the light fittings are designed to include Hathor's menat necklace rattle. As a horned, Sun goddess of music, pleasure, art and beauty, Hathor brings many blessings to Norfolk. When her wherry, now owned by the Norfolk Wherry Yacht Charter, sails up river into the city, people flock to visit and admire her.

There are further echoes of this Lady too. Thorpe Hamlet, the area just to the East of the city (where, incidentally, Alan Cozens-Hardy Colman is buried) is an anagram of Hathor Temple. Here there is a small open place, known as Cary's Meadow, which is rich in magical herbs, supports both Pyramidal and Bee Orchids, has Lizards hiding amongst the Brambles and is thronging with Fair Folk. It is situated beside the river, squashed between a main road and the railway line which takes people out of the city and into the lands of waterways and reeds. It is fitting that, in recent years, during the warmer months, cattle are brought here to graze the rich vegetation. These are Hathor's creatures, for she is often depicted with a Cow's head, and here is an excellent place to call upon her, for those who seek better understanding of her ways and her gifts. The Egyptian Sun God, Ra, may also have found a place in the Norfolk Broads. Britain's first solar-powered boat, which bears his name, has now joined the Hathor on the county's waterways, and regularly takes passengers on boat trips around Whitlingham country park, on the outskirts of Norwich, as well as being seen at Barton Broad and elsewhere.

Of the exotic deities brought to these shores, the Christian God cannot be ignored because the culture which has been built upon his worship has influenced all our upbringings and education, to a greater or lesser extent. The music, the art, the poetry and the craftwork of Christianity are part of our very being, and churches grace the horizon in all directions. Besides, many of those who worked their magic here in the past considered themselves to be Christian and used Christian magic in their spells. As the Venerable Bede tells us, when the Wuffing King Raedwald was baptised, he just added, to his temple, an extra altar to the Christian God, but continued to honour all the others as well. Bede, it has to be said, does not approve of this, but Paganism allows people to work with any number of deities or other spiritual beings.

Of Saints and Heroes

Saints have always had an important role to play in the magic of the land, because those which become popular with practitioners of the esoteric arts usually have significant links to their local landscape or culture, and are often manifestations of spiritual forces which predate Christianisation. Saints are also easy to work with because they have their roots in human experience. They have magical skills, expressed as the working of miracles, and there is an expectation that they will be petitioned for assistance, through Christian prayer, if not by other means. Nigel Pearson has already discussed the importance of saints in East Anglian magic generally, as well as re-telling, amongst others, the tales of St. Fursey, St. Felix, St. Edmund, St. Botolph, St. Etheldreda, St. Walstan and St. Withburga (Pearson, 2015). In the contemporary Nameless Tradition in Norfolk, it is St. Walstan and St. Withburga who resonate most closely with the needs and style of our magical workings (see Chapter Two), defying categorisation as either saints or heroes, and joining us willingly in the timeless, liminal realms of our spellcraft and ritual.

Julian of Norwich

There is another hero who plays a significant role in our magic, and who is spoken of as a saint, although, technically, she was never beatified. Beloved of Christians, Pagans, magical practitioners and mystics of all kinds, is Julian of Norwich, who lived at the end of the 14th and the beginning of the 15th centuries. She was an anchoress, one who had died to the world and lived a solitary life in pursuit of spiritual perfection. She was one of many holy and mystical women in Medieval Norwich, but is the best remembered of them because it was she who wrote Revelations of Divine Love (Spearing and Spearing, 1998), making her (as far as is known) the first woman writer in English.

Her text is the result of a number of "showings" or visions, which Julian received, in 1373, when she was near to death as a result of a serious and painful illness. In what would be regarded, in magical terms, as a shamanic experience, she understood herself to have come into direct contact with God, receiving information which was not just for herself, but meant to be conveyed to others as well.

Julian recovered, and probably lived into the 1420s, not only to write her Revelations, but also to give advice and comfort to many the visitors who sought her wisdom and healing. The most well-known recipient of her valuable guidance was the King's Lynn mystic, Margery Kempe, whose Book of Margery Kempe is said to be the first autobiography in English. Margery made the journey from West Norfolk to Julian's King Street anchorhold, and the two women spent many days together in "holy conversation" (Staley, 2001).

Julian's Revelations resonate with many people today because they emphasise the feminine aspects of divinity and insist that God is our Mother as well as our Father. The best-known, loved and most quoted line from the text tells us that "All shall be well; all manner of things shall be well." This is no trite, sentimental message, but a spiritual challenge to espouse such an optimistic understanding of the human condition in a turbulent world. In Julian's lifetime, two waves of the Black Death nearly halved the population of the city; in 1369 there was a failure of the harvest, leading to serious starvation; eleven years later, during the Peasants' Revolt, there were outbreaks of violence across Norfolk, including an attack on Carrow Abbey, with which Julian was associated (Upjohn, 1989; Ramirez, 2016). This was a time when it was forbidden for women to preach. So, perhaps even more of a threat for people like Julian and Margery, who gave expression to their unconventional experience of religion, was the risk of being linked to the Lollards. They must have known all too well the gruesomely fatal consequences of being found guilty of such heresy. In 1428, according to Foxe's Book of Martyrs, three Lollards were burned at the stake in what is now called Lollards Pit, just a quarter of an hour's walk from Julian's cell.

It is possible to visit Mother Julian's cell, which is now a single room attached to the church on St. Julian's Alley, just opposite Dragon Hall, on King Street. It is a calm and peaceful place, which offers Julian's healing to anyone who is prepared to sit and listen for a while, regardless of their spiritual perspective. This is especially remarkable, given that the original cell was pulled down during the reformation, and the church bombed during World War Two. But Mother Julian's magic is both complex and flexible, and the church and cell were rebuilt so that future generations would be able to benefit from this haven of quiet, so close to the bustle of the city.

Hazelnuts are often used as a charm to help us retain the gifts of Mother Julian. In her Revelations, Julian tells us:

> *In this vision, he [God] showed me a little thing, the size of a hazelnut, and it was round as a ball. I looked at it with the eye of my understanding and thought, "What may this be?" And it was generally answered thus: "It is all that I have made." I marvelled how it might last, for it seemed it might suddenly have sunk into nothing because of its littleness. And I was answered in my understanding: "It lasts for ever, because God loves it."*

The Hazelnut is the microcosm, filled with the potential for understanding all things. It contains the essence of truth and beauty and the mystery of love within creation. So, it can help us both to learn and to teach others, as we follow our intuition and seek, as did Mother Julian, direct communication with divine forces. Meditating with one or a number of Hazelnuts can enliven the spirit and bring either exhilaration or calm, as required. A simple rosary in honour of Mother Julian can be made by stringing together as many Hazelnuts as is numerologically appropriate for a particular spiritual or magical purpose. This can also be worn as a necklace and will become shinier and richer in colour the more it is worn, as the glossy nuts are polished with the oils in the wearer's skin.

Of course, Hazelnuts are well known in many traditions as givers of wisdom, the fire of the creative force, poetry and communication. In the Irish stories, for example, Cormac, on his quest to rescue his wife from the Otherworld, finds a pool surrounded by nine Hazel trees, whose nuts are eaten by the Salmon of Wisdom. From this pool flow the five streams, which are our senses, through which we obtain our knowledge. Yet Hazelnuts also have very down-to-Earth, simple uses, quite apart from being a food of considerable nutritional value. They can enhance the power of healing, be carried as good luck charms and represent wishes. A double Hazelnut carried in a pocket will give the bearer protection against toothache. With its amazing range of grand and everyday magic, it is natural that Mother Julian should choose to use this intensely magical item in her imagery. The Anglican church of St. Julian also uses the Hazelnut as a charm. Near the entrance to the cell is a bowl, made at the Pilgrim Pottery in Trimingham, filled with Hazelnuts for worshippers and pilgrims to take with them as charms.

Some images of Mother Julian show her stroking a Cat. There are two clear reasons for the feline connection. Firstly, the 13th-century guide for anchoresses, Ancrene Wisse, specifically states that "unless need drives you and your director advises it, you must not have any animal except a cat". Secondly, a stained-glass window in Norwich Cathedral shows the Lady Julian with a beautiful ginger Cat at her feet. However, for the magical practitioner, the image of the Cat is multi-layered: it speaks, amongst other things, of the familiar, the magical assistant, a fierce protector, psychic sensitivity and a guide for shamanic journeying. In Julian's case, it also hints at an unexpected and mysterious link to the Goddess Freya.

Will Kemp

In Chapelfield Gardens, in Norwich, there stands an Oak pillar, depicting Tudor musicians and dancers. It was carved by Mark Goldsworthy, in 1999, to mark the 400th anniversary of Will Kemp's "Nine Daies Wonder", in which the comic actor, jester and one-time friend of Shakespeare, "performed in daunce from London to Norwich". His own story of his lively journey, which took him through Bow, Stratford, Brentwood, Ingatestone, Chelmsford, Sudbury, Melford, Clare, Bury, Thetford, Hingham and Rockland, was written in 1600, to refute the slanderous accounts penned by some of the ballad writers of the time.

It contains "many things merry, nothing hurtful", which is key to the essence of the magic offered by this airy and enthusiastic character.

Kemp is a being of the Springtime, for his travels began on the first Monday in Lent and were full of fun and merriment. When he arrived in Norwich, it was to a rapturous welcome. The City Waits played for him, and the Whifflers helped clear onlookers from his path. Nevertheless, in the market place, a hapless "homely maide" came too close, and Kemp accidentally trod on her petticoat while fetching a leap. Much to the woman's embarrassment, the garment fell off, revealing her coarse under-smock, which as Kemp notes, was fortunately clean. At one point, so many people were thronging close to see him, that he was forced to leap over the wall of the churchyard of St. John Maddermarket to escape the crowds, an incident which is now commemorated with a plaque.

Kemp remains a popular and well-remembered character. One of Norwich's Morris sides, Kemp's Men, is named after their famous predecessor, and this side were amongst many from all over the UK who re-enacted the Nine Daies Wonder, in 1999.

For all his frivolity, there is a more serious aspect to this character, which can be useful to draw upon. At various points along the way, he is forced to show considerable determination, in order to continue with his plan. Quite apart from the physical rigours of the feat, of which he complains little, he has to avoid well-meaning crowds which often block his way and risk stopping his dance. He avoids alcohol and over-eating, and refuses to give in to various distractions which present themselves. Kemp makes light of all this in his tale, stressing his gratitude for the attention and kindness he receives in the places he visits. So, when we need to be resolute, and persevere with a project, without making heavy weather of the situation, the energy of Will Kemp can help us dance our way to success. It is also not without significance that Will kemp was well paid for his efforts, being awarded

40 shillings annually, for life, by the Mayor of Norwich. Magically welcoming Will Kemp is easily done, with bells, ribbons, music and dance and poetry, especially when it is in rhyming couplets. Writing one's own verse is always good, but it also works very well to use the welcome written for him over 400 years ago by Norwich citizen, Thomas Gilbert:

With hart, and hand, among the rest,
Especially, you welcome are:
Long looked for, as a welcome guest,
Come now at last you be from farre
Of most within the Citty sure,
Many good wishes you have had.
Each one did pray you might indure,
With courage good the match you made
Intend they did with gladsome hearts,
Like your well willers you to meet:
Know also they'l doe their parts,
Eyther in field or house to greete
More you than any with you came
Procur,d thereto with trump and fame.

Robert Kett

An earthier and more serious-minded character, albeit with echoes of more famous and more Mercurial heroes, like Robin Hood, is Robert Kett. A somewhat unlikely hero, Kett was a respectable yeoman farmer and tanner, who espoused the cause of the disaffected peasantry, who were suffering from the enclosure, by the gentry, of the common lands, where people had been able to graze their animals and make a living. In 1549, in Wymondham, anti-enclosure rioters began to pull down the fences of one John Flowerdew, an unpopular lawyer, who was a neighbour and rival of Robert Kett. Flowerdew bribed the crowd to go and pull down Kett's fences instead. Kett was so moved by the "poore commons'" arguments, that he not only joined them in destroying his own fences, but also agreed to become their leader, in what was known, at the time, as the "comoyson in Norfolk", and nowadays, as Kett's Rebellion.

Kett and his followers marched towards Norwich, passing the tree which is now called Kett's Oak. Here, Kett is reputed to have made a speech in which he declared:

> *I want to subdue the power of great men and am ready to sacrifice my substance and my very life, so highly do I esteem the cause in which we are engaged. (Hoare, 2016)*

On July 12th, Kett set up camp on Mousehold Heath, overlooking the city, and occupied the deserted St. Michael's Chapel, which became known as Kett's Castle. These ruins are now a good place for meditation, ritual, or just for a picnic. The centre of the camp was another Oak tree, the Oak of Reformation, where justice was dispensed, and arguments settled. Sadly, that tree is not still standing, for it symbolised the idealism and morality of the 15,000 strong camp. Kett did not see himself as a traitor, and emphasised the importance of order, legality and fair play.

Initially, the rebels managed to capture the city and, at the end of July, even defeated the royal army which had been sent to crush them. In the process, they killed the army's second in command, Lord Sheffield who, when captured, removed his helmet, wrongly expecting to be ransomed. However, a second, more ruthless force, led by Lord Warwick, with his German and Swiss mercenaries, would prove too much for Kett's army. At a meeting on Bishop Bridge, Warwick's herald offered to pardon all but Kett himself. The herald's words and tone were so objectionable that a young lad bared his buttocks at the delegation. He was shot and killed by the herald's bodyguard, destroying any hope of a peaceful solution.

Fighting ensued, and by 25th August, Warwick's forces had control of the city. The following day, the rebels chose to move from their strategic camp on the Heath, to a place, probably to the North of the city, called Dussindale. (This is most likely not the area which is known as Dussindale today.) This decision may well have been guided by an ancient prophecy:

The country gnoffes, Hob, Dick and Hick
With clubs and clouted shoon,
Shall fill the vale of Dussindale
With slaughtered bodies soon.

However, after a seven-hour battle, it was 3000 of Kett's fighters who lay slaughtered. Many of the survivors were executed, and the reprisals were only halted when Warwick pointed out that, if the gentry killed too many of the peasants, they would have to plough and harrow their own lands!

Kett himself was captured and, with his brother, William, taken to the Tower of London. They were tried, on the same day as the leaders of the Western Rebellion, found guilty of high treason and condemned to death. On 7th December, Kett was hanged in chains, from Norwich Castle, where his body was left to rot in public view. William was hanged from the tower of Wymondham Abbey.

400 years later, Robert Kett finally received recognition, with a plaque on the wall of the Castle, which states:

...This memorial was placed here by the citizens of Norwich in reparation and honour to a notable and courageous leader in the long struggle of the common people of England to escape from a servile life into the freedom of just conditions.

Whether anyone was working magically with the spiritual energy of Robert Kett, at that time, I do not know. Nevertheless, it is often the case that calling upon the memory of significant characters from the past, causes tangible ripples in the mundane as well as the magical realms. After all, Odin's Ravens teach us the importance of memory in our work. So, fifty years after the plaque had been unveiled, a small group of us had been consistently including Robert Kett in our rituals, over a sustained period of time. Two members of the group submitted a joint design for that year's Norwich Beer Festival logo competition. The image depicted Robert Kett and a Norwich Dragon, drinking beer under an Oak tree. The design won, and Robert Kett was seen on glasses, T-shirts and stickers throughout the beer festival and beyond. Local story-teller, Paul Jackson, retold the tale in a moving performance at Kett's Heights, as the area where Kett's Castle used to be is now called. It was a beautiful August evening and, as twilight fell, Paul, standing on the ruined, Flint walls of the "castle", reached the story's dramatic and tragic conclusion. Many people in the audience were moved to tears, and few were unaware of the shadowy crowds who had been drawn to us, 450 years after they had lived this tale.

On December 7th that year, a number of us made a large, fragrant garland, including Ivy, Rosemary and Periwinkle, and in a simple ceremony that evening, placed it beneath the plaque at the castle. Each of us contributed a few thoughts, and Paul sang, his clear, deep voice echoing out across the festive lights of the city.

Energies of the past wax and wane, according to the needs of the present, and the attention paid to them, but their magic is always there, written into the earth and etched onto the walls which still bear witness to the events. In 2004, Kett's memory once more bubbled to the surface, demanding both magical attention and something in the physical realms to anchor his presence in today's community. This coincided with money having become available to erect a village sign for Thorpe Hamlet, the area of Norwich which includes the site of Kett's Camp, Bishop Bridge and the Oak of Reformation. Blacksmith, Dave Capes, was commissioned to make the sign, which includes a view of the cathedral, an image of the broken enclosure fences, and the leafy face of the Green Lion, who is the symbol of the Friends of nearby Lion Wood.

It was unveiled by the Lord Mayor of Norwich on 28th May 2004.

Kett's story is currently reaching a wider audience, with the publication of Tombland (2018) by the best-selling author of historical fiction, C.J. Sansom. The novel intertwines the tale of a murder investigation by the London lawyer, Shardlake, with a wonderful retelling of the story of Kett's Rebellion. Sansom says of his novel:

> *I hope that "Tombland", which is fiction but based on primary and secondary sources, may help carry the story of Kett's Rebellion and the 1549 rebellions as a whole to a wider audience.*

Needless to say, this novel is proving very popular among practitioners of the Nameless Tradition here.

Finding the Fair Folk of Norfolk

Norfolk Fair Folk can be shy and elusive, well-camouflaged against the background of plants and animals with whom they live in close proximity. They may be glimpsed slipping amongst the nodding Reed heads on a breezy day in Broadland, or standing as still as the majestic Heron beside the water's edge. One may dart away into the trees, like the rare Red Squirrel of Thetford Forest, or shuffle through dry leaves, making only the sound of a foraging Blackbird. They are there in the marsh gas of the Fens and sometimes in the play of light in pools or foliage, or even in the shiny paintwork of cars. Some love Ivy, especially that which reclaims the ruins of old churches. All around the long curve of our coastline, they may be concealed in the dunes, blend with the shingle or feed with the waders on the saltmarshes. They are as varied as the beautiful landscape of the county itself, and differ vastly from one another, in size, form, in their likes and dislikes and in their attitudes to humanity. Not surprisingly, they are known by a multitude of names, such as Pharisees, Frairies, Ferishers, Hikey Sprites to name but a few.

Seeking the Norfolk Fair Folk in the many published works available on the subject of fairy lore provides only limited information, since such writings tend to focus far more on upon the Fairy Faith of the Celtic lands. It has been suggested that it was the power of Puritanism in the East of England which led to suppression of much local fairy knowledge (Clarke, 2014). Indeed, The Fairies' Farewell by Richard Corbet (1582-1635), who was a poet as well as being a Bishop of Norwich, provides an interesting insight into the Fairies' dislike of Protestant ways:

Farewell rewards and Fairies
Good Housewives now may say
But now fould sluts in dairies
Do fare as well as they
And though they sweep their hearths no less
That maids were wont to do
Yet who of late for cleanliness
Finds sixpence in her shoe.
By which we note the fairies
Were of the old profession;
Their songs were Ave Maries,
Their dances were procession.

(Reproduced in Glyde, 1872)
The whole poem includes much of the popular beliefs about Fairies, in particular their rewarding of cleanliness and punishment of the slatternly housewife as well as the need for secrecy in dealing with them.

The loss of cooperation between the human and fairy worlds, again possibly due in part to Puritan influence, is encapsulated in the Fenland story The Stranger's Share. In this tale, the Strangers, Little People, Greencoaties or Earthkin are a mere handspan tall, with hands and arms as thin as thread, big feet and hands, long noses and strange faces. They wear grass-green jackets and breeches, and yellow bonnets which look like toadstools. They are a part of everyday life, running and playing and dancing, sometimes mischievous but not threatening. However, people back then were aware that, should they be upset, all green things would wither, harvests fail and the people go hungry. So, the first fruits and flowers, of field and garden were offered to them on the large flat stones, where they could often be seen dancing. But there came a time when the marsh people forgot them. As Kevin Crossley Holland (1997) says in his version of the tale:

> *Maybe they went more to church and thought less about the Strangers, and the customs of their fathers; maybe they forgot the old tales their grandfathers had told them; or maybe they thought they'd grown so wise that they knew better than all the generations before them.*

Inevitably, when the offerings cease, and the Strangers are left to hunger and thirst, harvests fail, people and animals fall sick and die, and everything anyone tries to do goes "arsy versy". It is not until the marsh people resolve to be reconciled with the Strangers that things slowly improve, although they are never truly the same again.

There is much practical advice in such stories, which the magical practitioner does well to heed. We make sure that we remember to set out food and drink for the Fair Ones of the garden, in special, attractive vessels, and to bring them small gifts if we have been out and about. Another very important lesson of The Strangers' Share story is that the Fair Ones should be given the first fruits of everything which is harvested. We always, therefore, make a point of setting out the first Radish of the season, the first Tomato, Blackcurrant, Pear or Apple, in a special place in the garden.

It is from the Fenland areas of the West of the county and into Lincolnshire and Cambridgeshire that some of the most popular and best-remembered tales derive, perhaps because of the difficulties of living in such a landscape, with its ever-present threat of being sucked into a bog or of contracting malaria. These stories are full of magical, faerie-like beings: the Lantern Man or Jack O'Lantern who lures people to their doom, Will O' the Wisps, Boggarts and Bogles. It is important to give them gifts to keep them friendly.

Tiddy Mun is a Fenland water spirit, said to have a call like that of a Peewit, although I have never heard it myself. He has long white hair and beard, all matted and tangled, and a long grey gown so that he can hardly be seen when he creeps about in the evening mist. He is more benevolent than many of the other spirits and often helps people by stopping the water rising too near to their homes. In a cautionary tale, not unlike The Strangers' Share, he is angered by the draining of the Fens and brings down a curse upon the people until he is pacified by offerings of water and prayers that the curse be lifted (Briggs, 2002). This is generally considered to be a Lincolnshire tale, having been "collected" there by Mary Balfour in 1891, but Tiddy Mun is certainly still acknowledged in West Norfolk. The Norfolk Green bus company's bus number 123 is even named Tiddy Mun. He was also part of a 2014 summer celebration of Fenland tales at King's Lynn Museum, where his stories were told, along with those of the Greencoaties, and children had the opportunity to make a protecting spirit mask to keep. So, the tradition continues, albeit in a modern form, although it is also worth remembering that the Fenland landscape spirits still take human lives, when they have a mind to. Fewer people may be so obviously lured into bogs by Will O' the Wisps, but many a traveller still meets a watery death in the dykes besides some of the most notoriously dangerous roads in Britain.

The making of images of Fair Folk is an important way for people to connect with the tradition. Artist, craftsman and writer Ray Loveday published Hikey Sprites, The Twilight of a Norfolk Tradition in 2009. At the Norwich Mind, Body and Spirit Festival of that year, he not only sold copies of the book, but also twig figures of these spikey characters, which proved very popular and really revived local interest in these entities. Not long after the publication of Ray's book, I found a Hikey Sprite made with twigs and Willow binding sitting on the step of one of the cottages at the Anglo-Saxon village at West Stow in Suffolk. The book and the figures have certainly helped fulfil the author's wish, expressed in the preface to the book:

> *Compiled from the recollections of many, mainly elderly, Norfolk people, it will hopefully offer a helping hand to the Hyter Sprites and give them a foothold into the future.*

From the recollections documented in the book, it is worth noting that the use of the word Hikey Sprite and its many variations (Hyter Sprite, Highty Sprighty, Hikey Pike, Sprikey, Hoighty Toight) is fairly widespread throughout the county, with particular hotspots, in Winterton and Acle, and with the exception of the areas to the far West, whose Fenland beings have more in common with those of Cambridgeshire and Lincolnshire. However, the Lantern Man and the Will O' the Wisps are sometimes linked to the Hikey Sprites in the popular imagination, even in the East of the county, which also has its fair share of treacherous boggy areas and potentially dangerous waterways. Some people associated the Hikey Sprites with the glow-worms which once adorned the hedgerows but are now sadly a rarity, others with a threat to children as something which would "get them" if they stayed out too late in the evening. Not surprisingly, they are most often seen at those liminal times of dawn and dusk.

In Secrets of East Anglian Magic, Nigel Pennick (2004) describes Hytersprites as sandy-coloured and green-eyed, as being helpful or destructive to humans depending on how they are treated, and of sometimes flying around in the form of Sand Martins. He also tells of the sprites who are the spiritual guardians of an area:

Each dusk, the sprites that compose the Ward assemble at a sacred place in the village, and then travel by way of their sprite paths to their watch places...At night, if it has human acknowledgement and support, the Ward creates a protective magical ring around the town.

Pennick goes on to say that most settlements are now wardless due to the failure of humans to acknowledge the Ward. However, in my own area, only twenty minutes walk from the centre of Norwich, I have often been aware of the twilight gathering of these helpful sprites, perhaps because we have consistently worked land-related magic in the same place for over two decades, and there are certainly others doing similar magical work in the vicinity. Much has now been written about the importance of wildlife habitats in towns and cities. It may be that urban gardens have also become an important refuge for some of the Fair Folk, who have been displaced from rural areas, rendered gast by agribusiness and by the turning of settlements into no more than dormitory villages, or clusters of second homes, visited only occasionally.

In complete contrast to Hikey sprites and the Ward, there is the 12th-century story of two completely green children, found in Woolpit, Suffolk, as reported by Ralph Coggeshill in 1189. They had crawled through a tunnel from another, twilight world and were unable to return when blinded by the sun. The only food they would eat was green Beans (reputedly the food of the dead and, in my experience, much loved by the Fair Folk as offerings). The boy pined and died but the girl grew up, lost her green colour and married a local farmer, although she was always somewhat wanton in her behaviour! I quote this famous Suffolk tale as Faeries are no respecters of county boundaries and there have been Norfolk incidences of Faery children entrusted to human care, as well as those of mortals kidnapped and taken to Fairyland (Glyde 1872). Norfolk also has stories of green people. The

Green Lady is a sinister Bluebeard type of story, in which a green-skinned mistress and her daughter decapitate disobedient servants until they are outwitted by the youngest and tricked by some Gooseberry bushes into throwing themselves into the river where they drown (Lupton, 2013).

No green beings appear in Glyde's 1872 account of Fairies or Pharisees who:

> *...seem to stand midway between the purely spiritual and the natural, being able to go through a keyhole, and yet perform manual labour that is of great service to an industrious man.*

He tells of a ploughman given a hot cake as a reward for mending a peel (a flat iron for removing bread from the oven) and a clean, hard-working man whom the Fairies reward with a shilling left under a chair leg, and with assistance in cutting and gathering firewood. However, when he ignores their warnings and tells of his good fortune, he never sees them again.

The ploughman receives a cake, but it is often a Fairy or Pharisee Loaf, which is given to a mortal out of charity. Such loaves remain fresh and are always the same size, so long as the source remains secret (Bane, 2013).

Another ploughman is given a shilling each day by a fairy, but eventually is unable to use the gift, which turns to a curse when he loses his job, as a result of people's suspicions of him (Lupton, 2013). Likewise, the apparent good fortune of Tom, the lazy farm labourer, who releases, from under a stone, Yallery Brown, a creature no bigger than a baby, but with long, tangled yellow hair, a beard, black eyes and brown skin, turns sour when other workers turn against him and the farmer sacks him. When Tom becomes angry with Yallery Brown and refuses further help, the Faerie turns against him and completely ruins the rest of his life (Crossley-Holland, 1997).

115

Working with the Fair Folk is not a straightforward or entirely safe matter. Just like people, these beings are all different, have their own likes and dislikes, and can be quick to take offence, with dire consequences. However, many of the cautionary tales about the terrible havoc that the Fair Ones can wreak are perhaps designed to deter people from benefiting from what can be a very fruitful relationship, if sensibly and respectfully conducted.

Although caution and discretion in the matter of one's dealings with the Fair Folk, in whatever form they take, is necessary, I have been given permission to write about various personal encounters between them and local witches and magicians. These accounts illustrate the rich diversity of Fair Beings, still very much alive and active across Norfolk.

Traditional witch, Michael Clarke, was returning home from an astronomical lecture at the Seething observatory "in a completely scientific mood", not thinking about any esoteric matters, even though Seething Common is in a particularly charged-up area of many manifestations, not only of Faeries but of such threatening beings as Black Shuck and The Hateful Thing. Seething also suffers less than anywhere else in the county from light pollution. Michael caught, in his headlights, a being about the size of a ten- or twelve-year-old with a face "like a grown-up child", wearing a cloak and hood completely covered in white, grey and black scales. Having driven a further 100 yards down the road, he returned to the spot within 30 seconds to a minute, but all trace of the being was gone. There were no marks, not even animal tracks. What struck Michael most were the polished-scale clothes, which he described as being akin to the mithril suits in Tolkien's stories.

A completely different type of manifestation was experienced by magical practitioner Vicki Dolley who, as a child of ten or eleven years old, used to go out to seek the Faeries on East Rudham Common, which was near her home. She describes the Faeries as "quite orby, especially when the sun hit something." She always sensed activity in the place and never felt alone. Going there frequently made the spirits of the place respond more, not surprisingly, since paying proper attention to the Fair Folk is an important part of the tradition throughout the county. Recently, we visited East Rudham Common with Vicki, who had not been there for many years. We wandered through a dense area of trees near the water and out into a more open, grassy area, noting the changing atmosphere, the faces peering out at us, and some very impressive Stinkhorns. Vicki casually said that she had never found any bones on the Common but would love to have some from there. Clearly the Fair Ones were listening, and still favoured her, for we had not gone more than a few steps when she found a perfect Rabbit skull and some leg bones. They do not forget those who treat them properly.

Creating or restoring places can also work wonders, as demonstrated by the work of the Hermits previously of Mole End, whose Mid-Norfolk garden, created from a wasteland of concrete and rubble (see Chapter 2) became a Fairy haven. Once the plants became established, Faery beings about a foot high, clad in yellow and brown, could be seen dancing outside the kitchen window first thing in the morning. The Hermits considered this to be a blessing and enjoyed watching them, but never tried to communicate or interact with them directly. This account underlines not only the importance of the garden as a pleasing place for Faeries to enjoy, but also the power of the magical act of transforming a gast wasteland into a flourishing, enlivened spot, echoing of course the symbolism of the Grail Quest. It is a fascinating phenomenon that many of the places which have become Faerie "hot spots" are those which have been industrial, but which Nature has reclaimed, with or without the help of human hand. Many of these are now exquisitely beautiful, and some are even so full of wildlife that they have become Sites of Special Scientific Interest, but they all retain a strange and inexplicable quality, borne of the memory of destruction and restoration.

In my own experience, I have found that the performance of any kind of magical act, practical or ritualistic, can attract the Fair Folk. On a particularly memorable occasion in November 1998, I had performed a ritual in my garden, late one frosty night, with the Chaos Magician, Anton Channing. It was a beautiful two-part working, in which the energy of shooting stars, collected at the coast, was made into some much-needed talismans for an important, but difficult occasion. As we were leaving the garden, we both looked back at the Circle and saw white, misty beings dancing exactly where we had just been working. We watched, entranced, for a few moments, but felt that we should not intrude, so bowed our respects and left them to their work. I know these white beings to be closely connected with the Chalk, and with the Lady of Norfolk.

These same white, Fair Ones are often seen in a woodland area, now generally known as Lion Wood, which is only a short walk from the centre of Norwich. It is thought to be a remnant of ancient woodland and used to be called Bluebell Wood. Bluebells are strongly associated with the Fair Folk, as it is the ringing of the bells, inaudible to most human ears, which calls the Faeries to their meetings. Many local practitioners have seen, or at least sensed Fair Ones in Lion Wood. They are very close to humans, fascinated and attracted by our magical activities. At any time of day or night, it is possible to glimpse one out of the corner of your eye, as it flits between the Beeches and the Birches, or ducks under a gnarly Hornbeam trunk. My clearest visual experience of them here was in exactly the spot where Nigel Pennick had, not long previously, created a labyrinth for a Friends of Lion Wood event. It had been a labyrinth made of sawdust, which was meticulously cleared away at the end of the afternoon. Nevertheless, a little group of Faery revellers were following precisely the winding path which

Nigel had laid out and performing a much more agile and elegant dance than we had managed.

Faerie doctors have always been an important part of Celtic tradition (Briggs, 2002) and there are tales of healing carried out by Fair Beings in Norfolk. One such example comes from the grandmother of one of the aforementioned Hermits, who lived in East Norfolk, not far from Great Yarmouth. In the 1970s, she told her grandson the story of a time, years earlier, when she had been so grievously ill that the family had taken the unusual and radical step of calling the doctor. However, he was baffled and could provide neither diagnosis nor effective medical assistance, and the patient was expected to die. That night the girl was aware of Faeries dancing on top of the covers as she lay in bed. By the next morning she was completely well, as if nothing had ever been the matter. She was apparently a completely practical, down to earth, no-nonsense type of woman with no belief in ghosts or any other "superstitions". Nevertheless, she maintained that her life had been saved by these Faerie healers. Clearly the Fair Folk have not abandoned the people of Norfolk. However, we do need to remember to pay these beings due attention, make offerings to them, bring them gifts, honour the Ward and help to restore those places which humans have rendered gast.

Corbet in the 17th Century and Glyde in the 19th may have noted a decline in Faerie belief, yet these beings still weave the threads of their lore into the fabric of our everyday and our magical lives, providing a great source of help for the traditional practitioner working closely with the land.

Merfolk

Merfolk are important to the magic of most places with an abundance of water, and Norfolk is no exception. Every mere in the Brecks, every stretch of Broadland's waterways and all around our long coastline there are Mermaids or

Mermen to be found. However, they are mostly shy, secretive beings, who will usually only work with, or even reveal themselves to those who live in the vicinity and pay them attention on a regular basis. Neither would they wish to be spoken about openly. There are depictions of Mermaids to be discovered around the county, for example, the Mermaid carving on one of the Medieval stalls in the chancel of St. Botoloph's church in Grimston, West Norfolk (who has sadly lost her arms), and on a pew end of St. Margaret's, Cley. On one of the misericords in Norwich cathedral, there is a rather saucy Mermaid suckling a Lion. (It is also curious that the city of Norfolk, in Virginia, USA, chose the Mermaid as its symbol in 2002.)

However, the Mermaid of Sheringham, one of Norfolk's best-known Mermaids, welcomes attention and will work with those who can only visit her occasionally. She has many gifts to offer those who approach her with due respect, including holidaymakers who are lucky enough to discover her. A physical representation of this beautiful being is to be found in the church of All Saints, Upper Sheringham. This church is famous for its fabulous, carved, 15th-century pew ends, and offers an array of fascinating beasts of all kinds, including a wyvern, dogs in all shapes and sizes, a Cat with a kitten, and a swaddled baby. The Mermaid herself is carved into the pew end nearest the door, and hanging, in a frame, from the pew is one version of her story. It tells how the Mermaid made her way from the sea, all the way up the hill to the church, because she wanted to hear the sermon. The Beadle, who saw her peeping in at the door, became angry, threw her out and slammed the door in her face, declaiming loudly that he wanted no Merfolk in his church. The Mermaid was undeterred; she crept back and has been sitting at the back of the church ever since. There seems to be considerable wishful thinking in this Christian interpretation. Another story tells that she sought refuge from a storm at sea, but once again, this seems unlikely. Besides, there are churches in the town of Sheringham which are much closer to the sea. It seems far more likely that this magical creature would be interested in the music, for which Merfolk are known to have a great fondness.

The Mermaid is described as being exquisitely beautiful. Her face is the colour of moonstone, framed with silver green hair, and decorated with seaweed, pearly shells and tiny pink crabs.

Another interesting aspect of the story is that, directly outside the church, there stands a lovely water feature, known as Abbot Upcher's Conduit. It was made in 1814, from one of the many springs along the Cromer ridge, and was the sole public source of water in the village until as late as 1950. It has a circular brick wall, and a Flint and brick gateway, with a lovely, deep, wide pool, easily large enough for a Mermaid to bathe in should she feel a little dry while enjoying the music. Of course, her arrival in Upper Sheringham long predates the construction of the conduit, but there is a magical connection being made here between the sacred waters of the sea and the sacred waters which spring from the Chalk.

By working magically with the Mermaid of Sheringham and her stories, it is possible to enhance our determination to carry through a creative, spiritual or educational project, since she herself would not be put off from achieving her goal, even in the face of such rude rejection of her as was offered by the objectionable Beadle. The flow of sacred water outside her church also reflects the continuing flow of the creative force, which does not just run dry after the initial inspiration, but allows it to be continually refreshed.

It is a good idea to visit her first in the church, and offer her a gift, perhaps in the form of a song or a poem in her honour, or a tiny item which can placed discretely under the pew. This may then be followed by a simple ritual performed on the beach, using only items found there. It works best at twilight, when the Moon is almost full. On one occasion, when it had been cloudy all day, the Moon appeared at the opening of the rite, as if the Mermaid herself was smiling at us. As soon as the rite drew to a close, her face disappeared, and the rain began to fall: her tears perhaps at the cruelty and lack of understanding of so much of human behaviour?

Another way to honour the Mermaid is by sculpting her in the sand at low tide. Her hair can be made in seaweed and the best and pearliest shells sought out to adorn her. As with all offerings, the more effort which goes into such artwork, the better the magical effect, and the transitory nature of the finished piece makes it all the more powerful. It is often the case that even the least talented artist will be inspired under such circumstances to create something really beautiful. Nevertheless, it is better, magically, to resist the temptation to photograph the work. To retain the magic of the Mermaid, it is possible to make a small bottle spell, with a small Mermaid charm (ideally carved from driftwood) suspended from the cork, and some sand, shells and a little Seaweed placed within it.

The Mermaid of Sheringham is clearly closely connected to the Mermaid of Zennor, hundreds of miles away to the West, who was enticed out of the water by wonderful singing in the church, in particular by the voice of the chorister, Matthew Trewhella, whom she later lured away to live with her in the ocean. It would seem that the congregation of the Zennor church treated this Mermaid more politely than did the Beadle of Upper Sheringham, for they merely wondered at the mysterious stranger (Potts, 2000). Both Mermaids were carved into pew ends, although they are very different in appearance. The Mermaid of Zennor is carved, in relief, into a flat bench end, while the Mermaid of Sheringham is sculpted, in the round, on top of the buttress of a bench end.

Many of the spiritual beings with whom we work, have their special ways of making their presence felt when they wish to attract our magical attention for some reason. The day after writing (and to my knowledge, completing) this section on Merfolk, I attended a beautiful and moving lecture by

Norfolk archaeologist, artist and cunning woman, Imogen Ashwin, about the work and legacy of her late husband, Trevor. Among some of the lovely images she shared, was one of a spring, not far from Aylsham, called The Mermaid's Head, the source of the small Mermaid River, which is a tributary of the Bure. So, the story continues and there is always more to be discovered.

Dragons

The energy of Dragons provides Norfolk magic with much of its vigour and vivacity, and some Norfolk Dragons appear in many forms, some more and some less terrifying than the one which menaced the good folk of Ludham (see Chapter 2). The highest concentration and greatest variety of these fabulous beasts is to be found in Norwich, which is often referred to as "a Dragon City".

It is best to approach the Matter of Dragons by first seeking them out in their physical form. The effect of walking around the city, visiting them in the places they have inhabited for centuries (in some cases), then researching the historical background of each one, and the traditions associated with them, forms the foundation for later meditations, pathworking and ritual. My personal favourites among the city's Dragons include one in the spandrel to the right of the arched column, on the city side of the Ethelbert Gate. The crouched and snarling Dragon faces a bearded St. George, who leans forward and, with a long sword, menaces the Dragon, from the curve of the opposite side of the arch. The Dragon slayer is forever separated from his adversary by the road which runs between them and, these days, by a constant stream of cars driving beneath them, and onto the cobbles, to enter the Cathedral Close.

Another favourite is also a spandrel Dragon, intricately carved in wood, in the Medieval trading hall, built by Robert Toppes, in King Street, which is now known as Dragon Hall. The body and the fierce head of this Dragon are painted green. Her mouth is open to reveal six fearsome teeth and a long, undulating tongue. She has fabulous claws and a wonderfully elaborate tail and red wings (now somewhat faded). As is so often the case in Dragon lore, if you would work magically with her, you must first seek out her name.

The magical importance of Dragons in Norwich is paralleled by their long connection with the City's civic functions and pageantry. Every July, the City holds a Lord Mayor's Procession, which is headed by two whifflers, whose job it is to clear the route of people or of evil spirits, and Snap, who is a red and green dragon with snapping jaws. They are followed by the Lord Mayor, city dignitaries and numerous colourful floats, full of costumed characters, musicians and dancers. Huge crowds of people turn out each year to the line the streets through which the procession passes, to laugh and cheer, and to donate to charities.

This modern event is part of a long tradition, dating back to the celebrations of the Guild of St. George, a religious and charitable organisation, founded in 1385. They paraded from the Guildhall to the Cathedral, with the Dragon, St. George and sword-bearing whifflers and the musicians, the City Waits. The first written evidence for the Dragon is to be found in the Assembly records for 1408, and it is known that the early Dragons produced fire and smoke, using gunpowder. Since that made the operation of Snap a rather dangerous process, requiring considerable skill, the man inside received danger money (Pennick, 1997). Unsurprisingly, modern Snaps do not use gunpowder.

In 1532, St. Margaret joined the procession, and was sometimes referred to by the more magical names of "The Maid" or "The Lady". Another Dragon saint, the Christian Margaret was imprisoned by the Pagan prefect of Antioch, Olybrius, whose sexual advances she had rejected. He tried to force Margaret to renounce her Christianity, which she refused to do. While in prison Margaret was swallowed by a Dragon. However, from inside the Dragon's belly, she made the sign of the Cross, and was able to burst out unharmed, for which feat, she is now the patron saint of childbirth! In St. Helen's church, Bishopgate, there is a Medieval carving on a pew end, depicting Margaret's escape. The poor Dragon looks extremely sorry for itself, but fortunately, most of Norwich's Dragons fare considerably better.

Indeed, during the Reformation, in the 16th century, both the saints were banned from the procession, but the resolution stated that the Dragon would be allowed to remain "to come forth and shew himself, as in other years". He was never allowed into the Cathedral though, and when the procession went inside to attend the divine service, the Dragon was left outside on a special Dragon Stone.

The Norwich Snap is a tradition of "remarkable continuity" (Pennick, 1997). Whilst regular official ceremonies featuring him ceased in the 1850s, he was brought out on a number of important occasions in the 20th century, including the celebrations for the Festival of Britain in 1951. Today's Lord Mayor's Procession grew out of a Snap Festival in 1976, and he has delighted the people of the City ever since (Salt, 2010).

Snap has always been made of canvas, stretched over a wicker frame, and painted, so tends to be quite fragile. There have therefore been a number of them over the years, some of which have been preserved in Norwich Castle Museum. It is interesting to note that the sound of the Dragon's jaws is made by two horseshoes in its mouth, which snap together when the operator works the mechanism. This reinforces the magical connection between the Horse and the Dragon, and between Snap and the horse-skull "Ickeny" (see Chapter 8), which has made a much more recent appearance in the magical life of the City.

The suburbs of Norwich have also had long traditions of Dragons, such as the Pockthorpe Dragon, which was first paraded in 1772, another tradition which continued into the 20th century, but has sadly not yet been revived. This was a mischievous Dragon, by all accounts, who stole people's hats. The rhyme associated with this little piece of misrule, goes "Snap, snap, steal a boy's cap; give a penny he'll give it back" (Pennick, 1997). In Costessey, an extremely magical place to the West of the City, and home to many magical practitioners, past and present, the Guild had a Snapdragon, which took part in the Mock Mayor's events, the last one of which was in 1895.

A number of local artists have been inspired to make new Dragons. The Mighty Klang, for example, was created in 2000, to be the first new City Dragon for the new millennium. He is made of CDs, so is wonderfully shiny and reflective, and has had a number of attendants, including St. Margaret, Dick Fool, a Mock Mayor and two smaller Dragons. Dragon art has been an important feature of another Dragon-related tradition in the City, CAMRA's Norwich Beer Festival, which started in 1977 and has run every year since then, except 1978. The glasses for the event always feature a Dragon, and over the years, many delightful Dragon images have been produced.

Thus, the Dragons of Norfolk, and of Norwich in particular, span the earthly and the enchanted realms. They are much associated with wealth, but mainly the kind which comes from hard work, such as that which was generated by the merchant who owned Dragon Hall. Dragons are full of passion and creativity, but nothing comes from nothing, as the old story tells us, and so, like most spiritual beings, they demand commitment in both the magical and the mundane aspects of life.

Acknowlegements

Many thanks to Michael Clarke, Vicki Dolley and The Hermits-across-the-Water for sharing their personal experiences.

Bibliography and References

Aldhouse-Green, Miranda (2006) *Boudica Britannia: Rebel, war-leader and queen*, Pearson.

Bane, Theresa (2013) *Encyclopaedia of Fairies in World Folklore and Mythology*, McFarland.

Briggs, Katherine (1978) *The Vanishing People*, Batsford.

Clarke, Michael (2014) personal communication.

Crossley-Holland, Kevin (1997) *The Old Stories*, Colt.

Coggeshill, Ralph (1189) *Chronicum Anglicanum*.

Dio, Cassius *Roman History* 62 (Loeb edition, 1925).

Garmonsway, G.N. (trans.) (1953) *The Anglo-Saxon Chronicle*, Dent.

Glyde, John (1872) *A Norfolk Garland*, Jarrold.

Harte, Jeremy (2004) *Explore Fairy Traditions*, Heart of Albion Press.

Hoare, Adrian (2016) *On the trail of Kett's Rebellion in Norfolk 1549: Places, people and events*, Adrian Hoare.

Heslop, T. A., Mellings, Elizabeth, and Thøfner, Margit (eds.) (2012) *Art, Faith and Place in East Anglia: From Prehistory to the Present*, Boydell.

Jackson, Kenneth (1983) The Inscriptions on the Silver Spoons, in Johns and Potter (1983), pp. 46-8.

Johns, Catherine, and Potter, Timothy (1983) *The Thetford Treasure: Roman Jewellery and Silver*, British Museum.

Kemp, William (1600) *Kemps nine daies wonder: performed in a daunce from London to Norwich* Nicholas Ling (Larks Press edition, 1985).

Loveday, Ray (2009) *Hikey Sprites, The Twilight of a Norfolk Tradition*, George R. Reeve.

Lupton, Hugh (2013) *Norfolk Folk Tales*, The History Press.

Marsden, Adrian (2012) Piety from the Ploughsoil: Religion in Roman Norfolk Through Recent Metal-Detector Finds, in Heslop *et al.* (2012), pp. 50-65.

Marsden, Adrian (2014) Satyrs, Leopards, Riders and Ravens: Anthropomorphic and Zoomorphic Objects from Roman Norfolk: A safari through the county's religious landscape, in Ashley, Steven, and Marsden, Adrian (eds.) *Landscapes and Artefacts: Studies in East Anglian Archaeology Presented to Andrew Rogerson, Archaeopress*, pp. 45-72.

Nash Briggs, Daphne (2012) Sacred Image and Regional Identity in Late-Prehistoric Norfolk, in Heslop *et al.* (2012), pp. 30-49.

Pearson, Nigel (2015) *The Devil's Plantation: East Anglian Lore, Witchcraft and Folk Magic*, Troy.

Pennick, Nigel (2004) *Secrets of East Anglian Magic*, second edition, Capall Bann.

Potts, Marc (2000) *The Mythologies of the Mermaid and Her Kin*, Capall Bann

Ramirez, Janina (2016) *Julian of Norwich:* A very brief history, SPCK.

Rudd, Chris (2011) The Eye of God, *Treasure Hunting*, September 2011, pp. 21-3.

Salt, Peter (2010) Snap: *The Norwich Dragon*, Snap & Co.

Sansom, C.J. (2018) *Tombland*, Mantle.

Spearing, Elizabeth (trans.), and Spearing, A.C. (1998) *Julian of Norwich: Revelations of Divine Love*, Penguin.

Staley, Lynn (trans. & ed.) (2001) *The Book of Margery Kempe*, W.W. Norton.

Upjohn, Sheila (1989) *In Search of Julian of Norwich*, Darton, Longman and Todd.

Wood, Chris (2014) Hathor: Death on the Nile, Life on the Broads, *Quest* 178.

Wood, Chris (2017) Boudica: Britannia Victorious? *Quest* 192, pp. 27-32.

The Quest of the Year

Norfolk magic is so closely linked to the land, that the passing of the seasons and the significant events within the natural world are an integral part of our practice. Even those of us who live in the larger towns, like King's Lynn, Thetford, Great Yarmouth or the city of Norwich itself, spend as much time as we can outside. Indeed, in Norwich, we are blessed with many beautiful places within easy walking distance of the city centre.

Each year that passes is a magical quest through the changing landscape around us: a journey through light and dark, through growth and decay, through warmth and the cold. We mark and celebrate certain points as seasonal festivals. Very often we choose those eight major compass points of the Wheel of the Year, corresponding also to times of day and phases of our lives. These have the advantage of having been adopted by most of the modern Pagan community, so there tends to be a magical focus then, and a combining of the powerful intent of many groups and individuals, not just in Norfolk, but across the country and beyond. However, there are those of us who choose to celebrate a particular harvest or natural occurrence which is of more local or personal significance. This could be anything from a special saint's day to the first blooming of a favourite flower, the opening of the leaves of a totem tree, the shearing of one's own flock of sheep or the departure of the last swallow.

Another significant aspect of the Quest of the Year is the acknowledgement that the seasonal celebrations are only part of this annual journey. They generally occur every six weeks or so, but the magical and practical work undertaken during that intervening time is of great importance. What, after all would be the point of celebrating the harvest if none had been gathered, or the coming of the first frost if no preparations had been made for the dark and the cold months ahead? The work required of us may not necessarily be in the fields or the greenhouse, but it is of the land and the prevailing conditions, meteorologically and magically. It might involve spells woven, art or craft works created, poetry, music or articles written, a healing technique learned, or magical places visited. The important thing is that each of us has connected in some genuine, spiritual or magical way to natural currents of the county. Following the Quest of the Year requires more than merely attending seasonal rituals and parties, pleasant as that is. This is why our seasonal rites always involve the presentation of an offering of some kind to symbolise what we have achieved or contributed. Such an offering may be exquisitely simple or fabulously elaborate and complex, but it should be beautiful in the eyes of the deities and spirits to whom it is presented.

At every festival, and from one year to the next, our offerings will vary, just as our magical work will have done. On one level, every year follows a set pattern, but at the same time, each is unique, with its own special energy, its own form of abundance and its peculiar crop failures, be that of Apples, Cabbages, certain spells or magical projects. This is why, in the Nameless Tradition of Norfolk Magic, we never repeat a ritual exactly. Each one is written especially for that occasion, taking into consideration the prevailing energies. It is rare indeed for the details of a ritual to be fully determined more than a few days before it is due to take place. This helps to ensure that our magic truly reflects the emerging patterns on the great Tapestry of Wyrd.

The rhymes which precede the thoughts about each seasonal festival in this chapter were written for a special occasion in 2004, by Andy, Pammie and Julie, and are reproduced with their permission. The symbols are the East Anglian symbols for the festivals and were given to us by Nigel Pennick.

When the Year Begins

Almost any moment of the year could be considered its starting point, for every month embraces some form of planting, of harvesting and of clearing away, and the Sacred Wheel spirals through time with no beginning and no end. Some choose Samhain, the time of the ancestors, considered to be New Year by those on a Wiccan or Celtic path. Others prefer Yule, when the Sun is reborn. One could also select the feast of Imbolc, more or less in line with the Chinese New Year, or the Spring Equinox, when Iranians celebrate Nowruz. At various times we need to "turn over a new leaf", but any new Moon can provide us with that opportunity.

Twelfth Night

My first it is the upward spear,
Gifting the young for the coming year.

Practitioners of the Nameless Tradition usually regard Twelfth Night as the first step on the Quest of the Year, the time when work restarts after the Yuletide festivities. This mysterious but powerful festival has been forgotten or ignored by many who prefer the strictly eightfold Wheel of the Year. However, it is a moment of great potential power, which can set the tone for the coming months, and is therefore considered to be of great importance in Norfolk Magic.

This ninth festival has various names and may well be celebrated upon the day that the Yuletide decorations are removed. For many of us, those decorations consist

131

largely of greenery. Holly and Ivy festoon the ceiling and are draped from every available picture, bookcase or hook. There is also the Mistletoe and maybe a tree, but it all makes for a lovely bright bonfire, having been indoors for a couple of weeks and dried out to perfection. Casting the leaves and branches into the flames is a way of releasing their magic, through the power of transformation, and at the same time, a way of giving thanks for the abundance and joy of the festivities.

By the end of the Yuletide celebrations, most of us feel it is time to get on with ever-pressing tasks. Burning these symbols of the celebrations is a way of empowering the start of those tasks.

By Twelfth Night the lengthening of the days is clearly noticeable, and the bright flames remind us of that too. Many people feel, during the Yuletide period, as the Light begins to win against the Dark, that the creatures of darkness can be at their most dangerous – vampires and such like are on the loose. Only when Twelfth Night is reached is victory certain and the dark forces pushed back, for this season at least.

Thinking mythically about the ninth festival, in terms of the story of the God and Goddess, is another fruitful approach. If you think of the Sun/Son being born at Yule and each day after that representing one sign of the zodiac, by the time Twelfth Night is reached, he is twelve years old, almost grown up, ready to receive his magical weapons and set off on his quest through the year, which will lead him to union with the Goddess, kingship, sacrifice and descent into the underworld. This makes Twelfth Night a particularly important time for those who follow the Path of the Warrior.

Rituals which re-enact the arming of the young God can be moving indeed and can give all those present a feeling of courage about facing the challenges of the coming year. Drinking the "warriors' cup", a hot infusion of Thyme (Thymus vulgaris) and Borage (Borago officinalis), is a great help. Borage is a herb which is associated with bravery. Just remember the old saying, "A garden without Borage is like a heart without courage."

We think about our own magical "weapons" for the coming tide, or indeed for the whole year ahead. For a writer or student, this might be a pen, for a gardener, it could be a hoe to make war on weeds. We all have our personal magical weapons which give us power over our own lives and surroundings. Since the aspect of this festival is royal and expansive, its colours can be seen as purple or royal blue and gold.

The star is a powerful symbol for meditation and ritual work at this time, for it is the light which shows us the path ahead and guides us even when we ourselves are unsure of which way to go. It is not necessarily the brightest light in the sky, but it can give us wisdom, often heralding what is to follow, just as the Morning Star heralds the coming dawn. The star is also significant in the Christian tradition, since Epiphany (January 6th) marks the moment when the Three Wise Men arrived to honour the baby Jesus, having been led on their own quest by their guiding star.

Twelfth Night is also a time when people wassail the Apple trees, honouring their spirits and frightening away any evil which may damage next year's harvest. Drinking Lambswool – cider, cooked with Apples in it – provides a lovely warming moment after a chilly ritual and brings that glow back to the cheeks. It can be good to do this very early in the morning. That moment in the Winter when the dark recedes and the grey light of dawn spreads across the sky is a magical experience and well worth the effort of rising with the Blackbirds.

Closely associated with Twelfth Night is the important day of Plough Monday, which is when then men's work in the fields recommences after the Yuletide break. The ceremony of Charming the Plough involves the Plough being shown to all the inhabitants of a place so that they might better understand the miracle of bread which sustains us.

The need for dramatic change may also be demonstrated by the ride of the Wild Hunt across stormy skies. In various traditions, this exhilarating yet terrifying event is led by a deity or hero, such as Odin, Arthur or Gwyn ap Nydd. Here, it may be the Lord of Norfolk, in his aspect of the hunter, armed with Flint-tipped arrows, who can be seen expelling from his domain any who would harm this land.

There are so many ways to approach this festival. Sometimes we have re-enacted the giving of gifts to the young warrior, sometimes had a wild broom dance, a sword fight, or run with the Wild Hunt. On other occasions, we have been sombre in the face of the coming year, consulted an oracle or made solemn promises. Although this festival signals the end of festivities and indulgence in food and drink, we do sometimes eat Twelfth Cake after the ritual. This is made from a sweet, yeasty bun dough, usually shaped into a large ring, with balls of marzipan inside it. A lucky charm may also be included, much like the silver sixpence in a Christmas pudding. A whole Almond or a magical Bean may be used, or even an old-fashioned, Victorian "pudding doll", especially made for the purpose.

If the ritual is well-chosen, well-constructed and carried out with focus and true magical will, the work of the coming season is likely to run more smoothly, for as well as celebrating past work, any seasonal festival also looks forward to the next step along the path.

Twelfth Night to Imbolc

For many people this is a challenging point of the year, still dark and gloomy but without the major festivities to look forward to. We try to enjoy that sense of getting back down to work. There is always so much to be sorted out and a sense of urgency to get as much done as possible before it is time once again to sow seeds and nurture what is new.

Distaff Tuesday is usually the day after Plough Monday when the traditionally women's work of spinning and weaving begins again. There are taboos against spinning at Yuletide, for various reasons, and traditions vary somewhat in different European countries. We tend to be quite strict about not spinning or weaving at this time, and have had a few disasters when doing textile work over the Yuletide period.

The broomstick is an important domestic implement for the season, as the Cleansing Tide brings the tasks of clearing away that which is outworn and holding back our spiritual, magical and worldly development. Since the Snake can shed its skin and emerge renewed, Snake-like powers can usefully be harnessed at this time. Watching a Snake shed shows that it is not always an easy process. Before the event most Snakes do not eat and even appear to be blind for about a day, making them very vulnerable. The results though are magnificent to see – an amazing "new" creature with brighter and better colours, emerging hungrier and livelier than it has been for a while. A shed Snake skin attached to a besom can be part of a spell to allow us to go through a similar process.

Stormy beaches are wonderful to visit now. There are only a few other hardy souls around, and lots of fascinating things hurled onto the beach out of the Winter seas. It is a lovely Winter exercise to draw out a labyrinth in the sand and walk around it while flying a kite. In this way, we are joining Earth and Sky, as well as attuning ourselves to the four Elements of Earth, Air, Water and Fire, especially if the Sun blesses us by breaking through the cloud.

While it is still cold outside, this can be a good moment to repot and chat to some of our houseplant friends, who will begin to thrive better as the light grows and will rapidly reward the extra effort made on their behalf.

It can be exhilarating to work outside too, clearing and reorganising things in the garden, making some practical or magical rearrangements.

People often forget what a flower-filled and fragrant month January can be. The Rosemary often comes into bloom this early and many's the time you might be walking along and suddenly overwhelmed by beautiful perfume. This could be from a magical Witch Hazel tree (Hamamelis virginica), whose yellow flowers look like rays of the Sun against the background of an otherwise wintery garden. It might be Sweet Box (Sarcococca confusa), a common garden and municipal evergreen, with tiny but intensely perfumed white flowers, hidden amongst the leaves, and shiny black berries, or a Winter-flowering Viburnum. Mahonia japonica smells delicious, with its fountains of long, yellow spikes, as do some of the Winter-flowering Irises, like the pale lilac-coloured Iris unguicularis.

Imbolc/Candlemas

My second is the outstretched palm
Bringing Light and cleansing calm

The beginning of February is a time when the renewal of the Earth becomes visible with the appearance of certain flowers. Snowdrops (Galanthus nivalis), in particular, are associated with the festival, and the appearance of the first one, perhaps bravely thrusting up through a covering of snow, is often taken as the sign to begin the celebrations. Sometimes, this can prove confusing and unhelpful when they begin to ring out their silent melodies at Yuletide. In part, this can be a reflection of the changes in the seasons and generally warmer Winters, but there are plenty of varieties of Snowdrop which have been bred to bloom early or even in the Summer.

This iconic bloom is thought by some to be naturalised rather than native, but such distinctions are of little concern to those who have taken this delicate treasure to their hearts. There is no mention of the Snowdrop in Medieval writings, and it is little used in modern herbal medicine, although the crushed bulbs have been applied to frostbite to encourage regeneration of the tissue (Barker, 2001), an appropriate medical and magical expression of the power of this season.

Although so exquisite and tender in appearance, these plants are, like the Goddess herself, extremely resilient. The leaves around the flower head have thickened tips to allow them to push through the icy soil. Close examination reveals the leaves to be like long, green, witchy fingers, with a perfect nail at the top.

Norfolk has an excellent choice of Snowdrop walks, where the season can be celebrated by enjoying views of these lovely flowers stretching through woodland as far as the eye can see.

Perhaps one of the loveliest and most appropriate of these walks is in the grounds of Walsingham Abbey, whose story and ancient resonances draw together connections to the milk of the Goddess, the Lady of the Chalk and the power of resilience and renewal in the natural world and in the human spirit's striving for beauty and divinity. It is the perfect place to experience the meaning of Imbolc, with its symphony of echoes from the distant and recent past, and to face the brightening yet chilly days of February with a refreshed sense of optimism. This is the sacred site where, in 1061, the Lady Richeldis de Faverche saw her vision of the Virgin Mary and was instructed to build a replica of the Holy House in Nazareth. An anonymous ballad, published in the fifteenth century by Richard Pynson, tells the miraculous story of angelic assistance in the building of the house, which became a popular place of pilgrimage (Rear, 2011).

The Holy House was destroyed in 1538, during the Reformation, and the statue of Our Lady taken to London and burned. So, for four centuries, the enchantment of the place kept itself hidden from public view, until its magical current opened up again through the work of Charlotte Boyd, who bought and refurbished the Slipper Chapel, and Father Alfred Hope Patten, who revived interest in pilgrimage amongst Anglicans. In 1922, he had a new statue of Our Lady carved, based on the priory seal, to create a replica of the statue burned in London (Rear, 2011). The new statue was at first kept in the parish church but was translated to the new shrine in 1931. In keeping with centuries of spiritual and magical traditions worldwide, a well was discovered during the process of building the new shrine. Its water is delicious as well as magically effective.

It is difficult to put into words the feeling of sitting in the new Holy House, within the large Anglican church, looking at the statue, who is Our Lady, the Mother, the Goddess, regardless of one's chosen spiritual tradition, and experiencing the flow of magic which emanates from her. Such is the power of the message of Imbolc: frost and darkness may cut down much of our green world; people wreak havoc and destruction, yet the spirit of the land lives on. Memory is not so easily erased; life, beauty and magic will return when the time is right.

So, we return home from our mini-pilgrimage, to sow some seeds, to create something new, to write a beautiful ritual or to sing a new song. Often at this time, we melt down old candle stubs and reuse the wax to make fresh candles which, because of the mixture of colours in the wax, often turn out the translucent grey of the Lord of Norfolk himself.

Imbolc rituals are often the coldest of the year. On one remarkable occasion, there was deep snow in the garden, which had become packed down solid. All around the Circle we placed lanterns with coloured glass so that when all the candles were lit, the snow flowered into a rich carpet of greens, pinks, blues reds and yellows.

An Imbolc ritual will often focus on cleansing, in preparation for the coming growing season, with broomstick dances or aura brushing. It is a good time for making a new besom, with Birch twigs, a Hazel or Ash handle and a Bramble binding. Wands or baskets are also made, the wood being cut before the sap begins to rise again. There may be a lot of prunings too, from fruit trees and bushes, and these are useful for whittling spoons, knives, pokers and other small wooden items. Some of these may be used as ritual offerings or simply for practical, mundane purposes. They make lovely gifts too. On other occasions, illumination is sought as the days lengthen. Often, the Spring Maiden, bringing a dish of treasures, including some Snowdrops, Violets and early Irises, will give us the gifts we need for the next stage of the journey.

Celebrating the connection between humans and Sheep can be central to Imbolc rituals, as this is traditionally when the first of their young are born. This relationship is important for those of us who work with textiles and the magic of the spun thread, so around this time we normally try to get out into the countryside to see the new Lambs, who are so much a symbol of the hope of life returning, the abundance within the land and the blessing of the Lady of Norfolk.

Imbolc to Eostre/Ostara/Easter/Spring Equinox

This is a busy time, sowing seeds and trying to find enough space for them all on windowsills and in the greenhouse. In a warm year, the first leaf buds of the Lady Elder will begin to appear soon after Imbolc. These are not taken internally, but make an excellent oil, which can be used to anoint candles in honour of the Green Lady. It also makes an excellent wound salve: the perfect ointment for gardeners. Elder leaf oil can be made by simply covering new Elder leaves and buds in Olive oil and warming the mixture very gently, at a low oven temperature for several hours. Alternatively, they can be warmed in a bain marie on top of the stove and may be ready in an hour or so.

It is possible to see that the leaves have given all their "virtue" to the oil. They look shrivelled and spent. Strain them off and store the oil in sterilised, dry bottles.

If Sweet Violets (Viola odorata) are plentiful, their flowers these can also be made into a lovely oil for ointment and balms. It is surprising how early these shy, fragrant beauties appear, and they can just be left on a warm windowsill rather than heated, which would be too much for their delicate fragrance. A month is plenty of time to leave them before straining and bottling. If there is time, and I am feeling in a patient frame of mind, I may make some sugared Violets. This involves holding the flowers by their stalks, dipping them in egg white and then into icing sugar. They must then be allowed to dry and the process repeated several times. Although sugared Violets are a lot of work for a tiny result, they make exquisite gifts for the Gods, Fair Folk or other friends, and can be a perfect seasonal offering for any Spring rites.

The first Nettles will also be ready for harvesting, rich, green and delicious, containing all the love of the Green Lady and all the power of Mars. What a boon the Nettle must have been in those times before refrigeration and imported food, flourishing as it does before local fresh vegetables. Although despised by many as a weed, young Nettle leaves are good in soups, stews, stir-fries and sauces. They contain plenty of iron, which we so need in our blood and which gives us physical and mental/emotional fortitude, other minerals, including calcium, as well as vitamins C, B and K. We pick them for use now and dry them for later, when they can just be crumbled into whatever we are making, be that food or magical sachets for energy and courage. Nettle is very much of the God, strengthening, encouraging, empowering and well able to defend himself!

Medicinally, Nettles can be taken as a tea, vinegar, alcoholic tincture or powders, and are used for numerous conditions, such as anaemia, hay fever, arthritis, gout, heavy periods, skin problems and allergies. It is also excellent for the hair and fresh or dried leaves can be made into a hair-rinse tea, often in combination with Rosemary and a drop of cider vinegar. Later in the year, the long stems can be used to make beautiful cords for craft work and spells.

Jack Valentine is an important figure in Norfolk folklore and magic. The 14th February is not just for lovers, as the magical Jack visits with gifts, which are left on the doorstep for the lucky recipient to find. He is loving and generous, but can also be a trickster and, in more mischievous mode, he might attach a string to the gift and pull it away when his victim bends to pick it up (Maskill, 2013). We often give gifts to one another and to the Fair Folk, in the hope of enlisting their blessing for the growing and harvesting of the year. As the birds are singing their best, they too deserve gifts: extra seeds, nuts or fat balls, and warm water if it is still very cold. I always associate Valentine's Day with the Winter Aconite flowers, which are often at their loveliest and look like beautiful big yellow kisses amongst last year's fallen leaves. They are the gentle Spring sunshine kissing the Earth once more as She returns to her full splendour.

As the days grow longer and a little warmer, the Blackthorn fills the hedgerows with frothy flowers, which often coincides with the temporary return of colder weather. From across the North Sea icy winds whip coastline and farmland. It is a lazy wind, going straight through us rather than around, and discouraging us from venturing outside as much as we might like. That Winter is jealous of the Spring, and tries to retain his icy grip on the world, is recognised in many cultures, in story and in art. Here, we know this time as the Blackthorn Winter.

But wild Plums bloom, and Daffodils and Hyacinths appear. The Lady brings her colourful blessings, the atmosphere intensifies, and there is a special moment when we feel that the Wheel has turned again. Maybe we have been able to cover seven magical Daisies with one foot; perhaps it is just a faint perfume in the air, or a tingling in the blood, but we know that Summer is on her way. This is a time of drawing the light back into our lives. We clean the windows to let in as much sunshine as we can, adding a splash of herbal vinegar for protection and good fortune as the Growing Tide gains momentum.

The first hint of soft greens, as leaves begin to emerge, means that the medical and magical herbalists amongst us begin their gathering in earnest. We eat the "bread and cheese" of the first Hawthorn shoots. Seeds are now germinating and everywhere there are trays containing the precious potential of the seasons to come, while a good harvest of Nettle shoots is scenting the indoor atmosphere with their earthy goodness.

Cleavers (Galium aperine), or Clivers, Goose Grass or Sticky Willies, as they are also known, feature in our seasonal work as well. Their small shoots are often visible throughout the Winter, just waiting for light and warmth to enable them to loop their way through our gardens and dance all over the hedgerows. It is such a common plant and known to most us for its sticky little burs which attach themselves to our clothes and to the fur of animals.

This is a herb of the Moon and, in the Spring, it is full of a vibrant and magical green juice. It may appear difficult to extract, but all that is needed is to chop a pile of the plant as finely as possible and squeeze a handful hard over a glass. It is an excellent Spring tonic, as it has beneficial effects on the lymphatic system and is also a diuretic. It is generally a safe herb, but taking a glassful all in one go is a heady experience! Between one and three teaspoonfuls of fresh juice a day is plenty, but it is best to prepare it fresh on each occasion. It can also be used in tincture form, in vinegar, as a tea or eaten as a vegetable, although, typical of many plants which are ruled by the Moon, it doesn't seem to work as well in dried form.

Medicinally, it is used for swollen glands, skin problems, chronic fatigue, ulcers and numerous other conditions. It also has a reputation for helping people to lose weight and, magically, it is said that if a person takes fresh Cleavers every day for ninety days they will be so beautiful as to be irresistible. The herb is useful for any spells of a lunar nature, for the blessing of scrying equipment or magical mirrors, improving psychic ability or helping one attune to the waxing and waning flow of life and magical work.

According to a tip given to me long ago by the Hermits of Mole End, who have a vast knowledge of how to cultivate all sorts of plants, from the "humble" natives of the woodland floor to the most glamorous of exotics, March is the time to divide Mint plants. Most people tend to grow them in pots, and their long runners spiral round and round in a desperate attempt to escape. So, if they are to flourish, it is best to divide them and give them some fresh compost in which to grow. They will reward the effort by flourishing and providing teas, tinctures and vinegars, in addition to ingredients for incenses, potpourris and magical sachets. Mints are particularly beloved of local witches, who very often collect as many different fancy varieties as possible: variegated, curly-leaved, pineapple-scented and even chocolate-scented. There are so many to choose from. Magically they are, to my mind, ruled by Venus, although not all sources and not all practitioners agree on the subject. It is one of the herbs of Our Lady and can be used as a strewing herb around the Circle or in a temple, as well as in incense form. A sprig of Mint can be placed in your wallet or purse to increase prosperity, but also carried to ward off disease. Hanging it up in the house is protective. Peppermint, Mentha piperita, has numerous medicinal applications and can be used internally and externally. It is excellent for all sorts of problems of the digestive system, and has anti-microbial properties. It is great for coughs and colds as a tea, tincture or in the form of a balm rubbed onto the chest.

Along with the burgeoning plant life, animal products become more plentiful. Many in the Nameless Tradition have a strong connection with Hens and may keep feathered familiars, whose eggs they look forward to at this time. The egg is rich with symbolic meaning in many cultures, being everything from the World Egg, from which the Universe was hatched, to the Philosopher's Egg, which, in alchemy, is the seed of spiritual life and a place of great transformation. An egg placed on a post is used to mark an especially sacred spot (Pennick, 2004). Because they contain new life and vitality, eggs can be used in spells, including the drawing out of evil or ill fortune from a person or animal, or determining whether or not someone is under the influence of the evil eye. The egg can also act as a substitute for the victim, so that the evil is directed into the egg not the person. Good fortune and magical fertility can also be attracted by the careful decoration of eggs, especially those laid by Hens owned by witches. Sometimes it is appropriate to blow the egg, which in itself is a magical process, and wash it out so that it can be kept indefinitely. The whites and yolks can then be made into Tansy pancakes, which we traditionally eat as a cleansing food at this time, usually as part of our feast after our ritual to welcome the Spring. A golden egg laid by a Goose is a symbol of great wealth. A Goose egg can be blown and painted gold to represent this should it be required, although this is extremely hard work.

Eostre

My third is a circle sprouting two horns,
Bringing light and cleansing calm.

This is such a vibrant, colourful time, yet, it is not unusual to feel a little tired and out of sorts as the Spring Equinox approaches, which is frustrating as we want to feel filled with the energy of the light, warmth and growth. This is just the choppiness of the waves at the turn of any tide, and a few days to retreat and contemplate what the season of light holds for us may be no bad thing.

Protection charms are often prepared at this time, so a newly-woven God's Eye might be hung at each window and door, new Winter-storm-cleansed hag stones threaded on wool or wire, a Helm of Awe painted on a wooden disc or flat stone, or a new set of "running eights" patterns chalked onto a clean doorstep.

Whatever name we choose to give to this step of the Quest of the Year, around 21st March, when the Light and Dark are in equal balance, it is one of great beauty and sacredness. As the Venerable Bede wrote, from an Anglo-Saxon Christian point of view, referring to our Pagan ancestors:

Eosturmonath has a name which is now translated Paschal month and was once called after a goddess of theirs named Eostre, in whose honour feasts were celebrated in that month. Now they designate that Paschal season by her name, calling the joys of the new rite by the time-honoured name of the old observance.

Bede De temporum ratione (Reckoning of Time)

In Norfolk, as in East Anglia in general, the Anglo-Saxon influence is still strong and, in our Tradition, we retain a deep respect for their deities, their crafts, their lore and their light touch upon the landscape. Eostre is therefore much celebrated (although many name her Ostara, which is the Old High German version).

We often use eggs in our Spring ritual, making our own special nest for them and covering them with a cloth until they are revealed, in candlelight, at the right moment in the ritual, with words such as, "behold the mystery of life renewed". On other occasions we focus on the more outgoing aspects of the season by making and wearing outlandish Spring bonnets or colourful pointed hats, covered in flowers, fabric birds or rabbits. We also make a Spring arch decorated with coloured wool and feathers so that we can leave behind any problems of the Winter and step through lightly into the pleasures of the Spring. Sometimes we write a list of twelve magical tasks for the coming year, such as things to learn, plants to grow or magical places to visit. Saying them in a ritual makes it much more likely that we will actually fulfil them!

Thunder is very unusual at this time of year, so there is an old saying, "If in March you hear the thunder, by Summer you will see a wonder". Some years ago, we did indeed hear some March thunder and were suitably impressed by the wonder which unfolded during the course of the warmer times. In the year of writing this, March thunder has again been heard, this time on a Tuesday, during a very powerful ritual of deep learning of ancient symbols. It was a clear message about the importance of rune-working in our practice, but we also await with interest the wonder which is to come.

Eostre to Beltane
More and more time is spent outside, and this is often the season when we have our first "Summer kitchen" of the year, cooking outside over an open fire, with the cauldron on a tripod and the gentle smoke rising into the twilight sky. Herbs go straight from the living plant to the cooking pot, without ever having been taken indoors. Long, light evenings are such a luxury, especially as we need more time to be outside and yet to get all of our tasks done at home as well. We revisit some of our favourite places around the county, some of which we may not have had the chance to see since the Autumn. It is a kind of stretching out and extending our physical presence further afield. New ideas and inspiration are pouring in, and our spells and rituals often focus on nurturing and nourishing the progress of our latest projects, whatever they may be.

There are more seeds to be sown too. No light half of the year flows as it should without a good selection of Beans. They are a must to please the Fair Folk and to honour the dead once the year grows dark once more. Pumpkins too are sown with Samhain in mind, so that they are ready to plant out once the risk of frost has passed. It seems strange to think of the Autumn when the Summer has not yet begun, and it reminds us that we hold the entire Wheel of the Year in our minds, even though, physically, we dwell in only in one part of it at a time. Honouring the growing Sun by planting some stately Sunflowers adds energy and rapid progress to our lives, for they shoot up so fast with their huge leaves and solid, bristly stems. Their magnificent flowers may not come early in the season, but they will still be there as the air becomes chilly again. Even once the frost has ravaged their petals and sucked out their colour, their brown heads will remain, offering sustenance to hungry birds.

There is always something to harvest at any season. One important "crop" for us, is our Balsam Poplar buds (Populus balsamifera), which some people refer to as "Balm of Gilead", although there are a number of herbs and plants which have been given that name. The buds are extremely fragrant and are one of the best incense ingredients which can be grown locally because they are rich in resins. This also makes them extremely sticky to pick, especially just before the leaves open, which is when they are at their best for harvesting. It is useful to note that the resin is chemically very similar to propolis (Conway, 2001), which bees use to plug small gaps in the hive. The buds are therefore an appropriate addition to incenses or spells of protection, but also to any magic which draws on the magic of bees themselves: the sweetness they can bring, the wealth and warmth and cooperation within a community. I like to place five Balsam Poplar buds in a perfume ring or open wire bead, and carry the perfume and the sweetness with me. They are, however, very bitter tasting and have a number of medicinal uses, as they are analgesic, anti-inflammatory and antimicrobial, as well as expectorant and stimulating to the immune system. This makes them useful, when made into a tincture or a syrup, as an internal medicine for coughs, colds, sinusitis, various complaints of the stomach and as a gargle for laryngitis. The tincture is very strong though, and can be a skin irritant, so it is important always to dilute the tincture before taking it. The buds can be macerated in oil and used in ointments for bruising and swelling, and for arthritis or muscle stiffness and pain. It can also help treat various skin conditions, including ringworm.

Another herb, which also goes by the Biblical name of "Balm of Gilead," is the Canary Balm, Cedronella triphylla, a beautifully fragrant plant of the Mint family. I have grown this in the garden for many years, since first being delighted to receive one as a gift. They are originally from the Canary Islands, so flourish best in a warm Summer and will not survive a wet or very cold Winter. During a good summer, it will grow rapidly, with all the expansiveness of a plant ruled by Jupiter, and provide a huge quantity of fragrant leaves which make wonderful incense and pot pourri, and its pink flowers are a delicious treat for bees. A tea can be made from the leaves, known as Canary Tea, which some will also say is special for Norwich, given that this totem bird of the weavers has become the nickname of Norwich City FC. Many sources claim that this plant does not have medicinal properties (Bown, 2008), but given its fragrance, I would have thought it to be anti-microbial and good for the digestion and lungs, and must have traditional uses in its native islands. Some years I have had huge bunches of it festooning the ceilings and walls. Not only is it protective and warming, but it also lifts the spirits and improves energy levels.

March and April are amongst the most colourful of months, with all the bulbs, the blossom and the

Polyanthus in bloom. I often dye some wool in vibrant shades to match what is going on, as I feel I want to be the colours I see around me, and dress in honour of Iris of the Rainbow, who is so much in evidence here in the Spring. Most of the plants we grow here for dyestuffs are not yet ready for harvesting. However, it is possible to buy natural Indigo for blues, Madder for oranges and reds or Cochineal for pinks and reds (although this is not suitable for vegetarians, as it is the beetle, Dactylopius coccus, which must be dried and powdered to produce the carmine colour). There are also plenty of lovely colours which can be created using modern acid dyes, which are simple, quick and versatile to use. At times, I have tried to give them up and become an Old Ways purist, but my addiction to colour has always proven too strong in the end. I love to visualise my aura decorated with flowers of all kinds, which may sound rather "fluffy bunny", but is a useful exercise. It is a pleasurable thing to do, improves general health and mood and fosters a greater love of life. It always has a positive magical impact on those you meet, whether they are people you already know or complete strangers. When you need people to respond positively to you, try some Roses, Rosemary, Primroses, Marigolds or Lavender, or maybe some Cherry blossom. I generally avoid anything thorny, as that can have the opposite effect, making you seem like a "spikey" person, but the choice of flowers or herbs can be adapted to suit the requirements of the moment. At the very least, people will smile and chat to you in the street and at best, who knows what fabulous gifts and offers you might receive!

As the days become warmer and longer, and the leaves begin to burst from their buds, it always seems that there is a moment when the fabulous mix of Spring colour disappears, to be replaced by an almost overwhelming music of green and white, accompanied by the heady scent of Cow Parsley or Queen Anne's Lace (Anthriscus sylvestris). It all happens so quickly and suddenly the May blossom is out, and Beltane is upon us.

Beltane

My fourth it is the Maypole tree,
Bringing warmth and joy so lustily.

For most practitioners of Traditional Craft, and indeed Pagans of many different paths, the blooming of the Hawthorn, one of the most fabulous of the gifts of Flora, is the sign that Beltane is here, that it is time to "cast clouts" and put on our new finery which we have prepared over the previous season, and that the season's rites should now be celebrated.

The scope for the celebration of Beltane is vast, and depends very much on the guidance received from the beings who speak to us so very clearly as the burst of sprowl from the Earth tears back the veil between our world and those of the Fair Folk and the plant spirits. Sometimes we take advantage of the easier communication to learn more of poetry, music, dance or storytelling. We may be able to delve yet more deeply into the ways of our land, send our roots down further and so expand towards the heavens like the canopy of a great tree, or be rewarded with an increase in our skills at nurturing plants, for receiving the blessings of green fingers at Beltane is a gift beyond price. The Green Witch may instruct us in the ways of medicine and other uses of the herbs of her sacred garden. It could be that our rite would involve masking and shape shifting, to meet or reconnect with our totem animals or those of the land, or we may call into our Circle the power of the Horned One. There is a beautiful horned mask, which was given to me as a gift and which someone may be selected to wear during the Beltane ritual. Both wearing the mask and seeing its effect can be transformative. Sometimes petitions are made for fertility, of the land, of animals and people who have requested help in this matter. We always hope for some increase, and anticipate this with joy and expectation, but recognise too that it will almost certainly involve hard work as well.

To me, Bluebells (Hyacinthoides non-scripta), so beloved of all who walk in our woodlands at this time, are just as much flowers of Beltane as the Hawthorn. They are also considered dangerous. The Scottish name for the plant is "Deadmen's Bells" and hearing the bells ring means that you are hearing your own death-knell. According to Brian Froud (Froud and Lee, 1998):

> *The Bluebell is one of the most potent of all faerie flowers, and a bluebell wood is an extremely hazardous place to be – a place of faerie-woven spells and enchantments.*

I must say that I have never been deterred by such dire warnings and love the sight and scent of these exquisite flowers, especially as they grow so well in the company of our beautiful Lady of the Chalk.

Culpeper says that the roots of the Bluebell, when dried and powdered, are "balsamic and styptic in nature", but it is not, to my knowledge, used in modern herbal medicine, being somewhat toxic. The mucilage in the bulbs, which makes them feel sticky, has been used as a glue in the past by fletchers and bookbinders, but these days we would consider them too precious to dig up when there are adequate alternatives.

Beltane to Midsummer

The summer has not truly begun for me until the first of the Swifts have returned from their long journey. They are such amazing creatures, travelling all those miles every year and spending weeks at a time airborne. Often, a few days after the Beltane ritual, black sickle-like silhouettes will be spotted against a clear blue sky and before long, groups of them wheeling above the city, shrieking in those wonderfully eldritch voices, which have given them their reputation, throughout Britain, of being the Devils' Birds. Indeed, our neighbours in Lincolnshire say of the Swifts there that they are lost souls, circling church towers and expressing their regret about their failure to find redemption (Buczacki, 2002). These birds love Norwich because it has so many church towers, which they favour, not as places to express sorrow, but as their nesting sites. Some folk may still fear their diabolical associations, but those of our Tradition love them and welcome their return. They are with us for such a fleeting stay, spending far less time here than the Swallows or Martins, reminding us of the transitory nature of all things, inspiring us to make the most of the summer season, of their presence, and our own, all too brief visit to the world in this incarnation. We are reminded that Beltane is on the same spoke of the wheel as Samhain and there is a hint of delicious melancholy, even as we celebrate life in all its fullness.

One year we were reminded of this most powerfully when we found a fledgling Swift fallen on our neighbour's lawn. Their feet are tiny, meant only for clinging on to the places where they nest, so they cannot walk or relaunch themselves if they fall to the ground. There are no second chances for the young leaving the nest, no flopping around like baby Blackbirds with watchful parents keeping guard. It's fly or die. But this poor forlorn creature was not dead. We were advised to take it up onto a roof to give it some height for a second attempt. We were optimistic initially, but later on we found it dead on the ground: a stark reminder that we have to accept that not all young creatures are meant to survive, however much we may want them to.

When I see the first Swift, I throw into the air a wish or a project to be fulfilled while they remain here. It is the simplest of spells, but they are not called Swifts for nothing, and their ability to keep flying, sometimes for weeks without rest, can fill us with the enthusiasm we need and keep our attention focused on the task at hand.

They are nevertheless birds of the daytime and seem to work with the Ward, the Faery guardians of the area, who change their shift at dawn and dusk. All day the Swifts wheel over the garden, high or very low, depending on the weather, then as the Ward changes in the evening, they give way to the bats, who take their place. It is wonderful how their voices can fuel the magic and bring such a spell to fruition. Often now, we will light our Summer kitchen while the Swifts are circling the garden, then, as we cook and eat, we watch the birds disappear into the twilight.

Often on our outings around the county, we come across people with roadside stalls selling Asparagus, or "Sparrow Grass," as we often prefer to call it. It grows well in this area because it favours a light soil, and there are many commercial producers of this magnificently phallic Beltanetide vegetable, which can be eaten raw in salads, steamed whole to maintain its shape, or chopped into green, leafy soups. Not only is it delicious, but also of great benefit to the urinary tract.

It was always the case that, just after Beltane, I would walk with the Hermits of Mole End from the car park in Stow Bedon, not far from Watton in Mid-Norfolk, along the Pingo Trail. The Pingoes are remarkable landscape features, formed in permafrost conditions. Water, which seeped in from higher ground or from springs, formed mounds of ice under the frozen ground. By the time the ice melted, deep pits had been formed to contain the water (Williamson, 2006). The pingoes on the trail are full of Water-violets (Hottonia palustris) at this time of year. These plants, found mostly in Eastern England, are quite rare, so it is a treat to see them. Their leaves are fern-like and submerged under the water, and the flowers are a lovely pale mauve with a yellow eye at the centre (Mabey, 1996).

We would continue across, through the woods, past a ramshackle thatched cottage, with very friendly goats in the garden, then down a long, straight path towards Thompson Common. It was while we were on this path that we always heard our first Cuckoo of the year. There is so much lore attached this harbinger of the Summer, but the tradition that held true for us for a long time was that, where we were when we heard the first Cuckoo one year, we would return to hear the first one of the following year. I now always think of that footpath as my Cuckoo place, even when I am there at another time of year. The Sheep which graze on Thompson Common belong to the Norfolk Wildlife Trust, and I have an especial affection for them as have been able to buy some of their wool each year, for spinning and felt-making, so no year is complete without going to greet them.

Beyond the Common, we used to take the stream-side path through the Alder carr and wander on as far as Thompson Water. This is not a natural mere, but a 40-acre lake, constructed around 1847 (Clarke and Clarke, 1937) and so close to the STANTA army training area that it is often possible to hear firing from the ranges. Nevertheless, it is a wonderfully magical spot and a haven for Herons, Egrets, Terns and numerous types of Duck. We always picnicked on one of the fishing jetties which create a liminal space between the land and the water. Now the Hermits have continued with their own quest across another stretch of water, I walk here alone or with other friends, but the route of our wandering still holds the echo of their footsteps and whispers magical memories as I pass by.

The blooming of the Elderflowers is another marker of the season, their frothy, fragrant blooms echoing the wealth of the fleeces and the richness of the cream which have always been important early summer harvests: gifts of the White Lady herself. The flowers are best picked early, if possible, before they become infested with little black Thrips, and in time to make champagne or cordial for the Midsummer celebrations. Something new is learned every Midsummer. This year our friends in the Tamar Valley suggested using the leftovers from making cordial and champagne to create Elderflower marmalade. It does mean taking all the stalks out before making the drinks and cutting the citrus peel considerably smaller than one would otherwise, but having tried this out, we know that it is well worth the effort. I just added a pound of sugar to every pint in volume of flowers and fruit, and boiled it until it produced a good set. The result is fragrant, delicious and thrifty. It is also as well to dry some Elderflowers for teas, as they are excellent for treating summer colds and fevers, as well as hayfever and other allergies.

Midsummer

My fifth is like a Lion's mane,
The peak of the Sun and burning flame.

Midsummer celebrations have a bittersweet feel as we know that, while we are enjoying the Sun at the height of his power, the light will decline now and the year fold back inwards once again. This is sometimes marked by a re-enactment of the battle between the Holly King and his brother and rival, the Oak King, who rules the waxing of the year and must now accept defeat and cede his crown to the dark evergreen sovereign of the year's waning. We have, some years, made beautiful costumes for the Kings, with cloaks, crowns, masks and huge clubs, painted gold for the Oak King and black for the Holly King, and festooned with ribbons and tassels. If there a lot of people taking part, there can even be an element of pantomime, with some people cheering for Holly and others for Oak. At other times, the ritual can be a simple celebration of the treasures of Midsummer: the Strawberries, Redcurrants and Blackcurrants that are the ripening jewels in the Lady's crown. Other Midsummer rites have included walking the path of a pentagram, traced out on the ground within the Circle so that a pentacle is formed. In doing so we are working with this ancient five-fold symbol, which is the human body, the four Elements and Ether, five points of perfection, the Endless Knot and so much more. Walking the shape ritually can be another way of drawing Summer's power into the very essence of our being.

Divination is, and has always been, an important aspect of Midsummer for many people, including those with no particular magical inclinations. There are many spells which involve the picking of certain herbs or flowers and placing them under the pillow in order to be given prophetic dreams, particularly involving who one's future partner will be. One such important Midsummer herb is St. John's Wort (Hypericum perforatum), so named because it usually blooms on Midsummer's Day, which, in the Christian calendar, is St. John's Day. If people's interest during the year are particularly plant-focused, the Midsummer rite may involve each person representing one of the magical plants of the season and augmenting its power or learning some of its secrets by working with it magically in this way.

Midsummer to Lammas

Most of us like to pick a few of these intense yellow, pentagram-shaped flowers of St. John's Wort to dry for solar incenses or to make the rich red macerated oil, which demonstrates transformative magic in a visible way during its preparation and feels powerfully magical when it is used. This oil involves simply filling a clean jar with dry flowers, ideally collected on a warm, sunny day just before twelve. These are then covered with Olive oil, as Olives are also ruled by the Sun, and left on a sunny windowsill for a month, or perhaps until Lammas, to undergo a process described by some using the beautiful term "solarisation". At first, the mixture is a yellowy-green colour, but there will come a moment when you suddenly notice that it has turned to a vibrant red. Once the oil has been strained of the spent flowers, you have a precious product, which can be used to anoint candles, particularly for Midwinter rites, when we wish to bring the power of the Sun back into the Circle and into our lives. When white candles are used, the effect is powerfully cleansing and purifying, so this combination is excellent for exorcisms. A little of the oil can be placed in a dish and used to bless participants in a ritual by tracing an appropriate symbol for the occasion onto their foreheads or the palms of their hands. The pentagram is often favoured for this purpose, but we also use the symbol of the festival, a suitable rune, or maybe even a Helm of Awe, should a very strong magical protection be required. The oil can also be thickened with beeswax to make a wound ointment, perhaps mixed with Marigold flower oil, so it is important to gather enough for all the anticipated uses throughout the year. Tincture of St. John's Wort, made from the flowering tops of the plant, rather than just the flowers, is a valuable addition to the dispensary. These days it is associated mainly with its qualities as an anti-depressant, which are obvious, given its strong links to the Sun. However, it has long been used for pain relief and is a powerful liver herb, which is why it should not be used internally when taking many other types of medication, including oral contraceptives. (When using St. John's Wort on the skin, care should be taken about exposure to sunlight, because photosensitivity may be a problem and can lead to skin damage). There is plenty of time to harvest St. John's Wort as it usually can be found in flower from Midsummer right through to Lammas and sometimes even later, although I have found the herb to be more effective when picked earlier in the season.

Mugwort (Artemisia vulgaris) is another of the many herbs harvested during this warm and sunny season, just as it comes into flower "(although for some purposes it is better gathered in late August.) This is one of our most powerful magical plants, often seen in the foliate heads of Medieval buildings, so it is important to pick it from a suitably magical place. I hang many bunches of this silvery-green herb around the house as it is not only protective, but also enhances any magic which is undertaken there, and touches with magic, even the most mundane of activities. It makes a wonderful addition to incenses, particularly those which are focused on psychic work, and the tea can be taken before rituals or divination to facilitate the correct state of mind for the work. Some people also like to smoke it prior to ritual or psychic work. Medicinally, the herb is a bitter digestive, and is excellent in the treatment of some menstrual problems, which is not surprising given its association with Artemis, a Moon goddess. It is anthelmintic too, so helps to expel worms. Great care should be exercised in the use of this powerful herb of sorcery. It should not be taken internally for more than three weeks at a time and must never be taken by anyone who is pregnant, trying for a baby, or breast-feeding.

Another magical use of Mugwort is for the feet, which may be seen as an example of the Doctrine of Signatures, as the leaves are somewhat foot-like in shape. Putting a fresh leaf into each shoe is a common way of avoiding getting tired feet when going for a long walk, or even indulging in an extended magical shopping trip. Finely ground and sieved Mugwort therefore makes a lovely addition to foot powders. My own "Three Mothers Foot Powder" contains Mugwort, Myrrh and Mint, which makes it magical, deodorant, and anti-fungal (so, excellent for anyone suffering from athlete's foot).

Fragrant roses are often at their best on or just after Midsummer, and we all like to collect petals for pot pourris, incense, teas and for the making of rosaries and scented beads. Rose and Mint tea is a great Summer favourite, but the addition of just a few dried Rose petals to any herb tea will give it "lift", make it look more attractive and subtly improve the fragrance and taste. Powdered Rose petals are lovely in cakes and puddings too, and help to foster the magic of friendship, love and beauty. Fresh Rose syrup on ice cream is an exquisite sweet seasonal indulgence. By cooking Rose syrup at a slightly higher temperature for a little longer, it can be made into a delicious confection once it is poured into moulds and cooled. For the very best Venusian effect, a heart-shaped mould can be used, and the resulting sweets lightly dusted with icing sugar which has been scented by leaving a vanilla pod in the jar or packet.

Roses have medicinal applications too. The tincture of Rose is often referred to by herbalists as "a hug in a bottle" and prescribed to lift the spirits and help healing after a period of grief. It is an excellent nervine, improving the mood, easing both physical and emotional pain and supporting the liver.

The land often seems very hot and dry during this season, especially in East Anglia, with its relatively low levels of rainfall. For those of us with gardens or potted plants, watering can be a major task, sometimes in both the mornings and the evenings. Rather than being a chore, it is best to see this as a pouring out of love and blessing upon the plants we have nurtured, and perhaps to add a splash of water from one of our holy wells, or even, as an exotic treat for our leafy friends, sacred water from Chalice Well in Glastonbury.

This is a good time for taking cuttings of many plants, including our aromatic herbs, and experiencing and benefiting from the magic which allows the cells of a stem to produce roots. Lavender, Rosemary, Thyme, Sage and even Roses can all be propagated in this way and passed on to other practitioners, spreading the plant magic from one Green Chapel to another,

The gold which is now spreading across the land can be captured in some of the dye plants which are often at their best in July. For example, Golden Rod (Solidago spp.) is an excellent dye plant, which I have used on many occasions to produce a lovely yellow colour. Depending on the conditions in which it has been grown, it produces a rich mustardy yellow, with an alum and cream of tartar mordant, and a more greeny shade with copper.

Medicinally, this diuretic herb increases renal function and is used in a variety of urinary problems, as well as for the respiratory system, where it is helpful for nasal catarrh and sinus problems. It is the flowering tops which are used as a tea, tincture or in powder form. The type of Golden Rod we see most commonly these days is the Canadian one, Solidago canadensis. My research has not revealed a great deal about the medical differences between this and our native herb, Solidago virgaurea, although Mrs. Grieve tells us that the Canadian type is used as a vulnerary. However, a colleague assures me that the two can be used for exactly the same purposes, which is good for me as I have a much better supply of the Canadian one.

Cunningham does not mention either of the above Golden Rods, but says that Solidago odora (which looks similar to the others but is, as its name suggests, more sweetly scented) is associated with the feminine principle, with Venus and with the Element of Air. This might, at first sight, seem strange, especially as all the Golden Rods are called Aaron's Rod and have a sceptre like appearance, which could also be considered phallic. However, when one thinks of the watery connections, this association makes more sense. The magical herbalist always needs to work these things out for themselves, of course. It's all a matter of thinking through the connections and following the flows of energy along the Web. It is also fair to say that closely-related herbs will have similar properties, but that there may be some subtle differences. Cunningham says that S. odora can be used in money spells. Could S. virgaurea and S. canadensis also be used in this way? My feeling would be definitely "yes," because they all have gold in the name and the colours green and gold speak very much of the natural wealth of our planet, of the green energy that rises from the Earth beneath our feet and the golden power of the Sun which pours down from the heavens, and which the plants convert into usable energy through the process of photosynthesis.

Cunningham also says that Golden Rod can be used to find lost objects or hidden treasure. You hold up the flowering stalk which then points in the direction you should look. This is a lovely idea, and works something like an upside-down pendulum. You may find literal treasure (gold again) but, in my experience, it has more to do with an appreciation of and access to the gifts of Earth.

The Tansy, whose fresh leaves we sprinkled on our pancakes at the time of Eostre, is now some three feet tall and covered in solid yellow "buttons", which retain their colour well if the herb is hung in bunches around the house. It has a clean and rather pungent smell, much hated by Clothes Moths, so is a useful addition to sachets to deter them, perhaps along with Wormwood and Lavender. These creatures are currently on the increase, probably due to warmer temperatures and loss of predators like bats, which is particularly annoying for those of us who like to spin and felt, and have a lot of woollen items around the house, as well as bags of fleece, so we need as much help as we can get in combatting them. Wool dyed soft yellow with Tansy is somewhat less attractive to Moths while it retains something of the scent of the plant.

The silvery leaved, dusty-flowered Lavender seems to sum up this time, as the flowers which have not been harvested pass their best and fade in the bright sunshine. Now is the time to prepare our straw plaits and a corn maiden for the Lammas festivities. We may sit for hours in the garden, after work, with damp towels and plant humidifiers, plaiting the wet straw into "favours", some with two straws, some with four, five or six. We all have our preferences, but there must always be some of each and, in particular, the twelve-straw, East Anglian Glory Braid, which everyone loves to make. This is a flat plait, worked from one side and then the other, and then folded back on itself, and although it looks complicated, is quite simple to master. Spirals are rather more time-consuming, and we usually include a Norfolk lantern in our year's collection, hanging the pieces out in the trees. Straw plaiting is important for Norfolk, as an agricultural county. Norfolk also used to be the home of a lovely straw museum, which we sometimes visited at this time of year for inspiration, until the sad death of its owner, Ella Carstairs, in 2017. Sadly though, the stems of the grain that is grown here nowadays are not suitable for plaiting because they are much shorter than traditional varieties, and the first node is very near the ear, leaving little space for working before a great lump appears. Unfortunately, cannot buy our straw in Norfolk, but order it from the wonderful Rosemary Sault in Staffordshire. We do need quite a lot, because our Corn Maiden is usually quite dramatic, with over 400 straws by the time all her decorations are complete.

Lammas

My sixth is like the archer's bow,
The corn now cut, the fields low.

We generally hold our Lammas rites at the beginning of August, the time when, traditionally, the grain harvest would have begun, even though, these days, the combine harvesters are out in the fields by mid-July or even earlier. Nevertheless, the first week in August retains its feeling of creative magical tension, of hope and danger, of being poised on a sword bridge between achievement and ruin. Although harvesting is a matter of joy and celebration, we nevertheless recognise that it does involve sacrifice, as the Corn King is cut down to feed the people, and the Poppies in the fields, so strongly associated with sacrifice in the context of war, represent his spilled blood. We think too of all the small creatures who are killed during the harvesting process, even if they are considered by many to be nothing more than pests. There is the magical fruition of our own tasks too, set in motion when the days were beginning to lengthen, and nurtured as the seeds sprouted and the Sun grew to full glory. It is often easy to sow the seeds of projects and magical or mundane ventures, but to see the process through to a successful harvest, and then benefit from what we have achieved, is not by any means a simple matter. Harvesting on all levels, requires skill and, more often than not, courage too. Indulging in self-sabotage can sometimes be an easier option than coping with the challenges of success. There is also an acknowledgement of the fear that if the rain falls at the wrong time, the precious wheat can be beaten down and spoiled. Disaster can strike suddenly at Lammastide, and not just in the fields. There may be accidents, the spread of disease during the hot weather, or sometimes an unexpected death. Such patterns become noticeable when one looks back and considers events over a period of many years.

Our ritual, therefore, will take these issues into consideration and be tailored to suit the prevailing feel of any particular year. Sometimes our focus is on the Mystery of Bread, with each participant in the ritual representing one of the traditional roles involved in the long and complex process from seed to loaf. There may be a ploughman, a sower, a reaper, a thresher, a miller and a baker, who all speak of the part they play, thus building up a sense of community and what can be achieved when people work harmoniously together towards a common goal. Another year we may emphasise the sacrificial aspects of the festival, with a specially-baked loaf, a dagger and quantities of blood-red ribbon. On a more gentle occasion, we may simply use the ritual to express our gratitude to the land and to the gods for what is provided, and ask for blessing upon all our work.

Lammas to the Autumn Equinox

To my knowledge, few now working within the Nameless Tradition of Norfolk Magic are currently farmers or employed on the land, but we all have plenty of physical crops to harvest from our gardens and foraging.

The Yellow Flag Irises, which thrive in ponds, river edges and damp places, have now finished blooming and are beginning to set seed. Their long leaves can be carefully gathered and dried ready to make all sorts of magical items from baskets to dolls, hats or magical cords. Wemight also cut some small branches for whittling knives, spoons, wands or other small items, as it is lovely to sit outside in the sunshine creating something with just a sharp knife and some twigs, and makes less mess than doing it indoors. It is often while enjoying this simple task that we suddenly become aware of something missing. The sky is quiet and strangely empty, and we become aware that our Summer companions, the Swifts, have left us once again to make their arduous journey back to warmer climes. It is a poignant parting, and one which marks a turning point each year: a moment of pause and reflection, even at this busy time, for some of those things which have not be completed will now have to be left until another time.

Blackberries are abundant, and many hours are spent gathering and preserving them. Summer pudding is a seasonal favourite, combining the magical Lammas bread with the mysterious dark fruit, which spreads its deep colour through the dome of soft slices. Jams and syrups bubble on the stove, despite the heat, and some of the berries are used to make Blackberry vinegar, which is an excellent remedy for winter colds. Plums and the greeny-yellow Bullaces begin to ripen, and our first Apples are usually ready well before September begins. Richness abounds throughout the county and in the city.

So, the year sweetens as the days darken and as we begin, gradually, to look inwards and to assess our progress and achievements. Rowan berries are picked and necklaces made. It is also time to knit new gloves in preparation for the chilly times, and perhaps some larger items too. These should not be started too late in the season or there may not be time to complete them before they need to be worn. My old friends in Sweden always warned that if you were still knitting gloves in the cold, you would be tempted to make the wrists too short and, thus, the end product would never be really warm or comfortable to wear. Gloves are extremely magical items, and making and decorating them can of itself be a form of enchantment.

The Elder Mother now embodies the dark Wise One, who will guide and protect us if we pay attention to Her, sometimes harsh, lessons. Her gifts of the season are Her purple-black berries, which we harvest to make delicious syrups and wines, some of which will be used to celebrate the Autumn Equinox and the rest saved for treating coughs and colds throughout the Winter.

The Autumn Equinox

My seventh it is the wilting plant,
Toward the dark a downward slant.

We once held a simple open ritual for the Autumn Equinox in Lion Wood, a magical place not far from the centre of Norwich. The ceremony called on the power of the Elder Mother to protect us and our health through the Winter months and to bestow upon us the blessings of the Dark times. The communion was a chalice full of thick, dark Elderberry syrup, freshly made and brimming with the magic of the season. Rather than having one person offer the cup to everybody, we adapted the "Communion of the Elements" from the Golden Dawn Tradition. The first person blessed the cup and invited the next person to share with them the dark and protective blessings of the Elder Mother. The second person offered the cup to the third person, and so on. The last person then completed the Circle by offering the cup to the first person. Had we been doing this in our own group, we would have spoken from the heart as we offered the cup to each other, but people are often nervous about remembering words or knowing what to say in public, so the suggested words were written on a card and placed next to the cup.

Our Autumn rituals celebrate the return to the balance of Light and Dark, and we often wear a white band or ribbon on one wrist and a black one on the other, for there can be no light without darkness, no sound without silence, no life without death. But the equilibrium we seek now is not only twofold. Like the Magician of the Tarot, who points both to the above and the below, the beginning and the ending, we also acknowledge the equal but varied powers of the four Elements which, in terms of the four humours of Classical and Medieval medicine, must be correctly balanced in the body if health is to be maintained. As we face the coming of Winter and the dark, this seems to be of particular importance. On some occasions, one of us has played the part of the Magician, standing before the altar and magically creating the delicate poise between Light, Dark, Above, Below, Earth, Air, Fire and Water. We have also made a large, leafy and fruity garland, which is placed in the centre of our Circle and, at an appropriate moment, lifted and held high in everyone's right hand while we circulate clockwise. We then turn and hold the garland in our left hands as we walk anti-clockwise. Later the garland itself becomes a very special offering.

This festival also celebrates the mutuality of giving and receiving, as exemplified by the gifu rune. Someone might therefore take the part of the Spirit of Autumn

Fruitfulness, receiving gifts from all present, in gratitude for this harvest, but also giving everyone a physical gift and a blessing. There is an overwhelming sense of richness and abundance most years, and a joy in the celebration of all the sweetness which surrounds us. The air is heavy with the heady scent of ripening fruit, and every year there are those who declare that this is their favourite season. The light paints the Circle with its golden glow and the lazy wasps add their voices to the music of the moment, as they come to suck the juice from the delicious fruits, clinging to what remains of their little lives before the frosts come to take them.

The Autumn Equinox to Samhain

The energy of many our plants sinks downwards, back into the Earth which has nourished their growth. This means that it is the ideal time to harvest those plants whose roots we require for magic and medicine. One particularly magical herb whose root is extremely useful, is Elecampane (Inula helenium). This magnificent plant is a truly architectural addition to a garden and, when it flowers, mine is considerably taller than I am. It does, however, need good, rich, moist soil to thrive. Medicinally, Elecampane has a long and venerable history of use for chronic lung problems, such as asthma and bronchitis, and contains 40% inulin, which is a polysaccharide thought to support the lung tissue. Interestingly, it has huge, lung-shaped leaves, which are also lovely for placing offerings on. It is extremely bitter, so also very effective for the digestive system, in the form of a tea or tincture. Alternatively, the root can be candied and used as a sweet to help both digestive problems and asthma. Culpeper (1649) recommends the fresh root as a sugared conserve or a syrup as "very effectual to warm a cold and windy stomach and stitches in the side caused by the spleen and to relieve coughs, shortness of breath and wheezing in the lungs." He goes on to recommend various preparations for numerous other conditions. Elecampane is also one of the ingredients in Absinthe. It is also known as Elfdock and Elfwort, names which give us a clue as to its magic, and it is very much associated with the world of Faerie. An infusion can be drunk to help us contact Nature Spirits, or it can be burned as an incense, or thrown onto the ritual fire to attract them. The flower heads can be added to a pot pourri to give a splash of colour; they are a lovely bright orangey-yellow.

So, we enter the time of the darkening mystery. We feel drawn to the work of divination, of seeking advice about what is to come and finding our direction for the next Quest of the Year, which will come once the light begins to return. Some read the runes or the Tarot, the tree oracle or the witch stones. Others favour the black mirror for this work, delving deeply into its pool of hidden treasure, for it seems often the most appropriate form for the season, while those who are not fond of fancy tools scry in a dyepot, in the bubbling stew or in the Autumn puddles as the rain begins to fall.

Nuts are plentiful. We collect Hazel nuts, not only as delicious and nutritious food, but also to represent the wisdom of the darker portion of the year and in honour of that wise and gentle lady, Mother Julian. Walnuts are an excellent brain food, even being shaped like a brain, in a perfect example of the old "Doctrine of Signatures." This is the idea, dating back centuries, that each plant has some indication, in shape or habit, of how it can be used in our quest for health. So, it is useful to know where there are Walnut trees, especially as fresh green Walnuts have a milder, and more delicious flavour than those which have been dried. It is also possible to make a black dye from their fresh outer covering, which can be used for the hair or for magical cords.

The spiky-cased, Sweet Chestnuts (Castanea sativa) usually provide plentiful free, nutritious and delicious food. There is no need to travel long distances out into the countryside to find them, as they grow in many city gardens and churchyards, and drop their bounty onto the pavements for anyone to gather. This tree came to us with the Romans, but is just like a native now, and beloved as such, growing huge, living for many years, offering shade, beauty and healing. Sweet Chestnuts are associated with the power of the God because, in July, the long, yellow flowers, hanging like tails against long, green leaves, smell of his seed. Sometimes there are two seeds in just one case, so if both are good, one can be shared one with a friend or lover, to seal a bond. They are as lovely raw or roasted, but first you must brave their spiny covering, which will tear your fingers if you do not act with care. So, their magic speaks of generosity, abundance and of sharing, but warns against greed and benefits the brave and careful.

For those suffering from acute despair, the Sweet Chestnut flower remedy can restore control over the emotions and bring light to inner darkness, which sometimes troubles people as Autumn progresses.

Samhain

My eighth it is a trodden maze;
This signals the end of Summer days.

As Samhaintide approaches, we take a great delight in gathering Pumpkins and Squashes of all shapes and sizes, often from people who are selling their surplus vegetables at the roadside. We love to decorate our homes with them, either whole or carved into lanterns. We are aware, of course, that they are not an old tradition of our lands, the idea of using them having come from America. Our ancestors used Swedes or Turnips, but Pumpkins are such a wonderful colour, so dramatic and, it has to be said, a great deal easier to carve than the root vegetables. So, we have enthusiastically embraced the orange and the black as the colours of this festival.

169

In the past, Samhain was the time of the first frost, when communities would come together and it would be cold enough to slaughter those animals which were not to be kept over the winter, hence the old Anglo-Saxon term for this time as "Blood Month" (Bede, 725). These days though, Hallowe'en, on the 31st October, can still be rather warm, so we often put out our decorations for Hallowe'en, aware that many magical groups will be sticking to the exact date, and feeling all that energy beginning to whirl with the fallen leaves, but wait awhile before celebrating this time of the ancestors, at "Old Samhain", about a week and half into November.

Samhain rituals are always emotional, filled with tears and laughter as we remember our blood and magical ancestors, departed friends and beloved creatures. We often set up a spectacular altar, with black mirrors and bowls of water, which reflect the flickering lights of the candles lit to remember the special people who have passed to Summerlands. Occasionally, we choose to commemorate those who have died during the past year by lighting sparklers. This represents how brightly their star has burned during their lifetime, and it is a sombre feeling indeed when the final sparks fly, and we are left holding cold metal and a burnt-out firework.

Samhain rites usually include something to remind us of our own mortality. Sometimes one person will take the role of the Grim Reaper, sending shivers across our warm flesh and a chill into our veins. One person may take an axe and, with an eldritch shriek, sever into two halves a Pumpkin which has been waiting on a block for this moment. Yet the sudden violence also reveals the seeds of hope within, some of which are kept as charms, representing the hope of new life which will flourish during the next Growing Tide.

Something which is almost always included in our Samhain rites is the "toasting". This is an extension of the ritual communion, and we keep refilling the cup and passing it around so that each one of us can toast any departed person or creature. These could be family members or friends, or famous people, and even historical characters who have been dead for centuries. The toasting usually begins in sombre fashion, but the longer it goes on, the more celebratory it becomes!

At times it is considered acceptable, even appropriate, to evoke spirits of the dead, while the veil between the worlds is fine enough to allow this to be done relatively easily. The decision to include such work in a Samhain ritual is never taken lightly. There are two main reasons for doing it: one is out of love, and the other is to retrieve important information. Ritual methods are favoured for the process, although the dumb supper also works well at any time between Hallowe'en and Old Samhain. The latter method involves setting out a dinner table, for all who are to take part, including a chair, food and drink for the deceased person with whom one wishes to communicate. Much useful knowledge can be gained at such dinners, as well as magical assistance from beyond the grave.

Samhain to Yule

So many people dislike the darkest of days between Samhain and Yule, and complain about everything being dull and grey. Yet there is colour everywhere. There are still intensely red and orange leaves, particularly on the Field Maples, and even once the last of them have fallen, there are still plenty decorating the ground. The bright yellows of the Birch leaves lift the spirits too, and it is quite usual for some to remain, clinging to the twigs until Imbolc. As the leaves fall, we always try to catch one before they touch the ground. It is not as easy as it sounds, but such caught leaves are lucky indeed, for they have not yet been "grounded", and retain a very special kind of magic, as do feathers which can be caught before they fall. The type of leaf we catch, especially if it just falls into a basket or gets caught in our hair or on our clothes, as quite often happens, gives us a message about the type of luck we will have while we keep the leaf. For example, a Birch leaf might offer something new to try or to consider, a Sycamore might encourage us to expand on what we have already done, a Hazel leaf will give us wisdom in our thoughts and our choices, while an Apple leaf could herald a time of sweetness and nourishment, or of travelling safely to magical realms.

More colour can be seen in the magnificent sunsets, which can sometimes paint the sky at this time. There will probably still be one or two roses in bloom, and the odd orange Marigold flower, determined to live up to its botanical name, "Calendula", which means that it can be found in flower at every month of the year.

For me personally, the 25th November has long been of significance because St. Catherine, whose feast day this is, is the patron saint of spinners, due, in Christian terms to the grizzly manner of her martyrdom, being broken on a wheel. I tend however to think of her story more in terms of the Wheel of the Year and the "death" of Summer. I have loved spinning since I first learned this magical, yet practical skill, in 1982, in a little stone cottage, in South Glamorgan, in South Wales. On this special date each year, I try to spend the day spinning. I acknowledge my gratitude for being "led" to the right teacher at the right time, for my beautiful spinning wheel and for all the people who have given me tips or supplied me with wool. It is lovely to invite others to join in the celebration, to cram the living room full of whirring spinning wheels, and maybe even produce special cords to mark the day. These may then be kept to bring protection to the spinning equipment and the fleece for the coming year, and to help foster the skill and success of the spinners until new cords are created. Alternatively, they may be hung outside as offerings, or worn over robes in rituals.

There is usually something of a party atmosphere on this day, with peals of laughter, especially from the less experienced or first-time spinners, who enjoy getting themselves tangled in knots. The fun and hilarity flow out in sparkling waves, into the dark world, just like the tiny galaxies of stars flying from the spinning fireworks to which St. Catherine has also given her name. It is a delight to be together, for although we relish the quiet darkness, community has always provided safety and protection during the Winter months.

It is often on this day, exactly a calendar month before Christmas Day, that the Fire Faeries appear. We catch glimpses of them in candle flames reflected in mirrors, in the flash of a headlight on the shiny metallic surface of other cars, or a streetlamp in a window pane. They are the intensity of the sparks within the darkness, reminding us of our own divine spark within. Some years we encourage and celebrate them by dancing around a bonfire, throwing onto it pine cones which have been especially coated to flare with a greenish light. This was first shown to me by a very secretive, hereditary Norfolk witch, who specialises in the magic that is under the ground and under the hedge. She kindly gave me a bag of such Pine cones and giggled when I told her the wild results of our first experiments with them.

Spinning is, of course, not the only craft of the season. It is common to try a new indoor craft, perhaps with a view to producing Yuletide gifts, which is a major task, but a really enjoyable one, sitting alone and thinking about what others within the Nameless Tradition would like to receive.

December 1st has recently taken on a special significance, as Rod and Rue, the Mistletoe King and Queen of East Anglia have declared this to be Mistletoe Day, as it is in other parts of Britain. Those of us who are able to do so now meet at Mulbarton Common, not far South of the city, as this is an area rich in Mistletoe. We walk all around the Common, starting and finishing at the village pond, looking at the Mistletoe in the huge variety of trees it favours here, and speculating on how much it has all grown since the previous year. Finally, we honour the Mistletoe in a short ceremony, in which we toast this magical plant with mead from a horn, then throw into the pond an offering of a small sprig of it, which has been cut with a golden sickle.

As the month begins to reveal its dark secrets, we look to the return of the light, and begin to prepare our decorations, festooning our homes with evergreens and maybe a Christmas tree, as well as increasing the numbers of candles and oil lamps we use, not to mention burning rich and spicy incenses on very possible occasion.

Yuletide

My ninth it is the sheltering altar,
So the newborn seeds do not falter.

There are a couple of gardening tasks which are traditionally carried out on the Winter Solstice itself, before the ritual takes place. One is the planting of Shallots, which should then be harvested on the Summer Solstice. The other is the taking of Holly cuttings, an appropriate task indeed at a time when many people think of the Holly King being defeated by his brother the Oak King. I am reliably informed by an expert on the Holly that, however many cuttings you take on this day, they will either all survive and root or none of them will, depending on the year.

The ritual itself usually focuses on the return of the Light, the spark within the darkness, the birth of the new solar hero, both as the Shining One within the Heavens and as the renewal of that energy within ourselves. Sometimes the ritual may be dramatic and full of colour and drama. Other years we may feel quiet and meditative, and hold a simple colloquy, to share our thoughts and inspirations. One of my favourite rituals, versions of which we have done on a number of occasions, is the Calling of the Light. Each practitioner dresses up as an animal, a plant or some other aspect of nature. Once the Elements and the Lord and Lady have been invited to the Circle, each person in turn, speaking on behalf of the power they represent, explains why they wish for the Light to return. We then all call the Light together. An archway is opened in the Circle, and somebody, dressed in gold with a sparkling crown upon their head, enters the Circle and gives us all the blessing of the Light. It can be very powerful and very moving, especially if everyone has made an effort with their costume and meditated on what they need to say.

We tend to think of Yuletide as covering the entire period from the Solstice Eve until Twelfth Night. It is a time of serious magic as well as of celebration, when the Light has been born but is still vulnerable to the Forces of Darkness as it grows from babyhood through childhood towards its coming into power. This can be a time when difficulties or unpleasantness can suddenly flare up. Passions may run high, fuelled by alcohol, party food and possibly unrealistic expectations of what the festive season may offer.

This has sometimes been a couple of weeks where we carry out a number of rituals, for the purely practical reason that quite a number of us are free from our day jobs for a while and have the time and space to concentrate on magical work. It is not uncommon to celebrate the Solstice, Christmas Day and New Year, when we sometimes focus on the story of Gawain and the Green knight and look to the possible challenges which may be presented to us in the next Quest of the Year. There may also be time to do some experimental magical work and even some rituals in deep snow, which can be special indeed.

So, in a whirr of celebration and magic, we know that we have travelled full Circle once again. One Quest of the Year draws to a close and a new one begins, with all its promise of adventure and an abundance of materials with which to enhance our magic.

References

Barker, Julian (2001) The Medicinal Flora of Britain and Northwestern Europe, Winter Press.

Bede, The Venerable (725) De temporum ratione (Reckoning of Time).

Bown, Deni (2008) The Royal Horticultural Society New Encyclopedia of Herbs & their Uses, Third Edition, Dorling Kindersley.

Buczacki, Stefan (2002) Fauna Britannica, Hamlyn.

Clarke, W.G., and Clarke, R. Rainbird (1937) In Breckland Wilds, Second Edition, Heffer.

Conway, Peter (2001) Tree Medicine, Piatkus.

Culpeper, Nicholas, 1649. The Complete Herbal, Foulsham edition, 1983.

Cunningham, Scott, (1995) Cunningham's Encyclopedia of Magical Herbs, Llewellyn.

Froud, Brian, and Lee, Alan (1998) Faeries, Harry N. Abrams.

Grieve, Mrs M. (1931) A Modern Herbal, Jonathan Cape.

Mabey, Richard (1996) Flora Britannica: The definitive new guide to wild plants, flowers and trees, Sinclair-Stevenson.

Maskill, Louise (2013) Norfolk Dialect, Bradwell.

Pennick, Nigel (2004) Secrets of East Anglian Magic, Second Edition, Capall Bann.

Rear, Michael (2011) Walsingham: Pilgrims and Pilgrimage, St. Pauls.

Williamson, Tom (2006) England's Landscape: East Anglia, English Heritage / Collins.

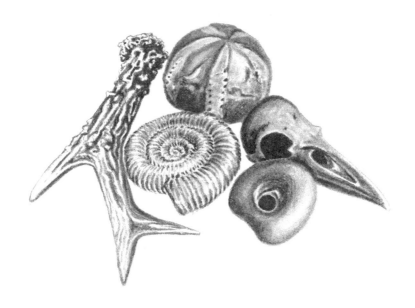

Materia Magica

The turning of the Wheel of the Year produces most of the materials we need for working our magic. Animal, vegetable and mineral material may all form part of these magical activities, be that as a focus for meditation, part of a ritual, something to place upon an altar or part of a charm or spell. These items help to draw through the magic from the astral to the mundane realms, providing a physical link through which spiritual forces may be channelled. They also have their own powers. Herbs have demonstrable pharmacological effects, which are often closely linked to their magical ones, but even more importantly, they have their own spirits which may advise and assist in sometimes surprising ways.

It should be remembered that each plant, animal or stone has its own individual spirit in addition to being a representative of its species, and that needs to be taken into account when selecting items for magical purposes. One piece of Flint is not the same as all the others and a particular sprig of Rosemary, from a special plant, may be chosen as especially apt for the purpose in hand. One Blackbird's feather could be useful whereas another is better left where it has fallen, to be tumbled across the damp grass in the spell of the wind, or to disintegrate calmly so that the magic of flight becomes one with the Earth in the ever-moving cycle of birth, power and decay.

Some of the plants, animals or minerals which provide us with physical ingredients for our magical work are county totems, which have a particular local resonance and act as spiritual intermediaries between our world and theirs, allowing us powerful insights, and providing very special forms of protection as we travel the sometimes tangled and uneasy paths of magic. In addition, those within the Tradition very often have one or more personal totems from any or all of the three physical realms. They may be kept very secret in some cases, never spoken of even to those working within the same group. The totem may be contacted during meditation, shamanic work or formal ritual, and may provide the practitioner with constant companionship and support. For others, a totem may be something which is shared much more widely, its image worn as jewellery, used to decorate the home or even forming part of a logo for a business venture.

Generally speaking, practitioners within Norfolk's Nameless Tradition prefer to use materials from the county and there are even some rites and spells in which everything used, including magical equipment and clothing, are best taken from a very specific local area. Sometimes we will seek out an item for a particular purpose, but we often gather things knowing that they will at some point be useful. Jars of shells, of herbs, of pebbles and of feathers commonly adorn our shelves, along with strings of berries, pieces of bark and numerous other interesting oddments.

178

We are nothing if not practical, however, and if we need something which cannot be found or grown locally, we may well buy it. Gifts from magical colleagues in other parts of the country may prove especially powerful, as may items collected on pilgrimages to distant places.

Whilst it is common for physical items to be used magically, there are those within the Tradition whose mental capacities are so well-developed that they prefer to do most of their work in a more cerebral manner. For most of us, the natural things mentioned in this chapter represent just a few examples of the most frequently-used materials in our magical endeavours.

Gifts from the Sea

With such a long coastline, sweeping round from the North-West to the South-East of the county, it is to be expected that the North Sea provides us with much of what we need on many levels. Besides, beaches are liminal places, between Earth and Water, and treasures collected from them contain all the spirament or sprowl of that very special "between the worlds" energy. Those of us who live inland, still feel the pull of the waves and make frequent trips to enjoy the landscape, to beachcomb or work magically where we can see the Sun or the Moon rising across the water. However, around the coastline, it is now forbidden to collect beach material, so it is important to be aware of what may or may not be taken, and work with items in situ, where appropriate.

Pebble, Pebbles, Pebbles

Take a photo of any square foot of a pebbly section of a Norfolk beach and you have an instant, exquisite work of art. All the pebbles are lovely and they all have potential magical uses. Of course, there is always a chance of finding a semi-precious gemstone, with specific magical uses, such as a piece of jasper or agate, some jet or even a little geode, which may look like a plain flint egg on the outside, but

179

suddenly splits into two halves, revealing a magnificent, miniature crystal cave.

However, the worth that the mundane world places on these things does not necessarily correspond to how much the witch will value it. A "worthless" pebble may have a special shape, colour or pattern which is just what is required at that moment. It could be a protective eye stone, a phallus, an animal statue, an arrow or blade of some kind, but it will be full of meaning and magic.

Sometimes, if the stones are removed, they are not quite as shiny and exciting as they were out in the sunlight, with the power of the waves still clinging to them. If this is the case, it is easy enough to take them back to the beach. Some witches in the area have a stone tumbler to give their pebbles a permanently glossy appearance. There are advantages to this and I do have, in my kitchen, a beautifully tumbled hag stone, which was a gift, but generally speaking, I like the pebbles just as they are.

Pebbles are often used for divinations of various kinds, to assess the magical currents and to determine the most fortuitous course of action. It is quite possible to select twenty-five or so pebbles which each carry a special meaning or piece of advice, according to their smoothness, shape, colour, and to cast them onto a clean cloth and "read" meaning from the pattern they create. Alternatively, one can be selected to provide a quick answer to a question. Three can also be used, one for past influences, one for the present situation and the third for the future.

A Grid of Nine is also popular. This looks like a noughts and crosses grid, in which the bottom row represents the past, the middle row the present and the top row the outcome. The left-hand column shows the hidden aspects of past, present and future, while the right-hand column shows the attitude of whoever is asking the question. The central column shows the effect of the past, the present situation and the best possible outcome. Grids of Nine, which are also a form of magical enclosure, in which the central position is protected (Pennick, 1999), are a particularly popular structure for a divination and can be used for Tarot, the runes or any kind of plant or twig divination. Of course, it is not necessary to take the pebbles from the beach at all. A circular, square or rectangular frame can be held, with a question in mind, over an area of pebbles and a reading made from the colours and patterns observed. This frame can be of any kind, one especially made for the purpose, or even a ring or bracelet.

Not everybody is happy to use stones for divination in their natural state, so many of us paint them with the runes of our Viking or Anglo-Saxon ancestors, the use of which is very much rooted in our landscape. When collecting stones for a rune set, on a deserted beach at dawn or twilight, it is easy to feel the presence of Odin.

Witches' runes are often made from smooth pebbles too, and these can be painted with images of the Sun, the Moon, waves, a tree, a hat, animals and other pictures which carry special meaning for the practitioner. As well as being powerful magical items for divination and spells, some of the sets which I have been privileged to see over the years are real works of art.

Holey Stones

Holey stones, hag stones or even holy stones, as we often call them, are very common around the Norfolk coast and particularly abundant between Cromer and Sheringham. They appear in all manner of shapes and sizes, some being small enough to wear as an earring, while others are so large that it would prove challenging to lift them. They are normally Flint, although there are some exquisite examples which are Chalk. The important feature is that they have a hole right through, formed by the action of waves and smaller pebbles constantly working away at the rock. Those who call them Adder stones say that they are formed of the hardened saliva of a ball of snakes, whose tongues create the holes.

We prize these stones highly and most of us wear one on a piece of cord around our necks, for luck and protection, but also to honour the Lord and Lady of this land, and as a constant reminder of our physical and magical connection to our beautiful surroundings. We also hang them up in our homes and in many places around our gardens. We sometimes make elaborate wire-work mobiles with numerous hag stones attached to them, which can be highly decorative and magical at the same time.

Sometimes people who are new to the Craft have trouble finding holey stones at first but, as with many kinds of foraging, it is just a case of "getting your eye in", after which one afternoon's stroll on the beach is likely to provide more than anyone would be happy to carry. It can be difficult to leave them behind though and, more than once (before the laws on collecting pebbles came into force), a walk turned out to be more exhausting than at first anticipated, due to the weight of stones in pockets, baskets and rucksacks.

Very large hag stones can have specific purposes. They are popular throughout the county with witches and plain folk alike, and are often placed attractively outside the front door. For the practitioner, though, these are used to "give birth" to spells, talismans and poppets, which can be passed through them to bring them to life before they are named and take up their tasks. If a poppet is particularly large, it may be necessary to go to the beach and perform the magic there, at one of the holy stones which are too big to move. We all have our favourites of these and know exactly where they are, although sometimes we arrive to find that sea has snatched them away. Another way of using these stones is to look through the hole in order to see things one would not normally be able to perceive with our worldly eyes. Certain hag stones with especially large holes are best suited to these purposes.

The use of these magical stones is ancient and widespread. Pliny's Natural History tells of holey stones being called serpent's eggs and worn by Druids, who obtained them at a certain phase of the Moon. One only has to handle such a stone to understand why they have been such a source of magical fascination for so long.

It does sometimes happen that our hag stones become a bit tired when we have had them for a while. In such cases the best thing is to take them back to the beach and wash them in the sea. This is not always enough and it may be better just to thank the stone, bid it farewell and return it to the water.

Carnelian

Small pieces of carnelian can be quite easy to find on the beach. They are usually a warm, orangey-red colour but often have some white in them as well. The important thing about them is their translucence, so that, when the sun shines upon them, they gleam far more than any of the other pebbles around them, as if they are calling out to be noticed. Carnelians help bring ideas to fruition, so may prove a useful addition to any spell designed to manifest an idea from the astral in the mundane world, which covers a huge range of magical work. They also have an energising and encouraging effect on those who wear or carry them, so many of us keep one close in a little charm bag.

There are numerous ways in which these lovely and versatile stones can be used, from healing jealousy and envy, increasing self-confidence and assertiveness to improving digestion. I know of several women who use large, red specimens of this gemstone to help ease menstrual problems, although according to one of the greatest practitioners of East Anglian Magic, carnelian operates "almost wholly on the spiritual level" and is used to cleanse the mind of unwanted thoughts. I personally find them very sociable and outgoing, which is perhaps why they are relatively easy to find. Apparently, the Prophet Mohammed and Napoleon both wore one (Holbeche, 1989).

Amber

Amber is one of our most prized gems and forms a mystical bridge, not only between land and sea, and ancient and modern times, but also between the mineral and plant worlds since it is the fossilised resin of the Pine tree, Pinus succinifera. Certain pieces of amber also provide a link to the animal kingdom, where the still-liquid resin trapped some hapless creature trying to escape its sticky flow. There it sits, perfectly preserved some 50 million years later, offering insights to scientists, and a special and curious type of magic to the witch who holds it in their hand.

Amber is very light, warm to the touch, unlike any other beach stone, and also develops an electrical charge, as well as a strong magical one. It comes in a surprising number of colours, from reds and oranges to the pure white which was so prized for use in rosaries in the 13th and 14th centuries (Hunger, 1977).

This warm, mysterious substance had been traded for millennia before that. Indeed, it was the search for amber and tin which, a thousand years before our common era, tempted the Phoenician seafarers away from their warm Mediterranean climes to brave the cold of Northern Europe. From even earlier times, amber beads and buttons have been found at Neolithic sites, dating as far back as 3700 BCE (Hunger, 1977).

Our Anglo-Saxon and Viking ancestors sometimes used amber in their sword fittings as, like many red stones, one of its powers is to the stem the flow of blood. It is known that they loved amber beads too, many having been found in graves, particularly those of the late 6th century, and I have even seen a most exquisite amber spindle whorl from the period. Naturally, amber is beloved of Odin and may be used as an incense in very special rites involving this powerful deity.

Classical writers have associated amber with tears: Sophocles writes of it as the tears of the Meleagrides, sisters of the hero Meleager, who were turned into birds. Another Greek legend, that of Phaeton's disastrous attempt to drive Apollo's Sun chariot, tells us that amber formed from the tears of the Heliades, Phaeton's sisters who wept for so long after Zeus had struck their brother down that even once they had been turned into trees, their tears continued to flow, and were hardened by the Sun into the precious gem (Hunger, 1977).

We often look to ancient legends to add to our understanding of the deep meaning and potential of natural materials, and these tales suggest an interesting aspect to the magic of amber, which is often used for its solar properties, of healing and protection, but is endlessly versatile. It has been used since the days of Pliny and Hippocrates to treat all manner of medical conditions, from impotence to asthma, ear, eye and stomach problems, as well as plague! It brings the warmth of the Sun to those who wear or carry it and is reputed to absorb negativity, so is particularly recommended for those living or working in an emotionally troubled situation. From my own experience, I find it helpful in shining light upon the pathways which lead us back to lost knowledge from the past. It most definitely should be worn, not hoarded, as the warmth and natural oils of human skin deepen its lustre, making it even more beautiful.

It is not that easy to find, and I had to petition the Gods for some considerable time before I was able to find a small piece for myself. It did not appear in the classic place along the strandline, amongst the Amberweed (Flustra foliacea), but was just at the point where the Chalk outcrop emerges from the sea: a gift from the Lady of Norfolk herself. It was so red and so brilliantly lustrous when I saw it, that I picked up this tiny, orange, glowing treasure thinking it was Carnelian, only realising, when I felt its warmth and texture, that I had in my hand, the thing I had sought after so long. It was confirmed to be amber by a local geologist, who also said that I was lucky to find a piece at all as, for the last decade, the tides and currents of these cold seas had been such that very little amber had been deposited at all. This made me extra grateful for the find.

Shells
Most types of shell can be used in protective and hearthside magic, as the shell has given a home and protection to the creature who once lived in it, though each type of shell has its own special magic.

Cockles
Beautiful rune sets can also be painted on the insides of Cockle shells. I have made lots of sets of these, as they make delightful magical gifts. They are light and easy to carry in a small bag or pocket, and make a wonderful musical sound as they come together in the bag or as they are cast. There are some Norfolk beaches which are covered in Cockle shells, and there are still many people who like to eat their inhabitants.

Sea Urchins
There are various beaches where small, grey-green Sea Urchins can sometimes be found, although lots of people don't notice them, so they often get trodden on. These definitely deserve pride of place on a mantelshelf or in a magical sprowl box. Some people consider them to be "fairy loaves" (although stones split open on the top, like a bread roll are also given that name), which will ensure that the household will never want for bread, and others place them on the windowsill to ward off lightning and the evil eye. However, one sees them, they are certainly treasure, and give a real sense of an abundance of good things in life.

Cowries
Cowrie shells can be found here, particularly on West Norfolk beaches. These are Trivia monacha (also known as Cypraea europaea) and Trivia arctica, which are found in

the Atlantic and in the North Sea and have tiny pinky-grey shells (Campbell and Nicholls, 1976).

Cowries have a long history of magical use worldwide, as amulets and in spellwork, mainly because their vulva-like appearance can be used to symbolise Love and Sea Goddesses. It is normally the Gold Ring Cowries (Cypraea annulus annulus) that are used (and these are the ones which have been used as money), but I much prefer our little native beauties, which are far better suited to our local magic.

Sea Glass

Glass is in itself such a magical material. Fashioned from sand with extreme heat and the very breath of life of the craftsperson, it is a special kind of solid, that is still capable of flow: a subtle shape-shifter indeed. When we add to this a lifetime of use, being discarded, broken and tumbled for years in the waves, we have not only a beautiful product, but something which holds within it all the power and insights of numerous transformations.

The glass we find is normally white (produced from the constant tumbling of clear glass) or green, although we do sometimes find blue or orangey-brown pieces. It is quite common to have an attractive jar in which to display them, but we also make them into jewellery or charms to assist alchemical or transformational processes. When working magically to improve local services and the environment, sea glass is of course an excellent addition to spells designed to encourage more recycling.

Sea glass, like pebbles, can make wonderful runic or other divinatory sets. For those of us who enjoy a little bling, gold enamel paint looks wonderful on the glass and is a reminder of alchemy at work.

Fossils

Fossils are just as much prized for magical work as are pebbles and gemstones, and form a link between the world of rocks and the animal kingdom. They are very common around the coast, particularly in the West Runton area, which is famous for its fossils. It was here that in 1990 the first bones of a Mammoth were discovered after a storm. The entire Mammoth was unearthed during the excavation of the site in 1995. In general, fossils can be used to aid memory, to ensure that something important is preserved, or to reveal a little nugget of ancient wisdom. However, each fossil has its particular traditional uses, depending on its shape and associations.

Belemnites

These pale orange, conical fossils once formed part of a long-extinct creature, which is supposed to have looked something like a cuttlefish (Blake, et al., n.d.). Small pieces of them occur very regularly, but the very best ones to find are those that retain their bullet-like shape and have a fairly sharp tip.

Some people describe belemnites as thunderbolts, actual, physical pieces of lightning which have fallen to Earth. They are therefore associated with the Norse god Thor, and are useful in rites which call upon his powers, though care must be taken when working with thunder and lightning strikes. Some people refer to them as Devil's Fingers, or even St. Peter's Fingers but we more commonly call them Elf Bolts, as do many people in Scandinavian countries, and we use them in magic to gain the favour of the Fair Folk. A particularly good specimen found during an outing might well be offered to the garden spirits on returning home. Because of their shape, belemnites make excellent pendants and lovely, weighty pendulums for dowsing. They have healing properties too and can be pointed at a specific area of the body to channel energy there. It is said that a powder made from a ground-up belemnite can be used to heal problems of the eye. It needs to be blown into the eye to be effective (Bassett, 1982). I have to admit I have never tried this, as it does not sound particularly safe! They also make excellent wand tips: far better for our kind of magic than a purchased crystal from the other side of the world. They work particularly well in conjunction with Elder wood and, if the shaft of the wand is carefully selected, the belemnite will slot easily into the hollow centre.

A very simple way to use a belemnite to speed a spell is to write your request on a piece of orange paper, fold the paper into a triangle and roll the belemnite inside it, forming a dynamic shape, like an arrow head. For protection of the project, this should be secured in place using linen thread. Just as the belemnite can be a physical piece of lightning from the heavens, so it can help focus the energy and bring your thought to manifestation in the mundane world, sometimes with the speed of a lightning bolt!

Ammonites

These are the fossils of a group of marine molluscs. Their lovely coiled shape has given them one of their common names, snakestones, so they are naturally said to protect against snakebite and to heal a bite when drawn across it in a special manner. There has always been a strong link between Snakes and Dragons and, in the Middle Ages, these fossils were sometimes associated with Dragons and the magic which attaches to them. They are also known as Ram's horns and the name ammonite derives from the Egyptian Ram God, Ammon, associated at various times with war, virility, invisibility and prophecy (Bassett, 1982).

These fossils can certainly bring luck to their finder and wearer, as well as beautiful, prophetic dreams. Due to their spiralling form, they can help the wearer to find the next steps along their path and provide focus in persevering once the correct direction has been established. I would say that, in Norfolk, ammonites are more difficult to find than belemnites, but of great magical value to anyone who happened to be blessed with such a find.

From the Birds of the Air

Norfolk is very much a county of birds, with its wide skies, long coastline, its salt-marshes, grazing marshes, woodlands and open agricultural areas. It is a magnet for professional ornithologists and amateur twitchers alike, all of whom flock to observe and record the common, the rare, the truly exotic, and the elusive. These people arrive in droves, at certain times of the year, migrating like many of the birds themselves. They are often armed with extremely fancy telescopes, binoculars, cameras and all the other paraphernalia which goes with their kind of magic, to dwell for a short time in the cosy wooden hides which can be found in all the well-known wildlife spots. The witches of the Nameless Tradition also enjoy spending time in these hides, as we are happy to sit for hours, watching, absorbing, adding to our knowledge and understanding. Sometimes a kindly twitcher will point out a special sighting or offer us a glimpse through a powerful telescope, which can be much appreciated. On other occasions, we may sit alone, in silence or perhaps muttering the odd spell as the mood takes us.

The flight of birds, their type, number, pattern and direction as they fly through a specific area of the sky above us can be used for formal divination, by those who favour augury, or just noted as a message, a hint or a sign of approval or disapproval of something. More important, is the feeling of the birds being out there over field, woodland and wave, even while we are indoors, at work or within the home. We may not be able to see them with our physical eyes, at any given moment, but we only have to reach out with our magical minds and there they are, constantly weaving their own invisible spells, filling the air with their own special magic. There are those who have particular totem bird who may fly above the county and bring them back word of anything they need to know. Others are talented in shape-shifting and their astral body may assume the shape of a bird, giving them, quite literally, a bird's eye view of all that is happening.

Feathers have always been an important part of magical work in many traditions. They are gifts which connect us to the special qualities of the denizens of the air, all the more special if they can be caught before they have touched the ground, which earths their magic somewhat. The choice of feathers for any magical task will depend partly on the preferences of the practitioner and partly on which feathers present themselves at any given time.

The Jay

The discovery of one of the distinctive electric blue feathers from the wing of the Jay is a delightful moment. For us, such a find usually indicates approval of a piece of magic or a decision taken. It can provide the creative impetus to tackle a difficult magical or craft project and renew enthusiasm which may have been flagging under the pressure of work.

Traditionally, the Jay has been associated with greedy or garrulous people. They can indeed be noisy sometimes and are not well-versed in the concept of sharing, especially when it comes to the Cherries in our garden, but we favour their presence nevertheless. In Shakespeare's time, chattery or gaudy women were compared with Jays, while the sombre, honest and virtuous women were seen as Turtle Doves. I know which I would prefer to be. Since the Jay utters a piercing shriek when danger threatens, finding a feather can be seen as warning of impending disaster, but my encounters with them have always been experienced as a blessing.

Migratory Birds

Swallows, Swifts and Martins are all important to the witches of the county for the joy they bring each Spring at their return, and the twinge of melancholy we feel when they depart for warmer climes, along with our gratitude for the blessings brought by their fleeting presence.

Swallows have long been seen as divine birds, and various parts of them have been used in magic and medicine over the centuries. Pliny held that young Swallows are blind at birth but that the parent gives them their sight by using the Greater Celandine plant, whose botanical name, Chelidonium, derives from the Greek name for Swallow (Grieve, 1931).

If we ever find a Swallow's feather, which is much more likely for those who live in rural areas, with the old brick barns in which they love to nest, we keep it for spells of vision on physical and magical levels, to ensure a safe journey with a happy return or to help us thread our way through a labyrinth of confusion. Mostly though, just sitting and watching their amazing flying skills, as they swoop at incredible speeds in and out of the small, dark spaces they choose to inhabit while they have their young to care for, is enough to lift the spirits and fill the heart with magical inspiration. Nothing is ever clear-cut though, and there is an old Sheringham saying that when the Swallows sit in rows on the church leads as they prepare to leave, they are settling who is to die before they come again (Rye, 1877).

House Martins were a particular favourite of one of the most gentle, yet powerful members of our tradition, who left us for the next life more than a decade ago. Every year without fail, they nested in the eaves of her house and she cared for and worked magically with them in her own special way. They somehow embody the intensity and creativity of the relationship which can develop between the witch and the wild creatures which live nearby. In order to benefit magically from this, it is not necessary to have feathers or any other parts of these creatures, but to spend time developing a relationship with them and learning from them what they have to teach. It is perhaps not surprising that, in the Christian tradition, it is said that "the Martin and the Swallow / Are God Almighty's birds to hallow" and that they are sometimes said to have been God's assistants when he built the sky (Rowland, 1978). It is interesting that the Swifts, their fellow travellers are associated with the Devil.

Craft Tools

Hikey Sprite

West Runton Chalk

The Author Spinning

The Ickeny

Rowan Craft

The Witch's Leg

Deer skull, deer foot bell and old sickle at the Autumn Equinox

Ethelbert Gate

Stockton Stone

Warham Camp

Warham Camp

Blackbird

Blackbird feathers are so easy to find. For those who are good singers, a spell made of their feathers can enhance their talents even more, and also help them to be appreciated more publicly, if that is what is required.

Not all of us have such ambitions, of course, so we use a little bunch of the feathers made into a fan with a yellow bead to make it easier to greet the morning with joyful enthusiasm. This is particularly useful in the Winter of course, when getting up in the dark can seem quite unappealing. The number of feathers can be chosen according to the hour at which you wish to rise: five for the really enthusiastic, seven for a normal working day and so on. When using this little incentive, it is wonderful how often the Blackbird's song is the first thing you hear on waking.

Blackbirds are easy to work with magically, even for city dwellers, because they are so close to us. We can spend time watching them and befriend particular individuals when they join us in the garden, and even have arguments with them when they insist on taking one peck out of every apple on the tree! It is quite remarkable how well they can adapt their behaviour to things which humans do. A pair of Blackbirds once even nested in the Christmas tree in Norwich station. Of course, the tree had to be left until the youngsters fledged. Later, an even cheekier pair (perhaps offspring of the Christmas tree couple), chose the wheel arch of a police car outside the main police station in Wymondham as their nesting site, much to everyone's amusement. They too were allowed to raise their family before the police car went back on the road.

Observing and really understanding the nature of creatures we work with, and interacting with them on a mundane as well as on the enchanted levels, is an important part of our magic. The more we know about the natural world and the creatures around us, the more effective our operative magic becomes.

Wood Pigeon

Pigeons are not generally among the most popular of creatures, being a considerable agricultural pest, to the extent that shooting of them is allowed all year round. As well as the mild winters, it is the Oilseed Rape production which has allowed them to thrive in their current numbers, providing them with a constant supply of nourishment. Indeed, Britain is the only European country in which they remain all year round.

There are plenty of folk who just wish they would go away, but those within the Nameless Tradition have considerable affection for them nevertheless, as totems of the Lord and Lady of Norfolk (see Chapter 1). They have much to teach us about simplicity and success. Their nests seem so sparse and so flimsy that it is remarkable that their eggs and hatchlings don't just topple out, and yet they breed prolifically and provide us with numerous feathers for fans and even cloaks. Their pattern of flight is beautiful too, as is their soothing cooing, the way they land in the branches, the clamour and clatter they make and the way they can look at you so intently.

From the Creatures of the Earth

Deer

Red Deer, Roe Deer and little Muntjac all thrive in Norfolk, and are honoured by those of the Tradition for their innate beauty and grace, as well as for their connection to the horned deities of the landscape, and to our beloved St. Withburga. Roe Deer and Muntjac are not infrequent visitors to the City, and many a time we have seen them in the evenings, wandering into gardens or negotiating the passageways between the rows of terraced houses near Lion Wood or Mousehold Heath. Pieces of antler are often used in the making of wands or to attach to the top of stangs, and a Deer skull may be placed on the altar for certain types of ritual. For divination, especially regarding local, rather than personal matters, it can be helpful to cast runes or twigs onto a Deerskin mat, while ringing a bell with a Deersfoot handle can be a powerful way to begin a ritual. To my knowledge, these bells are not made nowadays, but they were popular in Victorian times, and it is not unusual to find one in an antique shop, especially if we ask nicely.

Cat

Cats are the Lady's creatures, associated with Freya in particular. They make excellent familiars because they are so in tune with the currents of magic and have always been favoured companions of Craftspeople throughout the land, and associated with Witchcraft by the general public. Because it is their whiskers which enhance their sensitivity, those of us who have Cats always save these when they are shed and keep them safe to assist us in this area. White whiskers are much easier to find than black ones, of course, but to keep a mixture of colours, in a round bottomed bottle is a great aid to divination and to keeping the senses as finely-tuned as possible. They can be added to spells too, or be incorporated into wands, especially those made from Elder Wood, because they are hollow.

Cat's Claws are like little Moons, and they too are shed naturally. A bottle of them shaken at each New Moon, will confer fierce protection on one's own "territory", be that a physical space or of some other kind. They can also help us to relax, to enjoy the luxury of what we have and to remember the importance of making ourselves comfortable, for Cats have plenty of self-respect and know well how to ensure that their needs and wishes are met.

Sheep

So much of the history of Norfolk and of the whole of East Anglia has been connected with the wealth gained through the means of the Sheep. Wool gives life-saving warmth and comfort during a cold Winter, and is one of the most important raw materials from which we spin our yarns, both literally and figuratively. The great "wool churches", seen everywhere in the landscape, underline the connection between our gentle, woolly friends, who provide for our everyday needs, and the striving to express something spiritual and uplifting. They are also a case of earthly prosperity being channelled into spiritual purposes (taking a non-cynical view of the practice). Sheep are very much the creatures of the Lady of Norfolk, and often seem to have emerged directly from her Chalky landscape, so the very best Winter robes and cloaks are made from wool handspun from local Sheep. Not all practitioners want to go to such lengths, of course, but most will have at the very least, a cord which they have made from wool given to them by a local Sheep farmer.

Handmade woollen felt is also very useful for bags for magical items and as the basis of spells, as it can easily be decorated with symbols or have other items attached to it. Traditional witch's hats are felted from black Sheep's wool, and we do like to make them and wear them on the right occasion. Currently our best black wool for such purposes comes from a lovely farm in Terrington St. Clement, in the Fenlands, where Tiddy Mun flits through the mists and Tom Hickathrift defends the land from the encroaching Giant, using only a cart axle and an eight-spoked wheel.

Alpacas

In recent years, it has become very popular to keep Alpacas, and small flocks of these fabulous, exotic creatures have appeared in many areas of the county. Many people now favour their luxury fibre, which certainly has a glamour abut it. However, it is to my mind more difficult to spin than Sheep's wool, as its silkiness makes it rather slippery, and it is still the Sheep which have the ancient connection to the landscape.

Nevertheless, the Alpacas will no doubt establish their own place here and, in time, become part of the rich history of the place. Indeed, one of the Hermits of Mole End worked for a number of years with Alpacas and adored each one of his charges. He came to understand them and to appreciate fully their caring and loyal ways. At that time, much of the Hermits' magical and mundane craftwork was produced from Alpaca wool, and I even made a witch's hat which incorporated some black Alpaca fibre. It was a particularly tall and pointy hat, which took on a magical life of its own and migrated to become part of a local Wiccan Coven. Where it has gone now, I do not know, but it was certainly on a magical mission of some kind.

Snakes

Keeping a house Snake is traditional. In the past, it was often Adders which were favoured, but many practitioners now have a Corn Snake, as these are usually gentle non-venomous creatures. They provide a protective foundation for the home and for the magic which is created there, a kind of unobtrusive yet powerful presence, an undemanding solidity. We have had two Snakes in our home since 1999, and one of those was already seven years old when she came to us, so there is considerable consistency there. Yet when change is needed, the Snakes can provide the material and the know-how to help it to happen, because they are able to shed their skin and emerge renewed and gleaming. Such skins, if they remain whole are most valuable in various kinds of spellwork, and I have often been asked for them by practitioners who do not themselves keep Snakes.

Frogs and Toads

Much has already been written about the traditions of the Toadsmen and -women, who float the skeleton of a dead creature (often cruelly killed) on running water at midnight. The bone which floats back towards them is of great magical significance and is treasured, as it gives them power over animals and humans (Pennick, 2004). Some of those who currently practise within the Nameless Tradition are Toadspeople. Some have carried out the full rite, to the letter, while others have waited until they happened upon a dead Frog or Toad. However, commitment to such a path is not one to be taken lightly and, although it can confer great power, it also demands a heavy price. For this reason, many of us choose not to undertake the rite, which is by no means essential to the work we do in a 21st-century context.

The wearing of Frog or Toad jewellery or the keeping of Frog images or statues of Frogs around the home is considered lucky whether one is a Toadsperson or not, and can help to attract money. As amphibians which change their form as they grow and develop, these creatures help us to be flexible and to understand the deeper connections between Earth and Water, to move from one world to another and to allow ourselves to transform completely as life's labyrinth requires.

Ladybird

The Ladybird, or Bishee Barnabee, as it is known here, is most definitely a Norfolk totem and is used as a good luck charm by many. Our local occult emporium, Inanna's Magical Gifts, sells them in a variety of forms, including earrings and necklaces, as well as little wooden ones with sticky pads on the back. Lots of these have been placed strategically around the shop to attract luck.

Of course, most people throughout Britain love Ladybirds, at least the native ones, as opposed to the Harlequins which, since first being spotted in a pub garden in Essex in 2004, have posed a serious threat to our treasured "original" (Marren and Mabey, 2010). Indeed, throughout Europe they are considered to be bringers of good fortune. We like to think though, that in Norfolk we have an extra special relationship with them.

The name is generally considered to come from "Our Lady's Bird", a reference to the Virgin Mary who, although generally depicted in blue, as Queen of Heaven, is also painted in red, notably by Leonardo da Vinci, supposedly to represent the blood of Christ. The seven spots of the Ladybird are an example of the mystic number seven, the seven joys, seven sorrows, seven stars and so on (Chapman, 2007). Although they can have different numbers of spots, the seven and two spot types account for 80% of all recorded British Ladybirds (Marren and Mabey, 2010).

The Norfolk name for the Ladybird has been the subject of much speculation. Some have said that it refers to Bishop Barnaby, who is not a known historical figure. Others have said it is a link to the red cloak of a cardinal, or "the bishop is burning", meaning a holy man burned for his faith. More sinister, some claim that it may derive from "Bishop Bonner's Bee", alluding to Bishop Edmund Bonner, who was Rector of Dereham, in Mid-Norfolk, from 1534-8, and who, as Bishop of London, was later responsible for the burning of over two hundred heretics during the reign of Bloody Mary (Skipper, 2018). I find it hard to believe that such a delightful and lucky creature should have attracted such an ominous name, especially as Ladybird is a term of endearment and a group of Ladybirds is referred to as a "Loveliness".

From a modern magical perspective, it is worth remembering that, through two very successful companies, Ladybirds now have strong associations with books and clothes (Marren and Mabey, 2010) and may be used in spells connected with these items. However, we regularly wear a piece of Ladybird jewellery to attract general good fortune and to keep us connected to powerful, beneficial spirit of these insect gems. For those who do not like buying any of their magical items, Ladybirds are easy to paint onto pebbles or discs of wood, and the physical act of painting deepens the magical connection.

Shield Bugs

There are many different types of Shieldbug in Britain, including those associated with Woundwort and Birch. The most common is the Green Shieldbug, which likes

Raspberries and Blackberries. These beautiful insects are, as their name suggests, shield-like in shape and are thus great protectors of gardens and homes. They also form a link to heroic legends and are particularly associated with the Arthurian tales of Gawain, the Green Knight and the Green Chapel, often displaying the magical colours associated with the stories: red, green and gold. They are friendly too, and will sit for a long time on a finger, allowing their colour and shape to be fully appreciated. Taking time over this is a magical act in itself, and will certainly lift the spirits, as well as leaving us feeling that we have been granted the protection of one of the knights of old.

Another indicator of the protective power of this jewel-like creature is the fact that it secretes a fluid which discourages predators. This is a type of hydroquinone chemical, with the classic scent of Almonds, which is a warning of the presence of cyanide. In the past they were dried and kept in jars and could be powdered for use in both medicine and magic. Medicinally, the powder was a popular treatment for colic, fevers and urinary tract problems, often mixed with rosewater and/or honey (Marren and Mabey, 2010). Magically, the powder has been sprinkled around an item or place which requires particular protection or taken to enhance the practitioner's connection with our heroic mythology and to inspire creativity. However, I have never tried this personally as I feel sufficiently blessed and uplifted simply through contact with the living insect.

Magical Plants
There are no plants which are not imbued with magic and power. All have their uses and every practitioner has their own favourites, be those exotics or natives. I have mentioned just a few. The key to working successfully with them is to develop a good breadth and depth of knowledge about them, through reading, through listening to others talk about them, by using them and by paying attention and

forging relationships with the plants themselves. (Always be cautious when using herbs. Ensure that you have properly identified them and don't use them if you are pregnant, breast feeding or taking medicines with which herbs may be contraindicated).

Auriculas (Primula auricula)

Auriculas are wonderfully colourful and varied flowers. They were especially beloved of the Dutch weavers who fled to the city of Norwich in the 16th century to escape religious persecution in the Low Countries, bred them for their patterns, colours and textures, and used them as inspiration for their weavings: plants and textiles in a mutually beneficial cycle of creative magic. By the 18th century, Norwich was an important centre for growing Auriculas, as well as Tulips, Roses and Anemones (Heaton, 2017).

Modern Auriculas are descendants of Primula pubescens, a cross between Primula auricula and Primula hirsute. Tradition has it that Alpine peasants discovered this hybrid growing in the mountains beyond Innsbruck before 1583. It was taken to the garden of Maximilian II, where it came to the notice of the court botanist, Charles L'Ecluse, who is best known by the Latin name, Clusius. He developed the Auricula and took it with him when he returned to his native Low Countries. It was from here it spread to Britain (Baker and Ward, 1995). Gerard, in 1597, made the first mention of them in English, referring to them as "Beares eares, or mountaine Cowslips". He tells us that it is a "beautiful and brave plant", with a faculty of healing wounds, both inward and outward, as well as having "virtues in curing palsies cramps and convulsions". Particularly interesting from a magical point of view, he continues:

Matthiolus and other later writers have given names according to similitude, or of the shape that they beare unto other plants, according to the likeness of the qualities and operations: you may

*call it in English Beares-eare: they that dwell about the Alpes
doe call it by reason of the effects thereof; for the root is amongst
them in great request for the strengthening of the head, that
when they are on the tops of places that are high, giddinesse and
the swimming of the braine may not affect them.*

This is an excellent piece of sympathetic magic, which is
certainly be useful in charms to help those who are afraid
of heights but also, with a little imagination, in spells to
give courage to those who would like to live a more creative
life in art, poetry, music or in particular textile art, but feel
nervous or giddy about setting out on the arduous climb to
success in those fields (or mountain tops).

One excellent practical feature of the Auricula is that
it likes good light but not full sun. This means that an
otherwise unproductive shady area can become a blaze of
colour, ideal in a city of narrow streets. My kitchen roof is
always in the shade and I can see the Auriculas I grow there
out of the bedroom window. They are also so placed that
a couple of our neighbours have a really excellent view of
them, since the sharing of beautiful things is an important
part of our magic.

Auriculas also remind us of the practical and magical
connections with our Dutch neighbours, just across the North
Sea. The influence of these brilliant incomers, who became
known as the "Strangers", may be seen and felt in many places
in the county, from the gable ends of 17th-century cottages
to drainage systems of Broadland and the Fens.

Flax (Linum usitatissimum)

The Flax plant must be one of the world's most magical
botanical treasures. It is a delicate plant, with bluey-green
leaves and flowers the pure blue of a clear Midsummer
sky. It is known throughout Europe and North Africa
for its amazing properties and, not surprisingly, given its
flower colour, is said to have been a gift to humankind
from Isis, who also taught people how to spin it. We would

have needed divine assistance because the fabulous long fibres require a lengthy, complicated preparation process, before they can be spun and woven into fine fabrics for both household and magical purposes.

The Flax plant is well-rooted in the history of the county. Although it is more famous for its wool, Norfolk also had a thriving linen industry during Medieval and Tudor times. Those who contributed to it were independent craftspeople, weavers and smallholders, and it is interesting to note that after the industrial revolution, a complex combination of factors, from control of the spinners to cheap cotton imports, led to its decline, so that by the mid-19th Century, the growing, spinning and weaving of linen had effectively disappeared, apart from a brief revival in Sandringham during World War Two. Perhaps, as with many things in Norfolk, Flax works better in the care of individuals who are free to work in their own way rather than under the rule of those who would stamp their authority on people who wish to do things their own way.

Nowadays, Flax has made a reappearance in Norfolk and, driving through the countryside in June, fabulous blue fields can be seen. This time, the crop is not the fibre, but the seed, for the production of linseed oil and as a food.

In Norfolk magic, we use the stems of Flax, with the seed heads still attached, to fashion circlets which can be attached to the stang, to honour the connection between Earth and Sky, to request healing and protect our work. Linen robes are sometimes worn, and pieces of the fabric used to wrap magical items and tools for divination. Many of those who follow a high magic path prefer silk for such purposes, but linen is much more closely connected to our own land. Linen thread is favoured for much of the stitching or tying up of charms and talismans.

The seeds are powerfully protective against all evil and are often scattered around the outside of a property or in all four corners of a room which is troubled by difficult spirits. Growing Flax is also beneficial and it is said that the most powerfully magical seeds are produced from plants grown in a human skull. We eat the seeds on a regular basis, magically connecting to them, but also because they are physically beneficial to the lungs and the digestive system, being demulcent, healing and rich in beneficial oils. At Twelfth Night, it is the usual practice to scatter linseeds over the tools which will be used to help produce the crops for the coming year. Traditionally, this would be the plough, but for those of us who are not farmers we may bless gardening tools, paint brushes or pens in this way. This ensures that the harvest to come will be successful and will not be blighted by envy. An excellent meditation on the power of this plant is to take a small, very narrow necked bottle and place one linseed at a time into it until the bottle is full. This is not a quick process, but much can be learned from it and the bottle of seeds can be strategically placed in the home or car to provide very strong protection.

Should we wish to communicate with spirits of the dead, we do not use linseeds to protect the area because they can make it extremely difficult for the deceased to cross the barrier between the worlds. Indeed, one of the traditional uses of linseeds is to protect places from hauntings and to prevent those who have passed returning.

Rowan (Sorbus aucuparia)
One of the most commonly used trees of protection, in many British Witchcraft traditions, is the Rowan, and it is hugely popular within the Norfolk traditions, being grown in most witches' gardens for the protection the tree itself confers, for the wood and for the berries.

God's Eyes are simple, protective charms made from a cross of its twigs, wrapped round with red wool. Ideally the twigs should be taken from a tree one has never seen before. They need to be made every year, as their power does wane over time, especially if they are hung outside or in windows where the light is constantly upon them. Making new ones, which is usually done at the Equinoxes, is no hardship as the process itself is quite addictive. While the thread is being wound, a charm can be muttered and an appropriate visualisation carried out. Many witches love to string the berries on a linen thread, perhaps with the addition of a hag stone, and hang these necklaces around windows, doors and mirrors.

Although many people believe them to be poisonous, Rowan berries have remarkable health benefits, although it is best not to eat them raw. My old mentor, a cunning man in the Swedish forest, used to dry them carefully and grind them into powder, which he added to the flour he used for baking his bread and biscuits. He used to say that there was more vitamin C in one Rowan berry than in an Orange. In Britain, they are most commonly made into syrups or jellies. Indeed, for the meat eaters amongst us, Rowan berry jelly is an excellent complement to game dishes, going particularly well with venison.

The other health benefits of the berries come from the fact that they contain anthocyanins, tannins, flavonoids, quercetin and rutin. This makes them anti-bacterial, anti-oxidant, anti-inflammatory and an immune system booster. Mrs. Grieve (1931) recommends the berries to make a gargle for sore throats and the bark, decocted, for diarrhoea. Add to all that the magic of the tree and you have a powerful mixture indeed.

Lavender (Lavandula spp.)

Lavender, a much beloved herb of most magical practitioners, has a special place in the hearts of those of our Tradition, because Norfolk Lavender is so uplifting and so special to the county. The "tradition" of growing Lavender commercially here dates back to 1932, when the then famous Lavender growers of Mitcham, South London, were giving up their fields due to the lure of selling land at a high price for urban development and problems with disease. Linn Chilvers, a florist and nurseryman from Heacham, bought up six acres of fields and, in the face of doubts from local farmers, founded the now hugely successful Norfolk Lavender company. Chilvers, along with just three men and one boy, planted the land with 13,000 plants over a period of only 18 days (Norfolk Lavender, 2017). Now, a Summer visit to Heacham is a regular part of our annual calendar, and any essential oil of Lavender that we use for cosmetics, household products, medicine or magic will usually be bought from there.

Chilvers' story is a good indication of just how the Mercurial power of Lavender can help us to achieve what may seem to be impossible dreams, by providing the impetus just to get on and do something, even if others doubt us. Midsummer, when the gold of the Sun is at its height and the Lavender flowers are at their best, can be a good time to create a dream-achieving spell. It could be in the form of a cake or shortbread, to which a little powdered Lavender has been added, or involve a Circle cast in Lavender flowers. Alternatively, a plait or favour might be made, using the flower heads and stems in the same way as one would make a straw plait. If this is the case, the type of project which is the subject of the dream will dictate the number of stems and the type of plait selected. With any of the ways in which Lavender can be used for this purpose, it is a good idea to make a sachet to wear or keep in a pocket, so that the scent of Lavender remains with one in the background, as a reminder that this spell is "in the air". Other items might be included in the sachet: some gold if this is a project concerning wealth, some rose petals if it involves love, relationships or friendship, a Bay leaf if great success and recognition are required, some Eyebright or Clary Sage if clarity of vision is required, and so on.

Of course, Lavender also has a wealth of medicinal properties, and can help with nervous headaches, depression, stress, exhaustion and panic (especially if taken with honey). It is also a good antiseptic and can aid a sluggish circulation. It often works well in small doses, but can have the opposite effect is too much is used. This is particularly true in the case of insomnia. While a small amount of Lavender will aid sleep and relaxation, a large dose will be far too stimulating.

Juniper (Juniperus communis)

This evergreen conifer grows as a shrub anywhere from the Mediterranean to chilly Northern European climes, but it can in the right situation grow to quite a sizeable tree. The name comes from the Latin, junior, the young one, because the younger berries appear before the older ones ripen and fall. There are not that many growing wild in Norfolk, although they can be found on Scolt Head, an island and nature reserve with limited access by ferry from Burnham Overy Staithe, and also at Buckenham. We nevertheless use them a lot and plant one in the garden if we can. Numbers of Juniper trees throughout the UK have fallen dramatically in recent years, so it is important to protect and encourage them.

Juniper berries, which are technically not berries, but very small cones, are important in both magic and medicine. They have long been used for the urinary tract and as an external treatment for rheumatic pains and arthritis, as well as for flatulence and weak digestion, as Juniper is warming and relaxing for the digestive system. It can also be used for coughs and chest infections, and has been described as "truly a marvel among medicinal trees" (Conway, 2001). Indeed, for the witch or magician, it is a marvel indeed. It can be prescribed in the form of an infusion, a syrup or for external use as an oil or ointment. However, long term use of this herb is not recommended. It should not be taken internally for more than six weeks at a time, must be avoided in pregnancy and by anyone with a kidney problem.

The berries are excellent in spicy Winter incenses and the twigs and needles are useful in cleansing or exorcism. Juniper is one of the woods, along with Sandalwood and

Cedar, which are used, on a beach, to create the magical Fire of Azrael. (See Dion Fortune's The Sea Priestess for more information on this. Be aware, however, that it is illegal to light fires on beaches!) Both twigs and berries are highly protective. The twigs can be worn or carried to prevent accidents, and the berries can be strung into protective necklaces, much like Rowan berries. Using a single Juniper berry as the heart of a protective poppet, made of wax or fabric, can guard a home against theft.

In Sweden, Juniper wood is much prized for craft work. Fragrant kitchen utensils, particularly butter knives, are made from it, presumably because the oils have an anti-bacterial effect. I have had several of these for over twenty years and they still retain their fragrance, even after constant use and washing up. Sometimes the wood is even used for lamps which, when they are lit, have a wonderful red glow. They are often hung in the window, mainly because they look fabulous, but many people are also aware of their apotropaic properties.

Juniper berries are traditionally used when cooking game meats, such as Pheasant or venison. They are used for flavouring ales in some Northern countries and are most famously used in gin, which derives its name from the Dutch word for the plant. This is why some people believe that gin drinking is good for the kidneys! I wouldn't recommend it as alcohol is bad for the kidneys and should be avoided by anyone with any urinary tract problems.

Sweet Flag (Acorus calamus a.k.a. verus)

Sweet Flag, which is also known as Sweet Rush, Sweet Cane, Sweet Myrtle and Cinnamon Sedge, is a member of the Arum family and has a lovely fragrance, which made it an important strewing herb in the past. According to Mrs. Grieve (1931), the floor of Norwich Cathedral was strewn with it for the great festivals until not long before the time at which she was writing. The plant has long been used medicinally, and the genus name, Acorus, comes from the name used by Dioscorides, which derives from coreon, meaning the pupil of the eye, since it was used to treat eye problems. It was supposedly first brought to Europe, from its native Asia, in 1567, and by 1610 it was being cultivated here (Mabey, 1996). Gerard certainly cultivated it in his garden in Holborn, London, and Cardinal Wolsey was accused of extravagance for using it for his own floors, due to the expense of transporting the material from Norfolk or Suffolk to London. Indeed, at one time, Sweet Flag, known locally as Gladdon (slightly confusing as this is also the common name of the Iris foetidissima) was an important harvest on the Norfolk Broads, and many people went out in small boats to collect it (Grieve, 1931). The 17th-century doctor and alchemist, Sir Thomas Browne, wrote of the Sweet Flag, in a letter:

> *This elegant plant groweth very plentifully, and beareth its julus yearly by the banks of Norwich river... and also between Norwich and Hellsden-Bridge; so that I have known Heigham Church ... strewed all over with it. It hath been transplanted, and set on the sides of marsh ponds in several places of the county...*

Medicinally, the plant has long been used as a tonic, as it is an aromatic bitter and can stimulate production of digestive secretions. However, it has the opposite effect if given at a much lower dose (less than 5ml a week), so is very useful for treating people who suffer from acid reflux or who have a peptic ulcer. It is believed by some to be an aphrodisiac. It is also useful to give the dried root to babies to chew to help with teething (Grieve, 1931).

Magically, keeping pieces of Sweet Flag root in the corners of the kitchen can help prevent hunger and poverty and helps stop the Weevils causing a problem. The root can also be carried for luck, money, healing and protection, so this is a very versatile plant ally, and growing the plant brings particularly good fortune to gardeners.

Orris

Orris root is an essential magical material because it is a perfume fixative and can help incenses, sachets and other preparations retain their scent and their magic for some considerable time. It is also a very magical ingredient in its own right, and can form the basis of certain kinds of powder. This precious ingredient is made from the roots of Irises, specifically Iris pallida, I. germanica, the German Iris or Blue Flower de Luce, and Iris florentina, the White Flower de Luce. Orris root was important in perfumery in ancient Greece and Rome and was well known to both Theophrastus and Dioscorides. By the time of Gerard, all three of these Irises were well known in Britain, although they were not grown commercially, so that much of our Orris root is traditionally imported. Orris production takes considerable time because the plants do not reach maturity for two to three years. Then, when the root is first harvested, it is somewhat acrid and needs to be dried and left to mature before it is ready for powdering and use. Unlike many perfumes, the scent of Orris root seems to improve rather than deteriorate with age. Orris root contains a ketone called irone, which is what gives it a scent very similar to that of Violets, and it has been used as a substitute for "real" Violet perfume (Grieve, 1931).

Orris root is of course associated with the Greek goddess, Iris, who is quite popular here for her colourful rainbow associations, as a guardian of the dyepot and for bridging the expanse between Heaven and Earth, which means that the powder can be used in work for contacting the Higher Self. Some people use it in love attracting powders and others to protect against evil spirits.

White Bryony (Bryonia dioica)

Most magical practitioners associate White Bryony with its use as a false Mandrake, and remember the tales of people being sold Bryony roots carved to mimic the humanoid shape of the much-prized and more exotic roots of the true Mandrake (Mandragora officinarum), which have been used as poppets for all kinds of purposes over the centuries. However, this is to underestimate the power which Bryony has in its own right. The root, if hung up in the house is a good protection against being struck by lightning, and it can also be used as a medicine to treat coughs, catarrh and rheumatic complaints, although great care has to be taken with dosage as it is very poisonous, and many herbalists these days prefer gentler remedies for such ills, as there are plenty to choose from. For me though, the White Bryony is much more associated with wealth and with the gems so much beloved of the various Dragons who dwell within the county. In the Autumn, long after the Bryony's soft leaves and stems have withered, the berries remain, garlanding the hedgerows, gleaming and bright, in their reds, greens, yellows and oranges, like jewelled necklaces, string after string of riches beneath the fairy gold falling from the trees. Then when the new growth reappears in the Spring, the pliable shoots of the plant and its delicate tendrils belie the power driving its rapid growth and expansion. The greeny yellow, striped flowers appear early to the delight of bees and other insects who are drawn to it to gather their own treasures, filling the air with their music in exchange. So, the power of this plant can be used to enhance one's own wealth, if one of the berries is sown with a silver coin beneath it. As the plant grows, so will the wealth of the practitioner.

Some years ago, a White Bryony self-seeded in my front garden. Delighted as I was to have this plant nearby, I was worried about the poisonous berries being eaten by children passing the house, so reluctantly dug out the root, which was already quite substantial. I halved it and hung one piece up inside the house and gave the other to a magical colleague. The following year was financially disastrous, and I realised that this might well be connected to the loss of the Bryony. So, I brought a berry from a favourite Mid-Norfolk spot and sowed it in the back garden, with a suitable coin, of course. Not only did that plant thrive, but the one in the front reappeared, presumably from just a small slither of root left behind. This time I thought I'd better learn my lesson and leave it where it clearly wanted to be. Much to my amusement, it turned out to be a male plant anyway and although it produces an abundance of flowers every year, it never has any berries. The plant in the back garden, however, is smothered in berries every year, which trail along the fence where no children ever walk past. This was an excellent lesson, not just in the power of the Bryony in matters of wealth, but also in having faith in magical occurrences.

Plantain (Plantago major)

This apparently humble little plant is a powerful ally indeed, and, downtrodden as it is on paths, in lawns and on patches of wasteland, its virtues and usefulness should not be overlooked. The name given to it by our Anglo-Saxon ancestors, who had a wealth of herbal knowledge, was wegbrade or "waybread", and this is still a commonly used alternative name for the plant. It is, as the Anglo-Saxon Nine Herbs Charm tells us, a mother of plants. The Charm, addressing the plant itself, continues:

> *"Brides cried over you, bulls snorted over you, you withstood them all and you were crushed. So, you may withstand poison and infection and the evil which travels round the land"*

(Pollington, 2000).

Not surprisingly, this herb has a wide range of actions, both internal and external. It is anti-bacterial, anti-histamine, a lymphatic, a blood tonic, a wound herb, an excellent remedy for neuralgia, and is used to treat kidney and bladder complaints. It is interesting that many modern herbalists favour the use of the Ribwort Plantain (Plantago lanceolate), which is chemically very similar to Greater

Plantain (Bruneton, 1995), but which has spear-like leaves that stand well above the ground and tend to be cleaner and much easier to harvest than those of its downtrodden cousin. I have had much success using this herb, which has more of the warrior about it than its cousin. After all, its leaves are spear-shaped and, as children, we all used its tough stalks and seed heads to make little weapons to fire at one another. So, the Greater Plantain is gentler, and works much better for people who are oppressed, demoralised, ignored or have no idea how they are going to manage. Magically, the dried herb can be used in sachets to help those who find themselves in such difficult situations.

Poppies

In an agricultural county, the power of the Poppy is of great importance to the magical work. This is especially the case here, since part of North Norfolk has been known as "Poppyland" ever since the term was first used by the poet Clement Scott in the 19th century." It has been believed since ancient times that having Poppies growing alongside the cereal crops would improve the quality of the harvest, and Poppies have long been associated with harvest deities, not least the Corn King or John Barleycorn, who is cut down in order to produce food and drink to sustain the community, and whose blood is envisioned as the red of the Field Poppies (Papaver rhoeas), sprinkled across the golden grain. In other areas of the world there are goddesses associated with the Poppy, from whose stories we can learn much which is also applicable to our own magic. Ceres, for example, was said to have been too tired to care for her crops properly, so Somnus, the God of Sleep, gave her the Poppy to allow her some much-needed rest (Lavender and Franklin, 1995). An almost 80cm tall, terracotta statue of a pre-Hellenic Poppy Goddess, thought to date back to the thirteenth century BCE, was found in a shrine at Gazi, Crete, just to the West of Knossos. She has her hands raised, perhaps in invocation or blessing, an expression of ecstasy on her face, and a crown of three poppies on her head. This unnamed goddess has been thought to be a bringer of sleep, death, forgetfulness or drug-induced peace, because Poppies contain alkaloids which have narcotic effects. She is so beautiful and so simple, and a replica of her can enhance the tranquillity of gardens, and she seems quite at home here.

Opium Poppies (Papaver somniferum), sometimes known as the White Poppies, or Mawseed, grow very well in Norfolk, and can even be found thriving in cracks in the pavement or on stony driveways. Its reputation is dubious and mixed, since it is from this plant that opium is produced. This drug is hypnotic, sedative, anti-spasmodic and used as pain relief and to treat coughs. It has a long history of use in medicine, dating back to ancient Egypt and beyond, and was introduced to China by Arab doctors, who used it to treat dysentery and cholera. It is the juice of the plant which is used, collected from the seed heads, which are carefully cut to allow the milky white sap to ooze out. Indeed, the word opium is derived from the Greek opos, which means juice (Grieve, 1931). However, it is completely illegal and dangerous, as opium is highly addictive. Opium Poppies are still grown commercially, mainly in Asia, as such valuable orthodox drugs as codeine and morphine are produced from them, but heroin can also be made from morphine. It is often the case that plants which have great value and power also have a very dark side to them, and a chequered history. Laudanum, which is a tincture of opium, was hugely popular during Victorian times, and although an effective pain reliever and sleep inducer, it led to much misery and death amongst those who became addicted to it. Opium has also been the cause of various wars over the centuries. It is not illegal to grow Opium Poppies and we use the dried seed heads in garlands and other magical decorations. The stems are conveniently hollow, so wires or jewellery findings can easily be inserted into them. I have made lots of pairs of earrings from them, and I usually dip them in varnish to make them last longer. Not surprisingly, these seed heads can also be used as charms. Cunningham (1995) suggests gilding them and wearing them to attract wealth. If you write a question on a piece of paper, insert it into the seed pod, then place it under the pillow; your question will be answered in your dream. This is a very effective method for seeking guidance and can also help clarify a confusing Tarot or rune reading.

The California Poppy (Eschscholtzia californica), hardly a Norfolk native, nevertheless thrives here. Its bright orange flowers and blue-green, feathery leaves can be seen adorning gardens and roadsides all over the county, and it is the best and safest of the Poppies to use medicinally. It is sedative, soporific (sleep inducing) and analgesic, yet it is a safe herb to take and gentle enough to be used for children, allowing them to sleep if they have whooping cough, and reducing the pain of colic. It can also be useful for treating migraines, neuralgia, anxiety and depression, and can help children who continue to wet the bed. In 1893, G.S. Davis said:

"The effect of Eschscholtzia californica upon patients is the same as that of morphine, without the inconveniences of the latter drug"

(Bone, 2003).

Herb Bennet (Geum urbanum)

This native herb, also known as the Blessed Herb, grows well in our garden and brings its own understated but powerful blessings to our magical space. As a member of the Rose family, it has all the Venusian qualities one might expect, although the yellow flowers are too fragile to use for decorative purposes. More robust and very decorative are the fruit heads, which are a greenish purple and take the form of little burrs made up of lots of bristles, each of which has a hook on the end. It is very common to see the flowers and seeds on the plant at the same time. In Christian symbolism, the five flower petals are said to represent the Five Wounds of Christ, while the threefold nature of the leaves gives an image of the Holy Trinity. For this reason, the plant can be seen in 13th-century architectural carvings, on columns and wall patterns.

This is a herb of many names, including Colewort, Wild Rye, City Avens, Way Bennet, Harefoot, Minarta and Goldy Star of the Earth. Some people also know it as Clove Root, because the fragrant roots both taste and smell somewhat like that exotic spice, and have been used to add flavour to certain ales, acting as a preservative and enhancing their wholesome properties. The root steeped in wine, drunk first thing in the morning, was recommended by Culpepper (1653) as a way of avoiding the plague and poisons. In both Europe and America, the powdered root has been used successfully to treat malaria, with a drachm of powder being given every two hours (Grieve, 1931).

Magically, the root is used as an amulet to ward off evil. It can be hung up in the house or worn as an amulet, if one is feeling particularly vulnerable (Huson, 1977). Alternatively, it can be placed in amongst clothing to keep the Moths away. Traditionally, the root was dug up on the 25th March, when it was supposed to be at its most fragrant (Grieve,1931), although it is still effective if taken later. If you wish to use the powder, dry the root very carefully and only slice or grind it as needed, because the aroma can easily be lost.

In modern herbal medicine, the root is often combined with the aerial parts of the plant, which are collected any time between June and August. The actions of the herb are astringent and antiseptic. The herb stops bleeding and can reduce fever. This makes the plant useful for such conditions as diarrhoea, infections of the digestive system and inflammatory bowel conditions. It is also a useful gargle for the mouth, gums and throat, particularly if there is inflammation, and it also sweetens the breath.

Herb Robert (Geranium robertianum)

Herb Robert has lovely, delicate, pink flowers and feathery leaves, which are usually greenish red in colour. It thrives in our garden and, in this area, is much associated with the power of Traditional Witchcraft. Indeed, we have made a flower remedy from it which has helped us to uncover an enormous amount of magical information.

Some people suggest that the Robert of this little plant's name is a reference to St. Rupert, who was Bishop of Salzburg in the 7th century (Barker, 2001). Others associate it with the Robin Red Breast, with Robin Hood and with the Woodland Lord (Lavender and Franklin, 1996), who responds well to being called through the use of this plant, either as an infusion or a powder. Its other folk names, all of which offer clues to its magical use, include Bloodwort, Fox Grass, Fox Geranium, Dragon's Blood (not to be confused with the exotic resin often used in incenses and to make ink for spells), and Stinking Bob, because it does have a rather odd and not entirely pleasant aroma. Indeed, it is the rather strange smell that accounts for the traditional use of this herb for getting rid of unwanted insects, particularly fleas.

Traditionally, this herb has been used for a wide range of medical conditions, including for the treatment of cancer. The leaves, flowers and stems have astringent properties, so Herb Robert has always been considered an excellent wound herb. A strong infusion can be applied topically to cold sores, and makes a useful mouthwash for ulcers and inflammations of the mouth, as well as being good to gargle for a sore throat. It also has a history of use as a lotion for inflamed eyes, while as a snuff, it can stop a nosebleed. Internally it is used for diarrhoea and duodenal ulcers, as well as stimulating the pancreas. Indeed, research has shown that it is an excellent blood tonic and can help to lower blood sugar levels, providing a scientific justification for its traditional use in diabetes.

Heartsease (Viola tricolor)

Heartsease, our wild Pansy, has given its name to an area of Norwich and to a pub which has a lovely sign depicting this delicate and beautiful flower. Its long list of names gives us many clues to its magic: it is Love-in-Idleness, Meet-me-in-the-Entry, Kiss-her-in-the-Buttery, Jack-Jump-up-and-Kiss-Me, Three-Faces-under-a-Hood, Herb Constancy and Banewort, to name but a few. In Shakespeare's A Midsummer Night's Dream, it is the juice of this little flower of love which was squeezed onto Titania's eye. The flower, as its botanical name tells us, has three colours, yellow, mauve and white, which makes it beloved of the Triple Goddess, who will certainly bless the land on which it is grown. In Christian tradition this threefold nature gives the plant its association with the Trinity, hence another of its names, Herba Trinitas. The multi-coloured petals are not all the same shape, and so they are said to represent a stepmother, with her own daughters and her stepchildren. For this reason, the flower can help foster good relationships and soothe hearts in these sometimes complex and challenging situations.

Another association of Heartsease is with thought, as can be noted in its French name, Penseé, from which our word Pansy is derived. This is a gentle reminder, perhaps, to think carefully about how we use and relate to our herbs, and to give due consideration to the wisdom they have to offer us.

One of the lovely and useful characteristics of this plant is that it blooms throughout the season of flowers, from early Summer to late into the Autumn. It takes great care of its beautiful face too, drooping its head at night, and during wet weather, to protect the petals from dew or rain water. It does the same if the weather is too hot, to shield the flower from scorching by the Sun. It is an annual, though, so, to be sure of having some in the garden in each year, it is a good idea to sow some seed, although, once the plants are established, they usually self-seed quite freely.

Heartsease has a soothing, salve-like effect on the physical as well as the magical and emotional levels, because it contains lots of mucilages, as well as some saponins, which have an anti-inflammatory effect, both internally and externally. One of its main uses in medicine is for skin conditions, particularly eczema and psoriasis. Heartsease is a specific for "cradle cap" in babies. The infusion is used as a wash several times a day and, if the mother is feeding the baby herself, she can take the tea or the tincture, which will reach the baby via the breast milk. If not, 10-20ml of the tea can be added to the baby's bottle, although always consult a qualified herbalist before administering any herbs to babies or children, or taking themselves if you are pregnant or breastfeeding.

It is also possible to make Heartsease syrup from a strong decoction of the herb and flowers, which is helpful if people do not wish to use tinctures or keep making a fresh pot of tea. Decoctions can in some circumstances enhance a deeper and more rooted kind of healing than some other preparations, and a syrup of Heartsease is also a good way of administering this herb for the treatment of lung conditions, such as asthma and bronchitis.

Ivy

One of the very earliest cover photos for Nigel Pennick's ever-popular Secrets of East Anglian Magic, was a ruined church covered in Ivy (Pennick, 1995). Throughout Norfolk, this is a common image: a sacred building, constructed by human hand, in the stone of the Lord of the landscape, gradually transformed into a Green Chapel and a haven for wildlife, the Fair Folk and those who seek to delve into the magical relationship between ourselves and our surroundings. The Ivy is also closely associated with that great healing deity, known to many simply as the Green Witch. Wands or spoons fashioned from Ivy can be excellent for stirring medicines and other herbal potions, as well as for working ritually with this Lady and with the

Green Path she will open up to those who are willing to serve in her name. She has much to offer, and will show the seeker great wonders, although she can be a hard task mistress at times, and her ways are not for the faint-hearted.

Medicinally, Ivy has pain-relieving and anti-spasmodic properties and, if the leaves are chopped and soaked in vinegar for three or four weeks, the strained liquid can be used on the skin to relieve rheumatic pain, cellulitis or neuralgia. It is also a useful mouthwash for toothache. In the Anglo-Saxon Leechbook of Bald, there is a lovely, simple recipe in which Ivy shoots are cooked in butter and the resulting ointment used to treat sunburn (Cockayne, 1864-6). Ivy contains the soapy substances known as saponins, which are anti-inflammatory, so this is a very effective topical treatment. The herbalist, Julian Barker (2001), recommends adding the leaves to a hot bath, which is a lovely treat after a hard day's work preparing the garden or allotment for the growing season. In folk medicine, Ivy syrup has always been a popular remedy for coughs and can still be bought commercially, although it is so easy to make, and Ivy is so abundant that most people prefer to prepare their own.

As with all plants, the Ivy should be treated with care and respect. The beautiful, dark berries which ripen in early Spring, providing much-needed nourishment for Blackbirds and Pigeons, are purgative to humans, although they were used in many Anglo-Saxon remedies. They were previously used in medicine but they are toxic and some fatal accidents have occurred. Some people may be sensitive to the leaves and cases of contact dermatitis have been known, so always patch test an external preparation before using it.

Ivy is particularly useful in magical and practical crafts because it easy to find long, flexible stems which can be made into garlands, baskets or used to tie other items: one indication that this herb is ruled by the Lord of Time, Saturn, who binds and restricts. If you can bear to take them from the birds, Ivy berries can be the first natural dye of the year, producing various shades of green, depending on the mordant used to prepare the wool, but also on the acidity of the soil and the growing conditions of that particular year.

From a magical point of view, Ivy, which is associated with the deities Bacchus, Dionysis and Osiris, is carried for luck, as an emblem of fidelity, and to ward off negativity. It is reputed to prevent people getting drunk, although the sign of the Ivy bush outside a tavern was an indication that the drinks there were of high quality! The Ivy is hardy and tenacious. It is usually the first to bring wild nature back to ruined buildings abandoned by humanity, so it can strengthen our own connection to the ways of the wild. As Karen Cater (2011) points out, Ivy is also a tree of transformation because it changes the shape of its leaves as it grows upward towards the light and begins to flower, helping us to persevere and to fight through distractions to reach our goals.

Lime

There are many stately Lime trees throughout Norfolk. Those in the centre of King's Lynn are blessed with fabulous boughs of Mistletoe, which is a treat to see in the Winter. Some magnificent specimens are also to be found in Norwich, in Tombland, in the Rosary Cemetery and in the fields outside Bowthorpe Hall, a very short distance from St. Walstan's magical prayer cell. These latter trees are particularly impressive and, on sunny days around Midsummer time, when they are in full bloom, the bees and other insects play a symphony of delight upon them. These Limes have kindly provided low branches, which makes it very easy to pick the flowers. These are an important Midsummer crop because they make such a delicious tea, which can be drunk just for its own sake or can be used a medicine. Lime flowers are excellent for feverish conditions, colds and catarrh, but also have a nervine action, making them helpful for people who suffer from anxiety, insomnia, palpitations and high blood pressure.

Lime wood is very soft and light, so is traditionally used for detailed wood carving. It was also the wood from which Anglo-Saxon and Viking shields were often made (Härke, 1992), presumably because they needed to be reasonably light to carry and springy to deflect blows from weapons. This also means that Lime wood is useful for making "mini shields" for use in protective magic.

Magical Miscellany

It is so satisfying to find oddments of all kinds which may at some point be useful for a piece of craft work or some spell or other. Most of us have jars and boxes full of bits and pieces just waiting to be needed for a creative or magical purpose. Thus, it is unusual to find anyone within the Nameless Tradition who is a minimalist, and these collections of miscellaneous, potentially magical objects develop considerable power in their own right. Most of them are just found items, but some may have been bought from those great hunting grounds of charity shops and car boot sales.

Clay Pipes

Clay pipes have been used for centuries and some very beautiful examples, featuring plant or animal decorations, are still made. New ones may be used for smoking magical herbs, such as Mugwort (Artemesia vulgaris), Marshmallow (Althea officinalis) or Lemon Balm (Melissa officinalis), all of which are popular. Pieces of old pipe can often be found in the soil, particularly along the banks of rivers, and make useful magical materials. We often jokingly refer to the stems as "vegetarian bones", for they look like bone at first glance and, although they have not housed a spirit in the same way as bone, they have nevertheless been a pathway for the breath of life and the energy of fire and herb. Thus, their narrow air channels can be carefully cleaned of earth and they can be strung as necklaces to help provide insights into the past and the ways of the ancestors whose whispered wisdom they may help us to hear.

The stems also make beautiful, tiny wind chimes when several long pieces are arranged together with wire or linen thread. The subtle sound such instruments produce is particularly attractive to the Fair Folk and placing a few of these around the home or garden works wonders for enhancing Fairy magic.

Each item that we use in our magic enhances our connection to the world around us, and gradually the landscape offers up its treasures to those who watch its ways, heed its tales and meld their own lives to the pattern of its seasons.

References

Baker, Gwen, and Peter Ward (1995) *Auriculas*, Batsford.

Barker, Julian (2001) *The Medicinal Flora of Britain and Northwestern Europe*, Winter Books.

Bassett, Michael G. (1982) *'Formed Stones'*, Folklore and Fossils, National Museum of Wales.

Blake, P.W., Bull, J., Cartwright, A.R., and Fitch, A. (n.d.) The Norfolk we live in, Jarrold.

Bone, Kerry (2003) A Clinical Guide to Blending Liquid Herbs: Herbal Formulations for the Individual Patient, Churchill Livingstone.

Browne, Sir Thomas (1668) Dr. Browne to Dr. Merritt, July 13, 1668, MS Sloane 1833, reproduced in Wilkin, Simon (1836) Sir Thomas Browne's Works, Including His Life and Correspondence, Volume 1, William Pickering.

Bruneton, Jean (1995) Pharmacognosy, Phytochemistry, Medicinal Plants, Lavoisier.

Campbell, A.C., and Nicholls, James (1976) The Hamlyn Guide to the Seashore and Shallow Seas of Britain and Europe, Hamlyn.

Cater, Karen (2011) Ogham Sketchbook: A Diary of Tree Lore and Spiritual Growth, Hedingham Fair.

Chapman, Rod (2007) Seven: An Idiosyncretic Look at the Number Seven, Seven Star.

Cockayne, Oswald (1864-8) Leechdoms, Wortcunning and Starcraft in Early England, three volumes, Holland.

Conway, Peter (2001) Tree Medicine: A comprehensive guide to the healing power of over 170 trees, Piatkus.

Culpeper, Nicholas (1653) The Complete Herbal (Foulsham edition, 1955).

Cunningham, Scott, (1995) Cunningham's Encyclopedia of Magical Herbs, Llewellyn.

Fortune, Dion (1938) The Sea Priestess, self-published (various editions in print).

Gerard, John (1597) The Herball or Generall Historie of Plantes (Marcus Woodward (ed.) (1985) Gerard's Herbal, Studio Editions).

Grieve, Mrs M. (1931) A Modern Herbal, Jonathan Cape.

Härke, Heinrich (1992) Shield Technology, in Dickinson, Tania, and Härke, Heinrich, Early Anglo-Saxon Shields, Society of Antiquaries of London, pp. 31-54.

Heaton, Trevor (2017) Ten Norfolk-Dutch connections... Eastern Daily Press, 09 December 2017 (available at: https://www.edp24.co.uk/features/ten-norfolk-dutch-connections-1-5298780, accessed 1st December 2018).

Holbeche, Soozi (1989) The Power of Gems and Crystals, Piatkus.

Hunger, Rosa (1977) The Magic of Amber, NAG.

Huson, Paul (1977) Mastering Herbalism, Abacus.

Lavender, Susan, and Franklin, Anna (1996) Herbcraft: A Guide to the Shamanic and Ritual Use of Herbs, Capall Bann.

Mabey, Richard (1996) Flora Britannica: The definitive new guide to wild flowers, plants and trees, Sinclair-Stevenson.

Marren, Peter, and Mabey, Richard (2010) Bugs Britannica, Chatto & Windus.

Norfolk Lavender (2017) The Story of English Lavender, https://norfolk-lavender.co.uk/story-english-lavender (accessed 1st December 2018).

Pennick, Nigel (1995) Secrets of East Anglian Magic, First Edition, Hale.

Pennick, Nigel (1999) The Complete Illustrated Guide to Runes, Element.

Pennick, Nigel (2004) Secrets of East Anglian Magic, Second Edition, Capall Bann.

Pollington, Stephen (2000) Leechcraft: Early English Charms, Plantlore and Healing, Anglo-Saxon Books.

Rowland, Beryl (1978) Birds with Human Souls: A Guide to Bird Symbolism, University of Tennessee Press.

Rye, Walter (ed.) (1877) The Norfolk Antiquarian Miscellany, Part 2, Samuel Miller, pp. 297-8.

Skipper, Keith (2018) What links these Dereham cottages to a Norfolk ladybird? Eastern Daily Press, 12 May 2018 (available at: https://www.edp24.co.uk/features/the-story-of-bishy-barney-bees-1-5508672, accessed 1st December 2018).

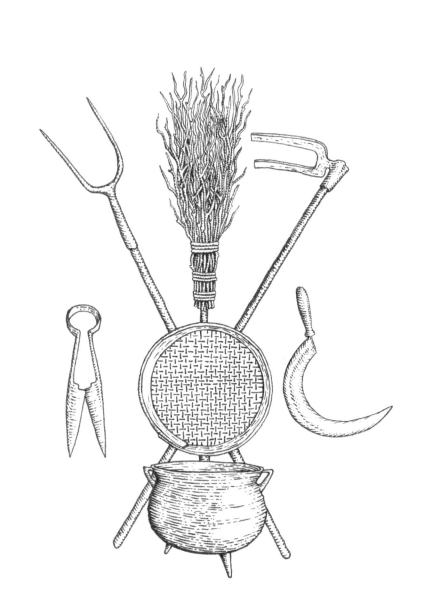

Magical Tools

A wide variety of magical tools is used within Norfolk's Nameless Tradition, depending on what is required for a particular piece of magical work or ritual. Rituals of community or those performed to ensure food harvests or prosperity quite often involve the use of agricultural tools and can be quite elaborate. Faerie rituals are often best performed with nothing which has needed fire for its creation, so we choose wood, leaves, bone, horn or shell items. The choice of magical tools is guided by the individual practitioner's magical style and preferences. They may be extremely costly pieces, handcrafted from precious materials, by experts. On the other hand, they may be simple, found within nature, made by ourselves or picked up cheaply in a charity shop. Some are gifts. Where possible, we choose items which have been made locally. Whatever the style of the tools we use, they vibrate with magical charge, built up over the years, become old friends and collect huge amounts of sprowl which enhances whatever work we ask them to assist with.

Of Earth and Iron: Tools of the Land

Agricultural tools are used in Traditional Witchcraft practices throughout the UK and beyond. Since a large part of Norfolk is farmland, it is fitting that we choose to use these things which forge a direct connection to those who worked the land before us. When we pick up a well-worn but still-sharp tool, we feel those other hands that wrapped themselves around the handle long ago, or lovingly ran a whetstone over the blade after a hard day's work in the fields. We work with many such tools, ever developing our understanding of their practical use and their symbolic and magical application.

It has been said that common items, found in most households, were used in more dangerous times to avoid attracting the kind of unwelcome attention which might be provoked by the wielding of swords or the flashing of jewel-handled daggers (Jones and Valiente, 1990). Whilst discretion is a perfectly comprehensible reason, along with the fact that not everyone could afford or obtain items from the shinier end of the market, there are many more magical layers to this practice. Were there not, we might question the wisdom of continuing to use such items today, except for reasons of mundane practicality: a sickle is, after all, a lot easier to take to a Lammas ritual than a combine harvester.

The knowledge and the means to till the soil have, through many mythologies been seen as gifts from the Gods. Osiris, for example, taught agriculture and showed people how to construct their tools, to grind grain, bake bread and brew beer (Dillaire, 2011). Meanwhile, in the Greek tradition, the demi-god Triptolemos is instructed in the art of agriculture by Demeter (Foley, 1994). Chinese mythology boasts many myths of this kind, a major one being that of Shennong, known as the Divine Farmer, who is not only credited with the invention of the hoe and the plough, but also with the discovery of the uses of herbal medicines (Yang, 2005).

The importance of smithcraft is another aspect of our relationship with these ancestral iron items. The magic of the smith, the closely-guarded secrets of the forge and the complex connection between the smith, the fertility of the land and human fecundity, are recurring themes worldwide, in the Ancient World and in some contemporary cultures (Blakely, 2006). The quenching water from the forge may be given to cure infertility and the blacksmith may be called upon to perform marriage rites at the anvil. These mysteries are still, albeit in a small way, a part of the mindset

228

of many in the U.K. After all, you do not have to be a witch, magician or magically inclined in any way to acquire an old horseshoe and nail it above your door for luck, or just to look stylishly rural.

That very basic farming implements have a special attraction is clear from the prices some of them now command in antique shops, appealing to a sense of nostalgia for a time when people were more in tune with the natural world and damaged it less. Of course, any kind of agricultural, or even horticultural, activity manages, alters or damages the Earth to some extent and has done for millennia. Very little of our world is "natural"; even the countryside that most of us love and wish to think of as Nature, has still been managed by humankind. In Old Testament terms, we were expelled from the Garden of Eden because of our desire for "forbidden" knowledge and must labour and till the soil. Few of us can now live as hunter-gatherers, or even as pastoralists like Abel. Indeed, we have moved so far along the road that farming or even industrial work have come and gone for most folk. Most of us live an urban lifestyle and work electronically. For now, it would be difficult to go back. Once Lucifer has ignited the Forge of Tubal Cain with the Divine Spark, iron has to be heated and shaped according to the True Will of the Divine Smith. "Progress" is unstoppable and the abuse of knowledge, power and skill is always possible. Not that the gifts of the Light-bringer are evil in any respect. Many witchcraft groups, including those who consider themselves part of the Nameless Tradition, revere Lucifer as the saviour of humanity, bringing the illumination of Gnostic wisdom and the fire of creativity (Jackson and Howard, 2000). It is just that, once entered into, the process is irreversible.

This mirrors one of the effects of the experience of initiation: once a dedication to the pursuit of magical knowledge has been made, life changes forever and we cannot return to our previous state of what most people consider to be normality. Nor can we pretend that we do not have magical knowledge and the responsibility which goes with it.

Just as humanity is challenged to discover better ways of using its technological power, so an important part of magical work, therefore, is to find a point of balance between the reckless or destructive use of what we have learned and the paralysing fear of doing anything with it at all, which is perhaps the fate of the armchair magician. There is also the risk of becoming complacent, of not going far enough, just reaching a plateau and stagnating magically.

One of the uses of simple iron tools in ritual is to help find balance, not in any sense as a naïve desire to return to some non-existent, idyllic, agricultural Golden Age, but because the tools represent a very direct contact with the land, its deities and spirits and with our pre-agribusiness ancestors. The tools are simple and comprehensible, yet effective. Some of them can be made by an amateur blacksmith with a forge in the back garden (a useful resource for many a magical group). They are easy to sharpen, can be used with a little practice, and they keep us in close contact with the Source from which food can be grown and clothing created. They form some of the many magical aids to keeping ourselves rooted in the Earth, like a tree, while stretching upwards and aspiring to the Shining Ones above.

The Pitchfork

Much has already been written and discussed about this versatile magical tool, as used in Traditional Witchcraft. Some people use it interchangeably with the stang. My personal preference is to use them somewhat differently since, to my mind, the iron tines of the pitchfork, while similar to the prongs of the stang in representing the horns of the God, between which the representation of the Divine Spark can be placed, produce nevertheless a very different type of energy, given that the tines are metal and wrought in the forge, while the prongs of the stang are part of the natural growth of the tree. Older pitchforks were made entirely of wood, but it is possible to find pitchforks where even the handle is iron, and indeed I know of a group who regularly use one of this kind. The pitchfork which our group uses was found in the basement of Tombland Antiques, in the centre of Norwich. It has a very solid, dark wooden handle and magnificent iron tines. At some point, a previous owner splashed flecks of yellow paint all down the handle. Far from detracting from the beauty and power of our pitchfork, this feature is all part of its appeal.

The pitchfork has been depicted in art, much as a broomstick, to be ridden, as in the paintings of Hans Baldung Grien. In the woodcut Witches' Sabbat from 1510, he also shows it in use as a potholder, and three of them placed on the ground to form a magical triangle (Grössinger, 1997).

The pitchfork can be used in the South as the direction of Summer and, in some traditions, the place of Fire. It is also useful for protection magic and for carrying things towards the central fire, or indeed in procession. It has been used traditionally to hold up the Neck – the last sheath, saved as a harvest amulet, as described by Ettlinger (1943) – after the wheat harvest (Hutton, 1996). I find it particularly appropriate for carrying our Brigid figure in Imbolc processions, given her associations with smithcraft.

Chris Wood has pointed out to me that the tines of the pitchfork represent polarity and the candle between them is the spark of life resulting from the creative tension between the two. The same may be said of horned deities, of course, particularly perhaps Egyptian forms, such as Hathor and Isis, who bear the Sun between their horns. It is noteworthy, in this respect, that Hathor is associated with metallurgy.

Interesting work is currently being undertaken to map the pitchfork onto the Qabalistic Tree of Life, the tines representing Binah and Chokmah, while the shaft represents the Middle Pillar. If one adds crossed arrows, which have many layers of meaning, to the shaft, one also has the four Elements and their corresponding Sephira (Damian West, personal communication).

The Sickle

As the implement used to reap the grain, the sickle has been used historically as a sacred cult instrument, for example in Greek festivals devoted to Demeter and also to Artemis. A copper or gold, sickle-shaped stick was known as an insignia of power from the third millennium B.C.E. in the Near East and the Caucasus (Gimbutas, 2007). Kronos too is sometimes shown holding a sickle, because of his association with Time and also because it was the weapon with which he castrated his father, Uranos (Stein, 2001). The sickle later became the scythe in popular depictions of Death.

Like many of the other tools, the sickle comes in various sizes, a small ceremonial one for cutting herbs and of course a golden one for Mistletoe. One might even carry or wear a small silver sickle charm, connected with the work of the verdelet, or magical herbalist. Whatever its size, the sickle has powerful connections to the crescent Moon and its magic, waxing or waning, depending on which way round it is held. It can therefore be employed as a tool in numerous lunar spells and in rituals of the first and last quarters.

It can be used in the West at the place of Water and as an instrument of sacrifice in Lammas rituals. Personally, I like to decorate the sickle with a Corn plait, Rowan berries and red thread, to protect the harvest from harm and in the hope of abundance for the following year. In Cornish magic, the sickle is placed at the foot of the staff during the harvest rite (Gary, 2010), but we normally place it on a flat stone or an altar.

The Shears

The shears we use are normally Sheep shears, which are lovely to hold and have a special and eerie music as they are opened and closed. They can be employed effectively in the North of the Circle, particularly if that is considered the direction of Earth, of Winter, of Midnight and of Death. In terms of the Fates, the Norns or Wyrd Sisters, they are the tool of She Who Cuts the Thread of Life, but as a tool for harvesting the wool, which has been such a source of great prosperity (see Chapter Five), the shears are a good implement to use in spells for increasing wealth, specifically for use in building or equipping a magical space. On a more basic level, without wool we would be hard pressed to survive the Winter, so we are also harvesting that which is essential to life. (If one places Earth in the South, it is equally powerful to use the shears there, as shearing usually takes place between Beltane and Midsummer.)

As a spinner and weaver, I was once given, by some students, a pewter pendant representing a pair of Sheep shears. It is most interesting how many people over the years have mistaken this simple shape for a stylised goddess figure.

The shears are also used, in conjunction with the sieve, as a divinatory tool (see below).

The Scythe

Because of the scythe's association with the Grim Reaper, it is often used in Samhain rituals, to remind participants of the tenuous nature of the Thread of Life and how easily and suddenly it can be severed. There is sometimes a point during the ritual when someone carrying the scythe, dressed in black and hooded, walks behind everyone in the Circle and touches their ankles with cold metal. This may sound simple, but on a dark, spirit-filled night, it can be a chilling reminder of the transience of life. The person wielding the scythe has to be careful not to press too hard, as the blade of the one we use is wickedly sharp.

The scythe is not always used in such a sinister way though. It is closely associated with St. Walstan (see chapter 2), and appears in many of the depictions of him, some of which, it has to be said, are a little reminiscent of the Grim Reaper. So, it can also be used in his rituals, especially around the end of May, to call upon his aid to protect and heal animals, to honour the hay harvest, and to ensure the healthy growth of crops. Indeed, it can be used to represent Walstan in the ritual, or be placed beside an altar constructed in his honour, which along with a depiction of the saint, would usually also include the horns of Oxen, Brambles, Roses and some water from his well at Bawburgh. Rituals involving St. Walstan should ideally be conducted in bare feet.

The Hoe
Since the hoe is used for weeding, it is usefully employed magically when one needs to get rid of something unwanted. It can also be used, under certain circumstances, to cast the Circle in a ritual. Because it has two prongs, connected by a blade across the top, it represents different worlds with the bridge between them, making it especially suited to creating a liminal space. It also symbolises the power of what we refer to as the Plant Pillar, the Animal Pillar and the Faery Bridge which joins the two. It is most effectively used for rituals around Plough Monday or at Imbolc, when soil is being prepared for the sowing of new crops, although of course "weeding" can useful be undertaken at any time of the year, and is perhaps most urgent around Beltane tide. Nettles, a dedicated practitioner within the Nameless Tradition is currently undertaking an in-depth analysis of the magic of this powerful tool.

The above-mentioned are by no means the only implements which might be used: rakes, axes, hammers, spades and many more all have their place in the magical toolshed. Using them with intent can forge a deeper understanding of the balance between creativity and destruction, tilling the Earth and raping her, weeding and wildlife, performing the spell and not interfering, and between Lucifer and the Divine Smith. In those rare moments when we strike that balance perfectly, magical creativity flourishes with abundance and beauty, and the Star Child is born anew.

The Sieve
The sieve is a tool much favoured in the Nameless Tradition, for its practical and magical versatility. Furthermore, it

encompasses the agricultural, the horticultural and the domestic. Sieves come in a wide range of sizes, some being metal and others wooden, with cotton or nylon mesh, but they are all round, like the magical Circle itself. A sieve can be used during the calling of the Element of Air, for it has an airy nature, being in its criss-cross pattern more Air than solid. It is also a tool which adds Air to that which it sifts, refining the soil to enable small seeds to germinate more easily, or enlivening the flour so that bread or cakes have an excellent texture. In this respect, it can symbolise work done within ourselves, as individuals: sifting out the "lumps" can remove some of the blockages we all experience in our lives, and enable creative ideas to take hold and flourish more easily. Equally, harsh as it sounds, a group will produce a finer quality of magic if those who have become unsuited to its work or style are identified and encouraged to continue their quest elsewhere.

Smaller sieves are also a useful part of the witch's collection of magical/practical implements, for straining out solid matter during the preparation of philtres, tinctures or vinegars. They are needed for refining cosmetic and medicinal powders, during the making of protection or banishing powders, or indeed any other of the types of powder that the operative witch might be called upon to produce. In these latter cases, the materia magica may be ground and sieved. That which remains trapped in the mesh is returned to the pestle and mortar for regrinding and re-sieving. The fineness of the end result will depend on the mesh size of the sieve chosen. A 20-mesh sieve has 20 meshes per linear inch and makes a no. 20 powder, which is considered coarse. A no. 40 powder (40 meshes per linear inch) is moderately coarse, 50 is moderately fine, 60 fine and 80 very fine. Such sieves are magically important, and the principles behind their usage are the same as for larger ones.

We occasionally find it useful to cast a double Circle for certain rites, sometimes using a figure of eight arrangement.

It is possible to use the sieve to represent one of the Circles, particularly if the purpose of having the second one is to contain some energy or spirit. This can be advantageous at Samhain, when less experienced practitioners may wish to evoke spirits of the Honoured Dead, but do not perhaps feel ready to stand right beside them in the main Circle.

A curious rite involving a sieve and shears or scissors as a form of divination is known to have been used in England, especially in the 16th century, as well as in Portugal, Brazil and Denmark, and may be even more widespread. It is especially useful for unmasking a thief. The open shears are stuck into the sieve (it would have to be of the kind either with a wooden frame or a rope binding around the centre). Two people hold the shears and the names of those who may have committed the theft are recited. In one version, the sieve turns until the right name is spoken and then stops turning, in another the sieve remains still throughout the recitation but turns only when it hears the name. This would not, of course, be very effective if the thief were a complete stranger. It is interesting to note that the 19th-century Danish version also had a hymn book and an heirloom (a silver tankard in the recorded case) placed upon the sieve (Levack, 2002). Some versions use prayers to St. Peter and St. Paul and there are other variations using a basket and shears (de Mello e Souza, 2010). The technique can be used to obtain answers to other questions or to contact spirits. It makes sense to use the sieve in such a manner because it represents a kind of sifting out of the truth.

I initially learned of the sieve and shears procedure through reading and, although I had long made use of sieves of all kind in my own practice, this was a magical operation which I had never seen in action, and was unsure of exactly how to carry it out for best effect, a fact which I mentioned in an article on the subject, in The Cauldron (Thomas, 2014). This came to the notice of the well-known Portuguese magician and author, Gilberto Lascariz, who was well versed in the technique and "just happened" to be visiting the UK from

Portugal, and staying in Norwich. He kindly offered, through a mutual friend, to come and demonstrate it for us, and his visit was a most memorable occasion. We sat out in the garden on an idyllic Summer's day, with Gilberto and various other magical practitioners, eating, drinking, swapping magical ideas and discussing potential future magical collaboration. We also spent a lot of time practising the sieve and shears technique. I have never seen a sieve rolling across the grass so many times or to the accompaniment of so much laughter. In the end though, we got it right and some very serious questions were asked and answered.

Given that the sieve may provide answers to an obscure question or puzzle, it is interesting to note that a synonym for the coarse, outdoor type is "riddle". A common phase in traditional tales is "Riddle me this…" or "Riddle me ree", as in the nursery rhyme:

Riddle me, riddle me, ree;
A little man in a tree;
A stick in his hand,
A stone in his throat,
If you tell me this riddle
I'll give you a groat.

The connection here with words and the cleverness of those who can solve riddles also serves to emphasise the sieve's airy nature and its possible position within the ritual Circle. I am, however, aware that the two uses of the word riddle are not thought to have the same derivation. The riddle which is a puzzle comes from the Old English rædan, meaning to guess or to read, while the riddle with the sense of Sieve derives from the Old English hriddel (Sweet, 1896).

The expression "carrying water in a sieve" is sometimes used to denote a futile task, but the Vestal Virgin, Tuccia, was able to perform this magical act, with water drawn from the Tiber, to prove that she was innocent of attending the rites of the Goddess in an unchaste condition (Holland,

2012). Again, there is the recurring theme of separating of truth from falsehood.

Keys

Another item which spans both indoor and outdoor use is the key. Old keys are wonderful to use in magic, although it is best not to know what the key was originally used to lock, and to separate the key from its previous use. Keys can represent so may things. They can unlock the Mysteries, open doors to our own future, enhance our understanding of our past and unlock the treasures which we have until now been unable to use. On the other hand, they can lock up safely something that you hold dear and, on or more mundane level, can be dropped down someone's back to stop them hiccupping. I have a particularly lovely old, iron key, which looks as if it must have once opened an ancient oak door or fabulously forged gate. It was a gift, and I have no idea even what part of the country it came from, and I like the fact that I do not know. It has an open oval shape at the top which is excellent for looking through. It can frame certain things and bring them into magical focus or temporarily capture an image that I need to work with. Sometimes it shows the most surprising things, which turn out to be of great importance. Cunningham and Harrington (2001) cite a number of lovely key spells for individual and domestic use. Wearing a gold key guards against the Evil Eye, and three keys on a chain bring health, wealth and love. Luck can be attracted by carrying a key which does not fit any locks in one's own home. If one is looking for a new home, workshop, studio or magical meeting place, adding a mystery key to one's key ring can help as part of the work to bring that about. A personal favourite of mine is to collect an old key for every door in the home. One key is touched to each lock in turn, while reciting a suitable charm to keep out thieves. While these spells are not specific to

Norfolk (although traditional, local key spells are of course used here) these have been adopted because we find them both attractive and effective.

Keys are also useful divinatory tools, the practice of using them in this way being referred to as cleidomancy. The easiest form is to hang one from a string or a chain and use it as a pendulum. There is another form, though, which is not dissimilar to the sieve and shears ritual. The key is placed between the pages of a Bible, preferably Psalm 50 (the one which begins "Our God shall come, and shall not keep silence"). Cord is then bound around the Bible so that it can be suspended in front of the questioner. If it turns clockwise, the answer is yes. This is usually employed to find a thief. Names of potential culprits are recited, and the Bible turns when the correct name is spoken. A version of this procedure has a tradition of use in Norfolk (Glyde, 1872). Personally, I am not fond of this procedure, mainly because it has a tendency to damage the Bible, so I prefer to use other methods.

The Cauldron
On a dark, chilly night, when all the ritual items have been set in place, there is nothing so atmospheric and so raising of one's magical personality as standing back and observing the Circle, anticipating the magic to come. A great iron cauldron, hung on a hand-forged tripod over the fire, sets the scene perfectly, and helps to awaken our magical senses. For the cauldron is a symbol of rebirth and of the Holy Grail, and as such, it can be a vessel to hold the Elixir of the Mysteries. So, it is often the case that in Winter ritual, the communion wine and herbs are warmed over the fire in our large, old cauldron and ladled into the chalice with a serving spoon, which is itself like a mini-cauldron. As a "humble" cooking pot, it has its own alchemical and sometimes life-saving magic. During the cooking process, a little of the iron enters whatever is being cooked, increasing its nutritional value. Our Anglo-Saxon ancestors knew this, and many of their medicinal recipes, especially for conditions linked to

anaemia, specify that an iron pot should be used in their preparation (Cameron, 1993). So, in the warmer months, when we favour eating outdoors, the iron cauldron is used for cooking over the fire of our Summer kitchen.

Cauldrons with lids are excellent for spells which need to be "cooked" for a considerable period of time before completion. This may involve being placed in the cauldron overnight, for one lunar cycle or, in rarer cases, for even longer. Once the spell is ready, the physical aspects of it are reverently removed from the pot in a birth-like process. The cauldron is usually placed beside a hearth, or if the home no longer has one, a suitable place which has been artistically created especially for the purpose. One of our magical colleagues, who lived in small flat with no fireplaces, or even chimneys, bought a small decorative, woodburning stove and filled it with coloured strips of fabric which looked very fiery indeed. As well as making a lovely focus for the room, it was very effective for use in spellwork.

Although cauldrons are basically feminine in aspect, in their shape and the fact that something is formed within their bellies, has the Divine Spark of Life bestowed upon it and is then brought out into the light, the Martian iron from which they are made provides a masculine balance. If one wishes to avoid iron for any particular reason, it is possible to use little copper cauldrons, which can easily be found second hand, are useful for small spells or love spells, and can form part of a mini-magic-set for travelling or for day trips.

From Woodland and Hedgerow

Dramatic and meaningful as working magically with agricultural and old, domestic tools can be, they are not suited to all types of magic or ritual work. Often wooden items are preferred for individual or small group work. The beauty of these is that we can craft them ourselves, using only a penknife, selecting suitable wood for the purpose and decorating the resulting items, often with runes, in paint or pyrography. Wooden knives or wands are not too challenging to make, even for those with only modest whittling skills.

Many pieces of magical equipment are made to fit the practitioner's own body. Wands, for example, are traditionally as thick as one's own thumb, with the length being measured from the tip of the middle finger to the elbow. However, in modern practice, we delight in making wands of various sizes, especially mini-wands, which fit discretely in a pocket or small bag. Spoons are a joy both to make and to use in ritual and spellcraft: Elder wood spoons to scoop out the incense for scrying, Sycamore for spells of the kitchen, Hazel to ensure the success of the magic of the dyepot, Rowan to scatter protective powders. The possibilities are endless, for woodland and hedgerow are a rich treasury of inspiration and of magical tools, which can be shaped for our purposes yet remain close to the Source, natural and untouched by industrial processes, the commercial or the environmentally damaging. They begin life as mere twigs, and when their work is done, they are composted or fed to the magical fire.

Besom

We all need a good besom, or broomstick, to sweep the magical space clear of leaves or unwanted energies, or to decorate with leaves, flowers, feathers, shells or skulls, and stand beside the altar or hearth to enhance the magical atmosphere. To be honest, broomsticks are rarely used for flight, in the Nameless Tradition, as most of us enjoy walking, or for longer journeys prefer the comfort of a bicycle or a car.

A besom is not hard to make, especially when working with a magical colleague. The most important thing is to prepare a good bundle of Birch twigs and hold them really tightly together while they are being tied. The traditional tie is made of either Bramble or Willow, but it is easier to make the first tie with a good strong garden twine then add the Bramble or Willow over the top. Even easier, it is also possible to use garden wire, which can be twisted to form a very secure binding and the ends curled into decorative and magical spiral forms. Only once the solid Birch bundle is ready should the sharpened point of the handle be inserted, and banged in firmly with a mallet. Hazel or Ash are often the preferred wood for the handle, but we are not prescriptive about such matters and individuals often have their own reasons for selecting a particular branch.

One of the loveliest of our group's enterprises, many years ago, was a day's workshop in which we all made our own besoms. We were a large group, so paying an expert craftsperson to come and teach us this skill was not a problem. We all gathered in our garden and Toby, our teacher, arrived with a selection of Hazel handles and a huge pile of Birch twigs. It was October. The ground was carpeted golden with leaves, and mist hung in the air all day, but it was warm enough or us to feel comfortable outside and to enjoy the rich scents of Autumn as we worked. It was a day of fun and laughter, which everyone still remembers fondly. It was remarkable that all the besoms which were made looked completely different, each one reflecting something of the magical colour of its maker. Some were neat and well ordered, others a little wild, with twigs pointing in all directions. But everyone was delighted with what they had produced and felt that their magic had been enhanced by the crafting process. To this day, many still have the brooms they made on that occasion, some left plain, others lavishly decorated, according to individual taste.

If the besom is to be kept indoors, it is important to allow the twigs and the handle to dry out well before assembling it. Otherwise, the whole broom may become loose and fall apart at a crucial moment during a ritual, which is both inauspicious and irritating. If the broom does fall apart, it is usually best to burn it, ceremonially, and to accept that these types of tool are ephemeral: they wear out in the mundane and the magical realms and should just be replaced.

Besoms are also used as gateways, placed on the ground to mark the entrance to the magical space or delineate between two Circles, where more than one is being used. Two besoms can also be held up to form an archway to admit a procession into a magical space or to allow a candidate for initiation to enter a Circle which has already been put into place.

The Fortune Basket

It is not unusual for those working within Norfolk's Nameless Tradition to be seen with an old-fashioned wicker or hedgerow basket over one arm, "just in case". Who knows what one might find while out walking? There is always the possibility of finding an attractive stone, an interestingly-shaped piece of wood, coloured leaves or items discarded by others, which have usefulness or meaning. Most of us have a foraging mentality, and not only when we purposefully set out to collect seasonal fruits or herbs. Carrying the basket provides far more than just a practical means of transporting found items: it is also a magical act in itself. Firstly, it is a means of constantly "touching wood", to enhance luck, and secondly, the openness of a nearly empty basket provides a space which draws items to it. I say, "nearly empty", because there needs to be something there to start the flow of good things, which is why we would never give anyone a bag or a purse with absolutely nothing in it, even if we are just returning one which has been borrowed. A coin works well, but an excellent way to attract benefits is to use a magnet, preferably with a heart on it, to ensure that only things which wish you well will enter the basket. The heart may be drawn in Chalk, to invoke the Lady, or painted more elaborately. Red is generally the colour most favoured for this. It works well either to leave the magnet in bottom of the basket or to make an attractive charm bag for it, which has the added advantage of stopping it sticking to your keys all the time.

Names are special, and discovering a new one adds more magic to the item or to the magical act it represents. The "fortune basket" is one such example. It has only recently been graced with this lovely name, which is yet another of those energetic links to Cornwall. Some of us first heard the words used by the Cornish artist, Mary Martin, a friend of our magical colleagues, Dave and Barbara, who now live on a farm in the Tamar Valley. Previously, we had used the specific traditional names for the different shapes and sizes of baskets made in Norfolk. There is the "Apple picker", the "Cherry picker", the "fishing crewel", and the more modern "shopper" – all part of the delightful poetry of genuine craft items. Of course, we have not abandoned these names. Loss of vocabulary undermines more than "just" the richness of the language, so this is a new and vibrant addition to our way of speaking about our magic. Besides, I would not be surprised to learn that the expression has been, or is, used here, by others outside our immediate circle, and that we have just travelled along the Mary and Michael Line to recover something which was really here all along. Such is the dynamic of learning, forgetting and remembering.

Stitched Baskets

It is a fun and magical experience to make one's basket, and most of us have done so on at least one occasion. However, Norfolk is blessed with some extremely talented professional basket makers, whose work we are delighted to support. Stitched baskets are much quicker and simpler to make from any long, slender leaves, such as Iris, Mombretia, or Maize. I have recently discovered how easy it is to make very small baskets using the fallen leaves from the common houseplant known as the Dragon Plant Dracena spp., which is of course highly suitable for working Dragon magic. Whatever plant the material is taken from, the leaves should be allowed to dry out, but then need to be moistened slightly, just before working with them, to make them pliable enough that they will not split or break. The dampened leaves are simply twisted together then coiled around, starting at the centre of the base and working outwards and upwards, stitching the spirals together as you go. More leaves are just added as required, ideally not too many at a time. These baskets make excellent bread or cake baskets for rituals, or can have offerings placed in them. Linen thread is the best to use, because it has so much healing and protective magic of its own, which it adds to the main material and intention of the basket.

The Fluidity of Glass

Glass is a truly magical material. It is, a blend of silica, sand, soda ash and limestone, transformed by the intense heat of alchemical fires, coloured and shaped by human skill. Yet, since this everyday material is so mysterious, glass items are especially suited to certain kinds of magical work. Glass has long been used as a bringer of light, and not just through the glass of the windows, which are the eyes of the home. The Victorians, whose houses were often quite dark, understood the value of placing lustres in dark corners, to create a sparkle and to chase out the spirits of gloom. These lustres (glass, umbrella-shaped stands, with clear glass points hanging from them), which we refer to fondly as "wand stands", can still be purchased from antique shops, although they are not cheap. However, individual glass points, which have become detached from their stands over the years, are not usually expensive, and if they are perfect and unchipped, make excellent wands for Dragon magic and for certain lunar operations. Glass knitting needles can be used in similar ways. Usually, they are the best tools for knitting spells, in which a square is worked while focusing one's intent into each stitch and muttering suitable charms. As soon as it is complete, the square is pulled from the needles and cast into the fire, its purpose being carried upward with the heat and the smoke.

Glass pens can also be used to cast small Circles, but their main use is for the writing out of charms with magical ink. Many such pens are produced these days, in a wealth of colours, and some of us have several different glass pens all used for different types of written spell.

Another popular glass item for the magical household is the twizzle stick. The main purpose of these highly decorative, but fragile items is to protect the house from sickness, to which end they are hung near the entrance and wiped daily with a soft cloth, which should then be discarded. Most good twizzle sticks are "friggers" from the glassworks of the 19th century, which were made from pot bottoms or as end-of-the-day wares, along with things like top hats or rolling pins. These items were often for the use of the glass-blowers themselves or to show off their decorative and creative skills. They are mostly associated with the glassworks in Nailsea, Somerset, but were certainly produced by glassworks throughout the UK (Vincent, 1975). For magical purposes, they do need to have a good "barley twist" pattern and to be completely undamaged. Woe betide anyone who breaks a twizzle stick! It is well to heed Nigel Pennick's warnings about the dire consequences of such a mishap. On several occasions, he has reminded us to take care when cleaning them. Twizzle sticks do appear every now and again in antique shops, but are expensive. A possible substitute is a glass candy cane, made for the Christmas market, and Langham Glass in Fakenham produce these. They are very attractive, but rather short for magical purposes, so having one made especially is another option.

Beads and Bloodstones
Glass beads were greatly loved by our Anglo-Saxon and Viking ancestors, and much can be learned by gazing at such necklaces in museum collections. Modern glass beads make excellent devotional rosaries, and are often added to spells or to offerings, the choice of shape and colour depending on the effect required. An old tradition is the use of the bloodstone to prevent cuts, or to heal them quickly if an accident should happen. They are sometimes seen on old scabbards, and were used by agricultural workers, who were always at risk of injury from sharp implements. Natural bloodstones are said to be the blood of warriors, whose battles are seen from Earth in the form of the Northern Lights (Pennick, 2004). However, these are extremely

difficult to find, so most people use the glass version, which is very effective, and also helps prevent nosebleeds. In the 19th century, Bloodstones were produced in King's Lynn, by a French glassmaker, but they are elusive, since those who have them treasure them and keep them secret, although Nigel himself does have one (Pennick, 2015). For those who wish to have one now, as with twizzle sticks, it may be best to ask a local glass artist to make one, and there are plenty to choose from in Norfolk.

Mirrors and Witch Balls

Silvered mirrors in all shapes and sizes are useful for deflecting unwanted energies, for capturing the light of the Moon and for looking at an object or a situation "the other way around", since a mirror image can often reveal a hitherto unnoticed aspect of something. It can at times be useful to carry a small mirror when out and about in order to have a discrete look at what is lurking behind. Mirrors are also powerful tools for self-reflection and self-knowledge, which is such an important part of any magical path, and yet so challenging. Magical practitioners within the Tradition differ in their attitude to mirrors in the home. Some love the increase of light that they bring to the indoor environment, whereas others consider them to be too much of a liability. They have to be carefully managed, of course, as they are openings, which can draw us into them or provide a route for other things to enter the home. Dark mirrors are also popular, for scrying and for plumbing the depths of the Well of Wisdom. Of course, it is just as easy to scry in a black bowl filled with water, or in water with a drop of ink or dye added to it, but a black mirror, with a suitably decorated frame, can develop a considerable power and attachment to the person who most often uses it.

Closely related magically to flat mirrors, are the mirrored spheres, known as witch balls. They are reputed to prevent maleficent witches entering the home, because the ill-wisher sees their own distorted reflection in the glass and is frightened away by it. Genuine Victorian examples, in silver, green, gold, blue or red, are much prized by practitioners of the Nameless Tradition, but modern versions, and even large Christmas decorations (which are derived from Victorian witch balls anyway) are equally effective, even if they do not hold quite such a quantity of memories as their older relatives. But that is always the way with magical equipment. There is a balance to be struck between that which holds a wealth of past memories, which may be for good or ill, and that which we acquire new, and holds only the story of its source materials and its making. Sometimes we laugh at the thought that some of the magical items which we have bought new or made ourselves, may one day be in the hands of our magical descendants, who may wonder about our lives and our work and feel the ancient touch of our hands on the physical things we have left behind. Such will not be the case with the very first chalice we bought for working with larger groups.

Chalice
We chose the chalice because it was made of recycled green-tinged glass and had an attractive Grail-type shape. From a practical point of view, it was inexpensive and large enough to refresh many participants in ritual work. It was also robust enough to be carried around in a shoebox to outside events. It lasted ten years. Then, on one fateful occasion, a small number of us were performing a Beltane rite at five in the morning, on top of Incleborough Hill, a high spot overlooking the sea at West Runton. It was a beautiful morning: fresh, bright and full of the promise of the coming season. The sparkle of the North Sea echoed from the glass of the chalice in the morning sunlight. The ritual focused on questing for wisdom, and a sword was firmly stuck into the soft ground, like an image from a Tarot card. The work proceeded well until, for no earthly reason, the sword began to fall sideways. On one level, that moment seemed to last forever, and yet it was too fast for anyone

to stop the sword falling onto the chalice, smashing it into a pile of uncountable glass shards. If ever disaster strikes during a ritual, it is nevertheless important to continue the work and to bring matters to a suitable close as far as is possible under the circumstances. So, we continued in spite of our surprise and shock, carefully clearing every scrap of glass from the ground once the rite had been brought to its formal end. However, we all knew that we had received an important, if disturbing message, although not everyone was in agreement as to its meaning. Had we all been able to interpret it correctly, to understand and to act upon it, we might later have been in a position to steer our own fate in a more auspicious direction. However, hindsight is a wonderful thing, and we did all realise that this was a portent of great change, although the threads of destiny would take a while yet to unravel.

The Solidity of Pottery

Magical tools made directly from the substance of the Earth itself often have a secure and homely feel to them, and drinking from an earthenware or stoneware chalice can be a very healing experience, especially if the hands of the potter who created it were gentle, and allowed the beneficent forces of the universe to flow freely into their work.

In this county, full of talented craftspeople, there is no lack of cleverly-fashioned pottery items to choose from, and it is easy to tell which have been imbued with the right sort of energy. It is always good, though, to have an understanding of the process behind the making and to appreciate just how much goes into developing and honing the skills required to produce work of quality. So, in the spirit of exploration, a few of us visited the pottery of the wonderful Andrea, at Wattlefield in South Norfolk. Her cottage is surrounded by open fields, yet totally concealed from the road by a tall hedge and the trees which look as if they form a copse but are in fact part of the long, wooded garden, with its ground cover of Periwinkles and Jerusalem Sage, and its narrow, well-trodden pathway to the pottery and the home. This is a haven for birds who frequent the feeders in the small, square courtyard which, situated between the kitchen and the pottery, is a cosy space full pots of scented herbs, climbing Roses adorning the brick walls, and a wooden table and bench, where we have sat on a number of occasions, enjoying tea and home-made cakes. The place so perfectly reflects the warm, gentle nature of the potter and the spirit of the work which she produces in this calm, magical space.

We spent the day under her watchful eye, and that of her Kiln God (see Chapter Three), learning to use the wheel and work the clay. We all managed to produce a bowl (glazed black for scrying) and a cup with a handle, although I suspect that our success was (at least in my case) as much to do with Andrea's discrete but expert assistance as it was down to any innate talent for this demanding craft. It was a most enjoyable and instructive experience, deepening our understanding of the creative connection between hand and Earth.

Witch Bottles

Witch bottles have long been a tool for operative magic, mainly as a means of preventing or diverting magical attack. Many have been discovered all around East Anglia, in hearths, up chimneys, in gardens or buried somewhere in the vicinity of the threshold. They are usually filled with pins and nails, as x-rays of many historical examples have indicated. One found in a garden in Hevingham on Mayday 1992, for example, contained two iron nails (Norfolk Heritage Explorer no. 28977). The metal items are often bent which, as Hoggard (2015) suggests, is a way of ritually killing them in order to activate a "ghost pin". This is more effective against an enemy who attacks in spirit form. Urine is an additional ingredient, but this of course rarely stands the test of time. One idea behind the spell is usually that, if someone is trying to attack you magically, their spell will find the bottle first, attracted by your urine, and it will then be deflected back onto them, often as a nasty attack of cystitis, caused by the sharp implements in the bladder-shaped bottle. In other versions, the bottle contains the aggressor's urine, if it is possible to obtain that, and is heated in the fire so that they are tormented with a terrible burning pain. This is somewhat explosive though, in all sorts of ways. Not all witch bottles necessarily contain nails or pins. One found in Welney had animal bones inside it, while another, found in a hearth in Hellington, South Norfolk, in 1976 contained Hawthorn thorns, knotted string and fragments from a 15th- or 16th-century breviary (Norfolk Heritage Explorer nos. 33778 and 20034 respectively). We all have our own ways of doing these things.

The traditional witch bottles were of course usually made in bellarmines, which have a bearded face just below the neck. The lovely old market town, of Swaffham, about an hour's journey from Norwich, has its very own Bellarmine Museum (http://bellarminemuseum.co.uk/), which can be visited by making an appointment with the owner and founder of the collection, Alex Wright, who is very welcoming, and not only has extensive knowledge of this subject, but generously shares the information he has gathered. Bellarmines are a kind of German stoneware flagon, found throughout Western Europe. Examples have also been found as far afield as North and South America, Africa, India and Australia. Most of those we have in England were from the Frechen area, from where they were imported from the 16th to the end of the 17th century, and were used to store acids, oils vinegar and mercury, as well as ale, cider and wine. Alternative names for these vessels include numerous versions of "beard man" (baartman, bartmann, bartmankruge, etc.) or greybeard, and these characters may be regarded as household guardians. The imagery is fascinating. Only a few of the exhibits show evidence of having been used as witch bottles, but the entire collection is magically inspiring. There is much variation in the design and decoration of the bottles themselves, and in the face masks, which have a wealth of different expressions, and often have interesting things hidden in, or peering out of, the beard. Some have ears of wheat, fruits or flowers, and have been considered to be harvest or fertility jugs (Wright, 2009-16). As is often the case, a single visit to this museum is not enough to appreciate the richness and complexity of the history of these "ordinary" household items, which have been (and still are) used as magical tools by many magical practitioners over the centuries.

Another type of bottle spell is the thread bottle, where you place all your offcuts of thread from embroidery, knitting or weaving, so that they form a fabulous swirling pattern, designed to baffle any witch or evil spirit who might be coming to do you harm. Nowadays, it seems to have become popular to make prettified witch bottles, usually in clear glass, with dried flowers, beads, ribbons and salt, which do look very attractive. Of course, once you start adding herbs, they can have any purpose you choose, though there is nothing to beat the old piss and pins trick.

Tools of Bone, Antler and Horn

Tools made from animal parts hold within them something of the melancholy poetry of life departed, which may be suitable for certain types of magic. A bone, unworked in any mundane way, can have powerful effects, the most well-known being the Toad bone, although many other types are also used, whether these are found, have been deliberately obtained or have been left over from a meal. Recently, at a dinner party, at which Partridge was served as the main course, I watched a fellow practitioner carefully collect all the wishbones, although whether she had some specific piece of work in mind or just wished to save them for later, I do not know. There is, obviously a different feel to using the bones once they have been cooked. A collection of small bones can usefully be used in divination and often speak, with considerable power, of hidden knowledge. Magical jewellery made from bone is also much sought after by those who are not of a vegetarian persuasion, and it works very well in combination with amber. I have an exquisite pentacle made from Cow bone by a very powerful and talented witch, Lynn, and I often attach this to a string of amber beads. Lynn was also kind enough to make me a drinking vessel from a curled Ram's horn, which gurgles charmingly whenever I drink from it, and has been known to make people laugh in rituals. For work with a flavour of the Norse Traditions or for toasting with mead, a Cow's horn works well. These are readily available in so many different sizes and in shades of brown, grey, black or cream, and look magnificent in a fancy stand on the altar.

Antlers are, of course, shed by Stags in March or April, so the top of a stang or the shaft of a wand may for a while have a connection to a creature who is still alive and roaming the woods or fields. Deer antlers are particularly special because they resonate with the power of our horned deities and finding some is considered to be a very great blessing.

Making, collecting and using magical tools is one of the great pleasures of our path. We realise that this is an approach which is very much of its time, and that most of our magical ancestors in these lands of Chalk and Flint are unlikely to have been able to amass anything like the quantity of magical paraphernalia which we gather and revel in like Dragons with their hoards. Neither is there any need for so many things in terms of operative magic, and without it all we would manage perfectly well. But it is a favourite saying of ours that you cannot have too many chalices or too many rune sets, and we appreciate the bounty and abundance of the world around us. The beauty of magical tools, their craftsmanship and the feeling of enchantment which emanates from them makes them irresistible on so many levels. Some practitioners' collections of them are as rare and precious as those of many a museum or gallery, more so indeed, for they are made up of living things, whose roles span the realms of being and whose thrum of power can guide and enhance our magical endeavours.

References

Blakely, Sandra (2006) *Myth, Ritual and Metallurgy in Ancient Greece and Recent Africa*, Cambridge University Press.

Cameron, Malcom (1993) *Anglo-Saxon Medicine*, Cambridge University Press.

Cunningham, Scott and Harrington, David (2000) *The Magical Household*, Llewellyn.

Dillaire, Claudia R. (2011) *Egyptian Prosperity Magic*, Llewellyn.

Ettlinger, Ellen (1943) Documents of British Superstition in Oxford, *Folklore* 54(1) (March 1943), pp. 227-249.

Foley, Helene P. (ed.) (1994) *The Homeric Hymn to Demeter: Translation, Commentary, and Interpretive Essays*, Princeton University Press.

Gary, Gemma (2010) *Traditional Witchcraft: A Cornish Book of Ways*, Troy Books.

Glyde, John (1872) *The Norfolk Garland*, Jarrold.

Gimbutas, Marija (2007) *The Goddesses and Gods of Old Europe 6500 – 3500 B.C.*, University of California Press.

Grössinger, Christa (1997) *Picturing Women in Late Medieval and Renaissance Art*, Manchester University Press.

Hoggard, Brian (2015) Witch Bottles: Their Contents, Contexts and Uses, in Hutton, Ronald (ed.) *Physical Evidence for Ritual Acts, Sorcery and Witchcraft in Christian Britain: A Feeling for Magic*, Palgrave Macmillan, pp. 91-105.

Holland, Lora L. (2012) Women and Roman Religion, in James, Sharon, and Dillon, Sheila (eds.) *A Companion to Women in the Ancient World*, Wiley-Blackwell, pp. 204-15.

Hutton, Ronald (1996) *Stations of the Sun: A History of the Ritual Year in Britain*, Oxford University Press.

Jackson, Nigel, and Howard, Michael (2000) *The Pillars of Tubal-Cain*, Capall Bann.

Jones, Evan, and Valiente, Doreen (1990) *Witchcraft A Tradition Renewed*, Phoenix.

Levack, Brian (2002) *Witchcraft in the Modern World*, Routledge.

De Mello e Souza, Laura (2010) *The Devil and the land of the Holy Cross: Witchcraft, Slavery and Popular Religion in Colonial Brazil*, University of Texas Press.

Norfolk Heritage Explorer: http://www.heritage.norfolk.gov.uk.

Pennick, Nigel (2004) *Secrets of East Anglian Magic*, Second Edition, Capall Bann.

Pennick, Nigel (2015) *Pagan Magic of the Northern Tradition: Customs, Rites and Ceremonies*, Simon and Schuster, Destiny.

Stein, Anthony (2001) *Ariadne's Clue: A Guide to the Symbols of Mankind*, Princeton University Press.

Sweet, Henry (1896) *The Student's Dictionary of Anglo-Saxon*, Oxford University Press.

Thomas, Val (2014) Of Earth and Iron: The Uses of Agricultural Tools in Witchcraft Ritual and Magic, *The Cauldron* 151 (February 2014), pp. 7-11.

Vincent, Keith (1975) *Nailsea Glass*, David and Charles.

Wright, Alex (2009-6) *The Bellarmine and Other German Stoneware* Volumes 1-3, Albion Antiquities.

Yang, Lihui (2005) *The Handbook of Chinese Mythology*, Oxford University Press.

Witch's Poppet – Moyse's Hall Museum

Operative Magic

Every common task which we perform can be a mere chore or, if we choose, the weaving of an enchantment, spider-silk fine and exquisitely beautiful, or flint-tipped and focused as a Stone Age arrow. It is partly an act of will, partly a feature of our relationship with our land, our tools and materials, and partly draws upon the aid of spiritual beings of various kinds. Beyond that, there is something more which is far less describable in words. It is an attempt to reach out to that great creative force, that wellspring of love and passion, which allows words to speak ideas into being, planks of wood to be transformed into altars, earth into vessels, seeds into great trees. It is also that which gives mere humans the ability to rise above the limitations of their mundane struggles and to know, albeit fleetingly, their true potential as Children of the Stars.

Most of us who are currently working in our Tradition also need to work in some mundane context to earn a living. Few of us have great wealth and the post of village (or these days, city) witch is hardly lucrative enough to pay rent or a mortgage, put food on the table or support a family of humans or other creatures. Some sell magical crafts; others charge a small fee for healing therapies or divination, but these are usually extra to some "normal" job.

A great challenge then is the time constraints this places on what we see as our real work: our magical studies (for we can never have enough knowledge) and our working of spells and rituals, with all the meditation, growing, crafting and writing which that entails. So, we need to see and work our magic in the context of the irritations and frustrations of modern life. This can seem, at times, an impossible task, if we are stuck in an office, a classroom or a hospital ward. However well and magically we try to do our work, it can still drive a wedge between us and our magical contacts. Such is modern life. Yet sometimes, the magic can flow into the most mind-numbing and infuriating of situations. We might glance through a window and notice a runic kenning in the shimmering vapour trail of aeroplanes or the bare branches of Winter trees; a few well-chosen words may, like a charm, calm a fractious situation, or the sachet of herbs hidden in the stationery drawer may begin to work its magic. All this helps to remind us, often just when we most need it, of who we really are and that, as Aleister Crowley wrote, "there is no part of us that is not of the gods". For a little while then, all runs smoothly. Tempers are good and people laugh and enjoy their work. You cut your lunchtime Apple across its equator so that the pentagram within it blazes out at you like a gift from the starry firmament.

Indeed, magic, like luck, is self-perpetuating. The more we actually work magic, the more we notice it in the world around us. Our connections with the deities, the spirits and Fair Ones are strengthened and deepened; our herbs smell sweeter; we capture the Moon in our scrying mirrors without even trying. Then somehow, the information we need unfolds effortlessly before us and we are able to achieve much that we desire. We relish such times, knowing that this buzz, this sparkling current of magic, is not constant and that there will be fallow times when progress is sluggish. We may even find ourselves doubting our magical abilities. Sometimes it is the weight of circumstances weighing us down, sometimes sackfuls of useless burdens not yet discarded, or lessons still to be learned. At other times, for reasons we may not grasp, the combined astrological forces may be at odds with what we perceive to be our magical best interests! Patience, at such times, and quiet contemplation, can ease the journey to the next twist of the labyrinth, when the small spark within can blossom once again into a Sacred Fire. This moment then finds us more knowledgeable, more skilful and wiser in our wielding of our magical power. Our lives, like the seasons of the year and the great tides of the North Sea, ebb and flow as we learn and develop. We build on each cycle, assessing, refining, adjusting and transforming ourselves into true alchemical gold and finding our rightful place within the Web of Wyrd.

There are those in the magical world who view the operative magic of Traditional Craft as "low" magic, suggesting that it is somehow inferior to the "high" magic of learned, ceremonial traditions. For us, however, the Great Work can as well be accomplished in garden, field, forest or home as it can in the most lavish of temples, much as we appreciate their power and beauty. By working with what is natural, by understanding the essence of things, we are piecing together the great pattern which is all of this world and the worlds beyond. As we perform the humblest of spells, mixing ingredients and focusing the mind, improving our own lives, or those of others, we are at the same time adding to the sum of our understanding and aligning ourselves more closely with the spiritual realms.

However, as Charles Leland wrote in Aradia, the discipline of faith is key to successful spell work:

> *It should be observed, and that earnestly, that the prayer, far from being answered, will turn to the contrary or misfortune, unless the one who repeats it does so in fullest faith, and this cannot be acquired by merely saying to oneself, "I believe." For to acquire real faith in anything requires long and serious mental discipline, there being, in fact, no subject which is so generally spoken of and so little understood. Here, indeed, I am speaking seriously, for the man who can train his faith to actually believe in and cultivate or develop his will can really work what the world by common consent regards as miracles.*

Within the Nameless Tradition, we use old spells discovered in books or taught us by past practitioners and adapted to suit our needs. We also share ideas amongst ourselves and seek assistance from the Fair Folk. Sometimes we fashion our own spells, using basic magical principles and the ingredients we have to hand. Each of us finds our own unique style, just as we all have our own handwriting, but we all draw together many threads and colours and patterns, not rigidly sticking to one form, but working fluidly to achieve the best results. Thus, the spells and rites which follow are not to be slavishly adhered to, but adapted and improved or simply used for inspiration. They can be performed in the context of a full-blown ritual, at an astrologically selected moment, or just mixed and muttered wherever and whenever circumstances require.

Magical Devotions

Most people who work this kind of magic have some pattern of rituals, however simple, that they perform on a daily basis. It sets the tone for what we are trying to achieve and keeps our minds clear and focused, allowing us to feel that we are weaving our own web rather than just reacting to what happens around us.

Probably the most common is some kind of morning ritual of dedication to favoured deities or spirits or a greeting to the Sun and to the new day, which may be conducted at a shrine or altar, with the lighting of a candle and some incense. A prayer or rhyme is often said, jewellery put on or holy oil applied to the forehead, as a single spot or tracing a particular symbol such as a pentagram, an appropriate rune or a Helm of Awe, should one feel in need of a high level of protection.

The kind of oil selected will depend in some measure on which spiritual beings we wish to align ourselves with, but also on the activities we expect to engage in during the course of the day. A rich red St. John's Wort oil will connect us with solar deities, boost our mood and our confidence and help us to shine out so that our work and efforts do not go unnoticed or unrewarded. Elder leaf oil will strengthen our connection with the earthy forces of green witchery, help with planting, harvesting, foraging or healing work. Basil oil may prove useful if the day requires financial transactions, while delicious Rose can sweeten any day by reminding us to love and to be loved. Should our thoughts be ranging further afield, exotic perfumes may draw to us the magic of deities from beyond these shores or open a pathway for us to travel to them. Blends are useful too, for most days have more than just a single focus, and the Fair Folk especially appreciate a lovingly selected and magically mixed fragrance. However, it is important to remember, when going out to meet the Fair Ones, that they also like to have some of the perfume for themselves, so it is best to take a small amount to leave as offering. I tend to pour the oil into a small egg shell or a Cockle shell, which is usually appreciated. If the giving of such an offering is forgotten, they may well decide to take something else that you are less willing to give.

Those of us with gardens will go out and greet them, first thing, acknowledging the ever-present Lord and Lady of Norfolk, plants, the spirits and the creatures. A long, elaborate eulogy may be declaimed or a cheerful rhyme spoken with love and respect, in acknowledgement of a long relationship with a place and its inhabitants. If one is going to be away for a while, and unable to do this, it is as well to make this clear to the garden beforehand, so that no one feels neglected or offended.

Although witchcraft is usually associated with night-time and the witching hour, in the counties of the East and of the rising Sun, we do some of our best work in the mornings. Quiet meditation or a walk around one's own magical patch, when the day is still young and fresh, before most other folk are awake, can bring surprising rewards. The night has hopefully soothed away some of the confusions, entanglements or disappointments of the previous day, and the results of meditation or observations often have a level of a clarity which may not be so easy to achieve once the concerns of the day begin to press upon us.

Other possible small acts of devotion throughout the day include an acknowledgement of the Sun at the height of his power, a twilight goodnight to the spirits of the daylight hours and a welcome to those creatures of the night who bring quiet blessings and protection.

Rosaries

The use of a rosary as an aid for prayer or meditation is a practice found in numerous religious or spiritual paths around the world and is much favoured in Norfolk magic too. Each bead on a string represents a particular focus of attention and can be held for as long or as short a time as we wish to direct our thoughts there. There are no set numbers of beads or specific points which should be included. We make our own and select each subject for contemplation according to our needs at any particular time. These might include the four Elements or directions, the Lord and Lady of Norfolk, the days of the week or seven classical planets, named heroes, deities or Fair Spirits with whom we regularly work, particular totem animals, trees or plants, the festivals of the year or the magical places of the county.

The beads themselves can all be of the same type, perhaps plain wood or appropriately coloured glass, or all different so that they embody physically the magical concept they represent. The bead for a totem animal might be a tiny wooden carving of that creature or a piece of bone or fur from one. The Element of Water could be represented by a tiny bottle of water from one of our holy wells, Earth a vessel of salt, Fire some red glass and Air a feather or sachet of scented herbs. The creation of such rosaries is both a meditative and artistic endeavour, which can be undertaken as a long-term project over a whole season or a whole year. I have some truly exquisite examples of such rosaries, some tiny and some quite large, with items collected from all around Norfolk.

The creation of a rosary is often used as a teaching exercise for those who seek our help in taking their early steps within the Tradition. For this we often use Rose hips, if it is the right time of year for them. When they are fresh, they have a lovely, rich red gleam to them and a glossy feel which is most conducive to contemplation. I am particularly fond of using them, as I live very near to Rosary Road, and one of my favourite local places for walking and collecting is a Victorian cemetery called the Rosary. For stringing the Rose hips and indeed any other rosary beads, my personal preference is to use pure linen thread, because it so protective, so healing and has such powerful and ancient magical resonance. Before using the thread, it is best to draw it through beeswax. This not only strengthens it considerably but also imbues it with all the magic and blessing of Bees, their warmth, their sweetness and the luck they can bring. The hips do often dry out in a rather attractive manner, but using a natural thread means that if the hips lose their shine and appeal the rosary can be left outside to find its way back to the Earth and possibly give life to a number of new Rose bushes.

When making a rosary around the season of Midsummer, it is a delight to use the old traditional method of creating the beads from Rose petals. Whilst it is considerably more fiddly and time consuming than using the hips, it is a very rewarding process. The beads are darkly fragrant and ooze magic. It is easy to understand why Rose petals are so favoured for making rosary beads and gave their name them.

The beads can be made in the following manner. Chop the freshly-picked Rose petals very finely. Put them in an iron pot with just a little drop of water, barely covering them, and heat for an hour without boiling. Repeat the process on three successive days, adding just a little more water if necessary. Oil your fingers (preferably with Rose oil) and roll the pulp into beads. These will take several days to dry out. Before they are completely dry, make holes in them with a suitably-sized needle, which can be heated if it won't go through cold. It's best to string the beads on plastic or nylon line, making sure they are not touching each other, until they are perfectly dry. They will be easiest to move like this, but if you object to using artificial materials, linen thread will also work well. Other recipes for making scented beads from powdered spices can be found in Jeanne Rose's (2001) Herbs and Things.

Other natural materials which can be recommended as rosary beads include Pine cones, for energy and clarity of vision, Alder cones for bridge-building between oneself and the other realms, Hazelnuts for wisdom or for working with Mother Julian (see Chapter Two), Cherry stones to focus on love and sweetness in life and Elder twigs for concentrating on healing, longevity and witchly ways.

Magic of Hearth and Home
For those of us within the Nameless Tradition, every room of the house or flat requires its special acts of magic, large or small. Spells of all kinds, depending on individual inclinations, may be secreted behind pictures or mirrors, hung from curtain poles or placed in vases. They may be hidden in the soil of pot plants, lurk in the corners of drawers or be invisible sigils painted onto walls or doors when they were being decorated, or drawn onto to windows as herbal infusions during the cleaning process. They may be general spells to attract luck, good health, success or money, or they may have a very specific purpose.

Altars
Most of us like to keep an altar in our homes. This may be done openly, in full view of guests, or secretly in a more private room. Such an altar usually has upon it a piece of Chalk and a piece of Flint as well as a pair of white or grey candles to honour the Lord and Lady of Norfolk. There will often be a green and a blue candle for the lush green Earth and the magnificent sky above, and perhaps one in a seasonal colour too. Other representations of the four Elements of

Earth, Air, Fire and Water are usually included, and there may be a censor or a dish of pot pourri if burning incense is impractical due to fire alarms. It is also quite common to have a small cauldron where spells, talismans or other magical objects may be left to cook or gestate for as long as they need. For those who are blessed with a real hearth, the cauldron is kept there. A large hag stone is also useful to "give birth" to magical items which have been created. Images of favoured deities or other spiritual beings are often included, and may have been painted or crafted by the practitioner themselves or bought from another craftsperson. As crafts play such a major role in our Tradition, some smaller craft tools may also be placed upon the altar, such as a drop spindle, a paintbrush, a whittling knife or whatever is significant to the work of the moment. Chalices are much favoured and at least one practitioner of our Tradition has an altar especially set aside for a magnificent collection of them.

Sprowl Boxes

If the altar is large enough, it may include one or more "sprowl boxes". Most of us have several of these, which contain collections of items from especially magical or significant places around the county. This allows a little of the energy, the sprowl or, spirament of a special location to be brought back into the home to help inspire and empower our work. Such boxes can also be used to form a physical link to elsewhere in the county. In other parts of the U.K., spirament or sprowl may be collected differently. In Cornwall, as Gemma Gary (2008) writes, the witch draws the essential, burgeoning energy of the Growing Tide into a magical staff, for later use. Our sprowl boxes perform a similar function, with "spent" items being returned to where they came from. New treasures are constantly being added, especially amongst those of us who live in the city and need to keep alive that current of connection with wave, woodland and farmland. We also keep sprowl boxes from distant lands with which we have a connection or an affinity. Personally, I have sprowl boxes from Cornwall and from Cyprus. Other practitioners with whom I work closely have boxes with sprowl items from places as far flung as Scotland and Japan. Equally, there are plenty of people living in various places around the world who keep Norfolk sprowl boxes.

The most common items to include in sprowl boxes are hag stones or any other attractive stones, particularly those which are perfectly spherical, shells, driftwood, fossils, seed heads, feathers and bones. Other bizarre, curious or remarkable items could find a place in a sprowl box, especially if they have a particular significance. The shape and decoration of the box itself is likely to be selected in accordance with the nature of the place from which the sprowl items were collected. Much of the treasure from East Wretham Heath, for example, includes Rooks' feathers which, for practical purposes alone, demand a reasonably long box.

Opening a well-worked sprowl box is always something of a special moment, as a tangible gust of sprowl often flies out and can catch the unwary by surprise. The collection and creation of sprowl boxes is a great magical joy which I would recommend to witches and magicians wherever they live. Magic is dynamic and evolving and, although Traditional Witchcraft is rooted in its own landscape, the flow of ideas to and from other times and other places nourishes us all and develops our practice.

The Hearth

The hearth, as mentioned above, is the best place for the cauldron and many other magical items are likely to be found on the mantelpiece above it. Wooden mantelpieces in older houses often have protective "daisy wheel" patterns drawn into them, for the hearth is a place of great power and magical focus, but is also fraught with danger, not least from fire itself. Bride's crosses, fashioned from straw or Rushes are much favoured here to guard against fire, as they are elsewhere in the country. One hearth may have many of them around it, not because a single one is not powerful enough, but because making them can prove a particularly addictive process.

The hearth is a place which is always open to the outside world, which renders it somewhat vulnerable to baleful influences which may enter the house via the chimney. There is an old tradition of placing a small shoe up the chimney for protection and good luck, and many people still do this. It was also common in the past to keep a mummified Cat in the rafters for protection against fire and other types of misfortune. Dire consequences have resulted from the removal of such guardians, as Nigel Pennick has documented in his Secrets of East Anglian Magic. Witches in this area today are generally not inclined to mummify their Cats, although when we lose one of these beloved creatures, we sometimes place their cremated ashes in the loft, next to the chimney breast, for the same purpose.

House Plants
House plants are much treasured, treated with respect and may be with us for many years, becoming firm friends and allies, offering as they do protection, inspiration, love and numerous other forms of magic. The placing of plants in strategic situations is essential for the plant's well-being but is also of magical significance.

On a front windowsill, a really spiky plant will help offer protection from unpleasantness from the street, which is especially important in the city, where front gardens are often small or non-existent and random ill-feeling (not directed at us personally) may need to be diverted. Some people like Cacti for this purpose, but my personal favourite is the dramatic Crown of Thorns (Euphorbia milii), whose stems are covered in long spines. One of the beauties of this plant is that it constantly produces bright red "flowers" (bracts, botanically speaking), which enhance the Martian look of the plants and can easily be collected, dried and added to banishing powders, should those ever be needed. These plants are very long lived and, although apparently aggressive, they reward good care and attention. House plant books claim they need little water, but mine is very often thirsty and can drink an enormous amount of water in one go.

Hoya carnosa, commonly known as a Wax Plant or Pentagram Plant, has lovely thick, dark green, oval-shaped leaves on long stems, which can be grown as climbers or trailing from a high shelf or basket. The flowers are really waxy-looking and borne in delightfully scented clusters. Because of their shape, the dried flowers can add power to any spell, particularly any related to love or communication. They need to be dried carefully or pressed, however, as they tend to shrivel up and go brown rather easily.

Many of our house plants have the power to improve the indoor environment, not just by making it more beautiful but also by removing some of the common indoor pollutants which are produced by such household articles as paper, foam, clothes, plywood, plastics, paints and various cleaning products. Numerous websites now list the powers of plants in this respect. The Peace Lily (Spathiphyllum wallisii), for example, as well as helping to maintain harmony in the household, also aids the removal benzene and trichloroethylene.

Philodendron scandens, or Sweetheart Vine, whose Latin genus name means "lover of trees", removes the formaldehyde at the same time as filling a room with the loving kindness which exudes from its heart-shaped leaves. Spider Plants (Chlorophytum comosum) also remove formaldehyde. They produce many small plantlets on long stems and are therefore useful to encourage fertility, be that of humans, animals or projects. It is obviously important to be clear which is intended if asking for assistance in these matters!

African Violets (Saintpaulia ionantha) make wonderful, inexpensive indoor companions. Their furry leaves can be stroked like an animal, which is very soothing, and the common purple-flowered types are often associated with spirituality because of their colour, but many other colours are available too and all have gentle, calming natures, as well as being protective.

There are Money Plants for those who seek wealth, Bead Plants and Lipstick Plants for the vain, Pelargonias for incense and flavourings, Rosary Vines for the prayerful, Aloes to heal kitchen burns and Dragon Plants to honour those great beings, whose name they bear. Indeed, the potential for growing house plants is endless and coming to an appreciation of what they have to offer is a fascinating voyage of magical exploration. Many of our house plants can easily be propagated by cuttings or offsets and sharing them with others is one of the great joys of both magical and mundane friendships.

Kitchen Magic

The magic of the kitchen is at once simple and yet complex. Any good cook performs magic by taking raw ingredients and combining them to produce something delicious, nourishing and pleasing to all the senses. Food is in itself magical, but the careful witch selects ingredients of appropriate colours and adds those herbs and spices which suit the occasion: linseeds to breads, pies or crumbles for all types of protection, Pot Marigold flowers in soups or stews to lift the mood, Lavender to aid communication, Rosemary to sharpen the mind and the memory, Turmeric or Cinnamon to soothe, heal and balance, Ginger, Pepper or Chilli to energise, warm and improve the physical circulation and thus move things forward magically too. Each one may be charmed before being added, but such words or rhymes are rarely written down. They are often of the moment, muttered into the pot through the vortex formed as the mixture is stirred, possibly by a magical spoon carved from a specific type of wood. Runes or other sigils are often written into the mixture and folded in, or, in the case of bread or biscuits, may be written onto the surface. It is also usual to have an ing or inguz rune somewhere near the stove.

To ensure plenty, a stone which looks like bread, or a Sea Urchin shell is often kept either in the bread bin or on the kitchen windowsill, along with fresh herbs for cooking, but also for their magical benefits. Pot Marjoram is excellent for the digestion and also maintains love within the home, while Basil is delicious with Tomatoes but can also help to increase wealth. Meanwhile Lemon Balm which, as a tea, soothes the nerves and digestion, is associated with the Bee Priestesses of Aphrodite and hence with love, beauty, success and healing.

We love to make our own wines and beers too. There are few sounds which are so gently magical as that of bubbles in the air lock of a demijohn full of fermenting must. But wine-making is a lengthy process with plenty of scope for things to go wrong, so charms are often employed to ensure a good result. There are rhymes which can be sung over the fruit or flowers as they are prepared or written down and hung onto the handle of the demijohn. They are simple though, and work best if the practitioner writes their own, varying them according to the blend of ingredients being used, although for those with a preference for verse, it is worth remembering that "wine" and "fine" rhyme. Other practitioners prefer to write bindrunes or sigils for success and protection onto the jar or bucket itself. I prefer to do this in blue but some use black. Alternatively, simply tie on a small hag stone. We each have our own way of working, and continued practice is one of the keys to mastery.

It is normal to hang a few charms around the kitchen to keep things running smoothly, keep food fresh, ensure that the bread rises and the jam sets, absorb bad energies, keep pests out of the food, and avert the Evil Eye. A cut onion, left on a plate, will rapidly draw any negativity towards itself. It will be obvious when this has occurred, because it will have an unpleasant look and feel to it. It is then best discarded completely, not even put in the compost. Lemons also work well in this way, over a longer period of time, and it is common practice to place them in black net bags and hang them discretely in the corners of rooms.

A simple general charm for a successful and productive kitchen requires a few miniature kitchen implements, such as a chopping board, rolling pin and knife. These can be whittled by the practitioner or, if that skill has not yet been acquired, bought as doll's house items. The items are suitably charmed, with petitions, rhymes and pledges, and strung together on red thread, along with a leaf of Bay, which is both a powerful, solar plant of victory and a common kitchen herb.

Threshold Magic

The threshold, as the border between the inside and the outside, is a place of particular power, but considerable care is needed with regard to who steps over it. For those of us with gardens, the back door is usually part of a gentle continuum between indoor and outdoors, perhaps with a conservatory or garden room as a transitional space. The front is another matter altogether, especially as many of our houses do not have a hall and the door may open directly onto the living room, in close proximity with the street. There is a long tradition here of growing protective plants across the front door, then only using it for weddings or funerals, and some people maintain this, although it is not always practical. I did try it once, but it upset the postman.

A good protective measure, which keeps the threshold magical, is to chalk a "running eights" pattern onto the step. Some people like to use lots of colours for this, but if the Chalk itself is that which is taken from the local Earth, it also confers the beauty and protection of our White Lady Herself.

It is usual to keep two large hag stones just outside, on either side of the front door. Somewhere in the front garden, it is not uncommon to bury a witch bottle, while just inside the threshold there will probably be a twizzle stick

Garden Magic

Gardening is itself an act of magic and, like many such skills, it is time and devotion which bring the most rewarding results. However, there are certain garden spells and practices which can enhance the physical work and improve the magical qualities of harvests.

It is usual to save some of the ashes from the Twelfth Night Fire. These are kept in a special jar and sprinkled as a blessing on the Earth when the growing season begins. It can be sprinkled on the soil or put into the compost to add essential nutrients and magical energy for the growth to come, for the future is always built on the foundation of the past. Other magical powders or holy water are sometimes used to bless the garden. Water from St. Walstan's Well is particularly beneficial, but if anyone travels West to Glastonbury, they usually return with some water from Chalice Well, which is highly effective too.

It is important to maintain the good will of the Fair Folk, so the first fruits of any crops are offered to them in a special place, with words of gratitude. If we travel anywhere or even go out for the day, we try to bring back a suitable gift: a shell, an attractive stone, a piece of fruit or a colourful leaf may all be found acceptable"(see chapter 3). We often make things for our garden spirits too, such as windchimes, mobiles or appropriate garden sculptures. Protective figures or outdoor poppets are often used. These are sometimes sticks which quite naturally have arms, legs and a head or require very little carving to bring out the figure hiding in the wood. Sometimes two forked sticks are bound together using Periwinkle, Honeysuckle or Clematis stems, which can also bulk out the body and form the head. Such figures closely resemble Hikey Sprites and need little encouragement to watch over flower or vegetable patches or particularly treasured trees. Bead figures may also be used. Wendy, of Worstead, created exquisite bead poppets to protect her garden from Snails, and an example of her work may be seen in the Witchcraft Museum in Boscastle.

Snails are wonderfully magical beings, and, as Gemma Gary (2008) has so beautifully explained, their presence should be honoured and revered. Of course, we love to collect the empty shells and string them on red thread, as a blessing for the home, but we still have something of an ambivalent attitude to them; Norfolk Snails, or Dodmen, are particularly voracious and can demolish an entire planting of magical herbs or vegetables in the course of a single evening. Reasoning with them is not always successful.

Blue is an important colour in the garden, since it is generally considered to repel the Evil Eye and to confer spiritual protection. We like to grow as many blue flowers as possible throughout the year: Rosemary, which traditionally flowers when the days are still chilly (often on Old Christmas Day), blue Anemones in the Spring, the Fairy Bluebells of Beltane, the Forget-me-Nots of early Summer, courageous Borage, fragrant Lavender and songful Larkspur, as the days become longer and warmer. There is also Hyssop, useful against lung problems and for purification.

Chicory, also known as Wild Succory, has flowers which look like tall, blue dandelions, and can be seen from July to September. However, the flowers tend to open very early in the morning and close again before noon. An infusion of the flowers can be used to soothe inflamed eyes, while the root is used for jaundice, gout and liver complaints. This lovely flower has a particular association with the area where I live. The late 18th-, early 19th-century botanist, Sir James Edward Smith, founder of the Linnaean Society, recalls tugging at the tough stems of the plant on his childhood walks on the chalky hills around Norwich (Kennett, 2016). Cunningham (1995) suggests various interesting uses for the plant, including anointing one's body with its juice in order to obtain favours from great persons, to remove obstacles or to encourage frugality. If cut with a golden knife, in complete silence, at Midsummer, at the hour of midnight, Chicory can confer invisibility, as well as opening locked doors or boxes. Not having a golden knife, I cannot comment on the effectiveness of this spell.

As many different blue flowers as possible are collected as the Summer unfolds, carefully dried, and set aside until the flowering season is over. They can then be powdered and mixed together. This delightful magical blend, known simply as "Blue Powder", can then be sprinkled around the home and garden to bring luck, prosperity and happiness throughout the year, but it should be made one year for use the next. Just as with wine-making, a certain amount of forward thinking is required. It is important to remember that some blue flowers, like Monkshood (Aconitum napellus), are deadly poisonous so these are best avoided if there are children around. Even Delphiniums are toxic, as are many common garden plants. Always wash your hands after touching them and don't spread the powder where it could harm people or animals. (If in doubt, don't do it at all: advice which is applicable to all uses of herbs and indeed to magic itself).

Some variety of blue Beans is also grown each year. Beans, which are ruled by the planet Venus, are in themselves magical, being the food of the Dead and of the Fair Folk. Many witches carry three blue Beans in their pocket, in a little blue packet or in the Bean pod (or bladder) itself. This is because they keep away malign spirits. Should one be troubled by such, all that is required is to rattle the Beans and repeat nine times:

> *Three blue Beans in a blue bladder,*
> *Rattle bladder, rattle,*
> *Rattle bladder, rattle.*

Because East Anglia has such strong connections to our Anglo-Saxon ancestors, we use many of their spells and charms, which are to be found in such old texts as The Lacnunga, The Leechbook of Bald, and the Old English Herbarium. Sometimes they require a little adaptation, but

274

we are fortunate indeed that these wise folk have left us such a wealth of medical and magical knowledge.

One charm is the Æcerbot or Field Blessing, taken from an 11th-century manuscript found in the British Library (MS Cotton Caligula, A VII). This is an elaborate ritual to be performed if fields are unproductive or if they have been magically attacked. Earth is dug from all four corners of the land, remembering where each came from. Oil, honey, yeast and milk are then taken, along with a twig from every type of tree growing on the land, except Hornbeam, and every herb except Buckbean. Holy Water is added and the mixture dripped onto the four clumps of earth while a succession of prayers, both Christian and Pagan are said, asking for abundance and riches from the land. The earth is taken to church where a priest says four masses over it before it can be ceremonially replaced on top of a Rowan cross carved with the name of the four Gospel writers (Matthew, Mark, Luke and John). More prayers are said after facing East and humbly bowing nine times and turning three times clockwise. The next stage requires seed to be obtained from almsmen, who are given twice as much in return. Frankincense, Fennel, blessed soap and salt are poured into a hole in the plough and the seed sprinkled on it. The prayer to the Earth Mother, which then follows, asks for the fields to flourish and be fruitful, to have tall, shimmering, glistening crops and all the Earth's abundance. When the first furrow is ploughed, an offering of bread, baked to the size of a man's palm and kneaded with milk and holy water, is placed into it, with a prayer which addresses the field as "the people's mother" (Bradley, 1982).

For modern use, the charm needs to be considerably simplified to be practical, but if the magical principles are retained it can be extraordinarily powerful. I have known it to be used with good effect on a city garden, an allotment, and to improve the atmosphere of a neighbourhood. The key points are the removal of the earth, its blessing with sweet, natural and precious things, the saying of appropriate prayers at each stage, replacing the earth in the correct place with a Rowan cross beneath it, and making an offering when the land is next dug over prior to planting.

Much simpler, but still both potent and moving is A Blessing of Plants from the Lacnunga:

> *Omnipotent, eternal God who from the beginning of the world has established and created all things, as with the species of trees so with the seeds of plants, which also by the blessing of your benediction you have sanctified the same, now may you deign to sanctify and bless with your benediction the herbs of the garden and other fruits, so that to those consuming them they may confer health of mind and of body and a protection of defence and an eternal life.*

(Pettit, 2001)

A garden protection charm which can be painted or chalked onto gates or fences is a square of "running eights" with a heart at its centre from which radiate three Ladybirds, facing outwards. This provides a defence against those who would harm the garden, a welcome for those who come with love, good luck and blessing as well as the natural destruction of predators.

Sheds and greenhouses are usually protected by placing a hag stone at each of their four corners. Sharp tools may have a bloodstone attached to them to prevent them cutting those who use them or to staunch the flow of blood should an accident occur (see Chapter Six). Such bloodstones are usually activated by nine drops of blood from someone of the opposite sex. Sometimes they are worn around the neck on a red silk ribbon with three knots, spaced three inches apart (Pennick, 2015).

The glass of greenhouses can be washed with water to which a splash of cider vinegar and an infusion of two solar herbs, St. John's Wort and Rosemary, has been added. This helps to ensure that light will prevail on all levels.

The Magic of Travel

Travel is not without its dangers, even in these risk-averse days, so we normally take precautions when travelling. Eggshells have an age-old association with travelling witches, and have long been thought to form boats in which they could sail out and often harm other ships. It is to prevent this happening that people tend to break their eggshells completely once the contents have been extracted. While I am unaware of anyone in the Nameless Tradition physically travelling any distance across water by eggshell, or indeed of having any desire to be a hazard to shipping, eggshell charms, or the addition of powdered eggshell to a travel sachet, are certainly effective.

Of course, vehicles are protected by various spells on a regular basis. Hag stones on Rowan necklaces or bunches of Feverfew, Mugwort or Wormwood are often hung around the rear-view mirror of a car, and it is common to keep a wand within easy reach of the driver's right hand, and to put a poppet or a jar of linseeds or other herbs into the glove compartment. I have a kilo bag of Valerian in there. This is not for protection, but because wherever I hide it indoors, the cats will find it, scatter it and cover it in drool.

A day or so before embarking on a long road journey, it is a good idea to clean the car outside and inside, and to burn some incense in there. I have noticed that this can make the difference between a smooth and trouble-free trip, and one which is fraught with delays, traffic jams or other irritations. It is also beneficial to write protective runes on the car, most effectively with one's own saliva. These quickly become invisible, unless the car is very dirty.

Bicycles perhaps need even more protection than cars, and similar charms and runes can be used. Even when simply walking somewhere, it is not a bad idea to place a Mugwort leaf in each shoe, to prevent one's feet from getting tired and to enhance the safety and enjoyment of the journey.

When we think about some of these simple measures of everyday magic, they can sometimes seem trivial or even a little silly. However, putting them into practice can make a huge difference to the way we experience our existence. They are the magical seasoning which ensures that our lives are varied, as safe as they can be and full of delicious flavour.

Poppet Magic

Poppet magic is a very important technique used within Norfolk's Nameless Tradition, probably because it so appeals to our love of handicrafts. It draws together the artistically creative output of the inspired hand and the mental focus of intent and spellwork.

Looking at old poppets can be useful and informative, and quite a few of us have spent many fascinating, but not necessarily comfortable, hours gazing into the eyes of the poppets at the Witchcraft Museum in Boscastle. Considerably closer to home is one of my particular favourites, to be found in Moyse's Hall Museum in Bury St. Edmunds, just over the border in Suffolk. She dates back to the 17th century, and has a wax head and a padded fabric body on thick wire. She was found behind a wall in Bury St. Edmunds, but may possibly have been made in Norfolk, according to curator Alex McWhirter (personal communication), who very kindly emailed me a picture of her. A bland description of her in no way does her justice. She has the most knowing and intense expression on her expertly crafted face, and her bonnet and clothing have been made with great skill, care and attention to detail. It is obvious that every stitch was filled with magical intent. In her left hand, she is holding a page of strange writing which, although I have looked at the poppet in the cabinet and an enlargement of the photograph, I have not yet been able to make any sense of.

It does seem to be the case that the majority of historical poppets which are available for study were made for the purposes of cursing. That is not necessarily our purpose in making them, although each practitioner makes their own choices about such matters and accepts the responsibility for, and the consequences of, their own actions. I am not aware of anyone having used a poppet to perform a "Grand Bewitchment", as described by Paul Huson (1970), in which the poppet is placed in a magical triangle and stabbed through the heart to bring about the death of the victim. However, if somebody had done this, I very much doubt they would be discussing it. I do, though, know of people who sometimes make a poppet image of a person in order to "bind" them, to prevent them doing something or making progress. Once certain rituals have been performed the poppet is firmly bound in a black box and buried or, for a modern, temporary version, placed in the freezer. Others have persuaded people to move a long way away by sending the poppet in the post to some distant location. The address does not have to be a real one, just look plausible to the post office! This need not harm the person and may indeed be to their benefit. It simply gets them away.

Other reasons for making poppets include protection for the home or personal protection if the poppet is suitable to be carried around discretely. Poppets can provide an extra pair of eyes, watching what is going on at home while you are not there and reporting back on your return. Beware the lovely poppet given to you as a gift by someone you do not really consider to be a friend. He or she may have been sent to spy on you, and of course, the more beautiful the poppet, the more reluctant you will be to part with it. Such things are unusual but they do occasionally happen.

A money poppet, small enough to be kept in a wallet, purse or money box, can help protect its contents from theft or unwise expenditure, and also attract more money. The poppet needs to be made of really tough material as, if it is to be kept in a purse, it is likely to be knocked by the coins. Finding a suitably-shaped stone and clothing or decorating it, is one approach, or providing the poppet with a protective padded bag.

Poppets are often created in conjunction with seasonal festivals, and some may be put away at the end of the season and brought out again the following year. I have over the years made Eostre poppets, Jack Frost poppets, Harvest Ladies, Pumpkin dolls, May Queens and many more. Poppets can also be especially crafted to give gentle support and encouragement to people who may be experiencing troubled times or who may require extra help to focus on something they need to do. To the imaginative witch, the possibilities are endless.

One of the most popular poppets in my possession is a tiny beaded witch, less than an inch tall, with black clothes and red and white, stripy legs, who is a dowsing assistant. To hone our skills at dowsing with a pendulum, we place her under one of a number of cups and somebody has to dowse to find her while repeating "Where's the witch?" It is both fun and serious at the same time, especially after a hearty feast. There are those amongst us who have become so good at this that they can find her a dozen or so times without once getting it wrong.

The choice of materials for a poppet depends on how long it will need to last and how it might need to be disposed of. There is a witch up on the coast in North Norfolk who always stitches hers from linen or cotton fabrics and has a special sewing basket kept just for that purpose. Other people knit them, making every stitch count. My personal preference is for handmade felt from local wool. If I want to put a written spell, a sachet of herbs or some other item inside the poppet, I often make a cone shape of thick felt for the body, which is then stuffed with more wool and the other items. Wooden poppets are also lovely because it is possible to choose a wood which is appropriate to the purpose. The carving need not be elaborate, especially if the wood is suitably shaped to begin with.

Although natural materials are preferred for most purposes, quite a number of practitioners make use of some of the new, but easy to use, materials like Fimo or self-drying clay for poppet heads or whole poppets. I have even used the wax covering from the outside of fancy cheeses on the odd occasion, and to very good effect.

One of the easiest types of poppets to make is the hankie poppet. I was first inspired to make one after reading about the beautiful Victorian church dolls, which were made of just fabric, cleverly draped and richly embroidered. They were light and easy to hold and, should the child drop the toy during the service it would make no noise. I adapted the idea many years ago for a poppet making workshop, using men's handkerchiefs and linen threads for tying the stuffing into the neck. Participants who were skilled with their needle stitched wool on for the hair and embroidered beautiful faces and symbols on the of rest of the fabric. Even among some Traditional Witches, sewing is a hated chore, so those who felt that way either painted on hair, face, symbols or rhymes, or simply used a biro. Seasonal versions of these can be made by cutting out a suitable square from appropriately patterned fabric and just adding coloured hair. Norfolk must be awash with these kinds of poppets, as so many people have now passed on the idea.

Working with Familiars
Most of us who embrace this kind of Norfolk magic love animals and enjoy working with them in a variety of ways. As well as companionship and support, our magical creatures provide a perspective on the world which would not otherwise be available to us. They have such a different balance of senses and sensitivities, and whisker, fur, feather and scale create a point of interaction between the physical individual and the surrounding world which is so unlike anything we experience through clothed skin. Having the poise, agility and elegance a tail can confer is something we can best appreciate by learning from familiars.

Cats are amongst the most common familiars, as they are not only relatively easy to care for, but are also so well attuned to magical currents and shifts in energy. They can also confer some of this sensitivity on us if they choose to do so. They love ritual too, bouncing in and out of the Circle with ease, for they have access to far more levels and worlds than we can ever hope to visit. They will patrol the witch's territory too, possibly working with the Ward, and bring back word of what may be occurring. Care is needed though because, if they have a genuine affection for the witch, they may also set themselves up as guards and can easily come to harm. Some practitioners give them a collar with a tiny protective talisman on it, while others find it helpful to write protective sigils or runes into their fur.

Ferrets are like little Earth Dragons and can be helpful in adding energy and enthusiasm to a working, particularly if it is fierce and Martian in nature, or indeed Mercurial. If you need to hunt something down, literally or magically, a good Ferret will enhance your efforts with speed and focus. Contrary to what many people believe about Ferrets, they can be very loving and loyal and have a great sense of community.

Ferrets have always been important familiars in East Anglian Magic, as Nigel Pearson has pointed out (2015). The infamous picture of Witchfinder General, Matthew Hopkins, with the witch and her familiars, shows a Ferret called Pyewacket. In fact, all the Ferrets I have worked with magically have had the surname Pyewacket. They have all been quick-witted, funny, affectionate and loyal. One of them, who went by the name of Birch, has the distinction of being the Ferret who Kissed a Rock Star. Ferrets have a great fondness for magic, so long as it does not take too long, and are talented assistants in spell work.

According to John Glyde (1872), one of a great many traditional cures for whooping cough involves drinking milk a Ferret has already lapped from. One of my Ferrets, Raedwald Pyewacket, had a great fondness for milk and was forever drinking from the milk jug. However, as (fortunately) nobody had whooping cough, there was no opportunity to try the spell. I do wonder though, if John Glyde realised what a drastic effect drinking milk can have on a Ferret's digestion! A lot of smelly clearing up is involved. Nevertheless, should I ever have a whooping cough, which none of my herbs could help me with, I would prefer this cure to the roast mouse or to torturing to death a frog, snails or a spider by hanging them over the mantelpiece or hearth in a muslin bag in order to take the cough away with them. The poor spider even had a rhyme to attend its misery, said while holding the creature over the child's head:

Spider as you waste away
Whooping cough no longer stay.

Guinea pigs are such steady, Venusian creatures, with wise little faces and a kind and calming influence. The Witch of Hethersett who was (mostly) gentle, calming and focused on healing, worked with and adored many Guinea Pigs over the years. They assisted her with such tasks as divination and the selection of flower remedies for those who sought her help. Guinea Pigs certainly seem well-suited to this kind of work. Ronald Hutton (1999), in Triumph of the Moon, mentions that Kilsey Nan, who ran an occult bric-a-brac shop in Skipton, Yorkshire, in the early 19th century, also told fortunes using her Guinea Pig and some dirty cards. I must, however, stress that the Witch of Hethersett's Tarot cards (and she had a considerable collection of different decks) were never even the slightest bit grubby.

Healing

The healing arts and sciences are a set of skills which most practitioners develop during their training to a greater or lesser extent. A basic knowledge of herbs is, as it always has been, an essential jewel in the witch's treasury. So, most will have a copy of Mrs. Grieve's herbal on their shelves and know to keep Elderberry syrup or Blackberry vinegar in case of Winter colds, to take Chamomile, Meadowsweet or Mint for digestive troubles, Hawthorn for the heart, Betony for the head, Rosemary to improve the memory, Marigold or Myrrh for wounds, Thyme, Liquorice, Elecampane and White Horehound for coughs, and Daisy cream for bruises.

It is very common to use magical herbs and spices in food, and so much is now known about the science of their beneficial effects. Garlic not only keeps away vampires but also fights off infection, thins the blood and lowers cholesterol. Cinnamon, an exotic spice which is considered magically to have healing properties and is traditionally used during the cold, dark times, helps those with cold hands and feet, soothes digestion, relieves nausea and may help to regulate insulin. It is also a plant of love and of raising spiritual vibrations, and if you are able to buy whole quills, they make excellent miniature wands. Turmeric is another super-spice, since it is anti-inflammatory, anti-oxidant, anti-fungal and cleansing. Its yellow colour is amazing and quickly adds a ray of sunshine to any dish, and it can be used to treat and to avoid numerous conditions such as arthritis, stomach ulcers, jaundice and high cholesterol. Various studies suggest it has potential in cancer treatment and prevention. Adding plenty of it to food becomes second nature. Scott Cunningham (1995) suggests sprinkling Turmeric on the floor in the magical Circle to give added protection. I would be cautious about this as, once it stains, it is very difficult to remove. It is after all, used as a dye as well as a spice and a medicine.

A magical spice grown closer to home, yet with all the mystique of the exotic, is Saffron, which comes from just the stigma of the Autumn-flowering Crocus. It is said to have arrived in Britain in the 14th century, during the reign of Edward III, just at the time Isabella was confined in Castle Rising.

Saffron was originally traded for tin by the Cornish, who were the first to grow it, probably in the area around Bude, which is why there is a tradition in Cornwall of baking delicious Saffron buns and bread. But the magic of Saffron is yet another of those delicate yet powerful threads which link East with West and West with East, across the Isles of the Wise, for this little plant of such huge value was also grown in East Anglia, most famously in Essex, as the town of Chipping Walden even changed its name to Saffron

Walden, so important was this botanical jewel. Norfolk and Suffolk were important areas for Saffron growing too. North Norfolk once produced enough Saffron to export it to the Low Countries. Since 1997 it has been grown commercially here once again, on a smallholding in North Norfolk by Sally Francis, a botanist who was initially given 20 bulbs as a gift from her mother and has now turned growing these plants into a thriving and award-winning business. She produces Saffron threads and smoked Saffron, as well as a "King Harry" Orange and Saffron liqueur and Saffron flour. In another little twist of the East-West connection, Norfolk Saffron's advertising stresses their product's suitability for use in such recipes as Cornish Saffron cake (www. norfolksaffron.co.uk).

Saffron is probably the most precious spice in the world. The threads are collected in September when the plants are in flower, and dried very carefully. It takes 60,000 stigmas to produce a pound of Saffron and it is more expensive than gold. The plant has been used in healing since ancient times. It is aromatic, bitter, stimulating and carminative, and its warming qualities are thought to occur because it begins to grow almost before the snows have melted, protected by the oiliness of the bulb (Wood, 2008). Medicinally, it has been used to treat headaches, digestive and liver problems, arthritis and psoriasis, amongst a long list of other ills. Although it is hugely expensive, only tiny amounts are needed and Mrs. Grieve (1931) recommends a low dose of the tincture: just 5 – 15 drops, since too much can provoke unpleasant symptoms. Over the centuries, Saffron has found its place in many myths and in poetry, and it has been much prized as a dyestuff: Saffron yellow shoes were part of the costume of the Persian Kings. Amongst the many magical qualities associated with Saffron is its use as an aphrodisiac and it has often been added to love sachets, or those designed to increase lust. Drinking the infusion is said to enable one to see the future, and in Persia it was used to raise the winds. It is also said to dispel melancholy, and there are warnings against eating too much of it, as there is a risk of dying from excessive joy, although I have no examples of this ever having happened. There is a tradition in Ireland that rinsing sheets with Saffron will strengthen the arms and legs of those who sleep between them (Cunningham, 1995).

One strand of Norfolk Saffron makes a princely gift for the Fair Folk, especially as a gesture of genuine affection and appreciation, for this is a herb of both love and healing.

Forms of energy healing are also part of the witch's skill hoard. Simple techniques are often used, such as drawing up the green energy of the Earth through the roots which extend downwards from our feet, and feeling the flow of light from the Sun, Moon and Stars into our being from the top of our heads. This can be used to heal ourselves or allowed to move through us and out again to help someone else. It need not be complicated. As our Dutch cousin from across the North Sea, Hella Gaddella (2016), says, "just plug in and do your job."

However, it is also the case that Norfolk witches are not only constantly curious, but also tend to be perfectionists (and that is not just the Virgos amongst us). So, many seek further training, some obtaining degrees or diplomas in herbal medicine, aromatherapy or massage, while others train with bodies like the Healing Trust or with a reputable Reiki master. We gather all the useful knowledge we can, wherever its origins may be. One young local witch even travelled to Kyoto, in Japan, to study Reiki with the teacher, Hyakuten Inamoto. She had chosen to go directly to the source of this wisdom: to Kurama Mountain, where Mikao Sensei had this spiritual enlightenment and healing ability bestowed upon him in 1922. She has brought back her knowledge and now shares it with others in the community (Vicki Dolley, 2017, personal communication).

Ritual Practice
There are so many ways in which operative magic can be conducted, but ritual workings are very popular within the

286

Tradition. Rituals may involve a lone practitioner or a group of people, and they have a myriad of potential purposes. They may seek the success of a project, strengthen the protection of a home, or of a wider area; they are a means of contacting the gods, of seeking knowledge or developing our magical understanding; they are a way of consecrating magical tools or talismans, or of formalising a divination, when we require guidance as to a future course of action. Rituals also provide a very special and focused form of celebration, which cuts right to the essence of the season in any particular year.

Much of magic is about story-telling, and ritual helps us to take our tangles of threads, colours and emotions, and fashion them into something of pattern, order beauty and power. As such, it is an act of creation. This, I think, is why our practitioners are so fond of it: a really fine ritual can take many hours of skilful crafting. The poet manifests the perfect selection of words from the vast potential of language, which now makes up our "word hoard"; the artist paints their picture from the chaos of colours on their palette; the whittler takes a cut stick, which might just be firewood, and transforms it into an animal or a useful tool. Likewise, the ritualist works with their desires, taking inspiration from the Starry Realms, fashioning it in the Place which is Between the Worlds, and manifesting the results in our mundane reality.

Thus, the work of the ritual commences as soon as the idea comes into the practitioner's mind. It may begin as a fleeting image, or just a feeling, but during the period of preparation, it is developed and refined. When working with others, it is very often the case that two or more people will "receive" the idea simultaneously: a sure sign that this is the right way to go. For a relatively simple ritual, very little may be required, but for the most elaborate and dramatic of our rites, weeks of work may be needed to create costumes, write poetry, gather materials or craft special items for this one piece of work. The sheer effort which goes into the preliminary work is all part of the building of power, which culminates in the ritual moment itself.

Ritual Structure

Our ritual structure is one we have used for over a quarter of a century. Its beauty is in its simplicity and flexibility. It has sufficient formality to foster the seriousness, focus and control of mind and body which are so essential to magical work, while at the same time allowing the freedom to respond to what happens, to extemporise, to be moved by spirits and energies, and to allow our wild natures to express themselves. We do not claim ours to be definitive, "right", the "only way", or even the best way. However, we have found it to work equally well for very experienced practitioners, performing a complex piece of magic, and complete beginners, taking their first tentative, and often nervous, steps on the ritual path.

There is always a clear opening to the rite, which alerts the gods and the spirits of place to what we are about to do. It also draws our own focus away from the mundane world, into that liminal space, in which we take on our magical personalities. At the close of the rite, we unwind what we have set up, in reverse order, gradually returning ourselves and the space to the world of everyday life. It is somewhat akin to putting up a tent on arrival at a campsite, then dismantling it when one is ready to leave, removing the traces of having been there. It must be said though, that when an individual, or group, works consistently in the same spot, year after year, there is a building of energies, such that the place takes on a sacredness, and it becomes ever easier to work there and to attract those beings with whom we wish to communicate.

The Lottery

The roles which people are to take in the ritual are normally chosen by lottery, because we have no High Priests or Priestesses, or even permanent officers, as one might in a ceremonial lodge. The lottery allows the gods to choose, and is a magical act in itself. It rarely turns out badly, even if initially people are not happy with what they have been given. In the days when we worked with a very large group, the lottery was always a moment of nervousness, and some hilarity as well. There were those who did not want a part which they perceived to be "difficult" and others who only wanted to take either masculine or feminine roles, as they interpreted them. Some people even tried to swap, which was not really within the spirit of things. What easily gets forgotten, in such circumstances, is that although one person stands in a particular role, everybody should be doing all the work together, concentrating and visualising as the Circle is cast, the Elements called, the communion blessed and so on. So, we are all responsible for the power and success which is vested in each part within the rite.

At the Circle's Edge

Before the formal part of the rite begins, we set up everything we need within the sacred space, ensuring that nothing has been forgotten, and that everyone knows what they will be doing at which point in the rite. We then leave the Circle, taking a few moments to view the space from the outside, acknowledging that perspective before we step into the midst of it. It also allows us that moment of thrill and excitement, as we anticipate the magic which is to unfold. Those new to the path sometimes struggle with anxiety prior to ritual. But nervousness is all part of the work. It never goes away, however experienced one becomes, nor should it. If there are no butterflies, the ritual is unlikely to be successful. Processing towards the ritual space is carried out slowly and reverently, in single file, each person taking their place around the Circle.

Casting the Circle

After a little time of time of reflection, we all take a step towards the centre, to give space for the person who will cast the Circle, to walk behind us. The Circle is created from an intensity of light, energy and sprowl, gathered and placed so that it surrounds us. It begins as a hoop, but extends above and below so that once it is complete, we are surrounded by a complete sphere, which places us at one of the many intersections between our world and those of the Fairies, the Gods and the Spirits of the Dead. The person who is casting the Circle may speak aloud of the sacredness, the magic and the protection of the Circle, or may carry out the work silently, walking clockwise. I have a white Holly stang, made by one of the Hermits of Mole End, which most people use to cast the Circle when we are in my garden. However, some people prefer to use their own stang or wand, of a wood which is suitable for them. Others favour a besom for casting, while there are those who just walk and visualise the process.

When performing open rituals, where the Circle is very large, it is often appropriate for the Circle to be cast from its centre. For the inexperienced ritualists present, it can be very helpful to be able to see and hear clearly what is going on, and some people may lose focus if the witch who is casting takes a long, slow walk behind them, and they do not fully comprehend what is happening.

Calling the Elements
The Elements of Air, Fire, Water and Earth are the essential building blocks of magic, ritual and of life itself. They are in everything, in different proportions, including ourselves, sometimes balanced, sometimes not. In the ritual, we invite them to join us and, like the Magician of the Tarot, maintain the delicate poise between them, which is necessary for the work, and which builds a creative tension, like trying to balance on a wall without slipping off.

The Elements, and their physical representations, are placed at the sacred directions, usually Air in the East, Fire in the South, Water in the West and Earth in the

North. There is nothing dogmatic about this placing and on occasions we will do it differently. The reason for the choice is that this arrangement seems to be familiar to most people, and therefore the most comfortable for beginners and for visitors. Of course, if we are working on a beach, or beside a lake or mere, the stretch of water determines the direction for the Element of Water, usually with Earth opposite it. Likewise, if the wind is blowing strongly, this may decide the direction of Air. These matters tend to be decided as appropriate to the work, to the place and to the moment.

It is normal to speak aloud when calling the Element. We each have our own special understanding of its power and meaning, because working with each Element in turn is a large part of magical training. This knowledge needs to be distilled into just a few sentences, which will have meaning for everyone else present, as well as honouring the Element we are calling.

For Air, we usually light some charcoal and burn incense in a thurible, wafting it gently, so that its perfume is carried on the breeze. Everyone turns to the East. A typical request for Air to attend the ritual might include the words:

Element of Air, we ask for your presence and protection at this ritual. You who are the breath of life, our first and our last, inspire our words and our magic. You who are the fragrance of Spring blossom, bring us the joy of your promise. You who hold the birds in flight, help our thoughts and our words to soar to the great heights of the clear blue heavens. Element of Air, we bid you, Hail, and welcome.

This is an example only. What people say will never be exactly the same each time. Mostly, we do not plan this in advance, but extemporise, although those who are new to this kind of work may well write something on a piece of paper, which they can read out. It is a matter of confidence and trust in oneself and in the world of gods and spirits, which can take a little time to develop. Although magical work should be challenging, it is counter-productive to push people too far beyond what they feel comfortable doing.

Fire is usually represented by a lantern, although we also have a rather lovely iron chimenea, which is sometimes lit for special occasions. The structure of what is said follows the same pattern as for Air and all the other Elements. Fire is warmth and passion, the energy which drives our projects and maintains our lives. It is both destroyer and healer: the gentle warmth of the candle flame, the roaring of a hearth fire on a chilly winter's night, and the ravaging of a heathland fire, burning the lovely Gorse to blackened skeletons, and killing any creatures in its path. It is the power of the Sun and the Divine Spark within each one of us.

We have a small hand-crafted bowl for Water. It is usually filled with water from one of the sacred wells of the land. This could be from St. Walstan's Well, St. Withburga's, Walsingham or St. Helen's, or from Chalice Well in Glastonbury, if we have any available. Water is our emotions, the raging seas, the playful stream or the cold, dark depths of lake or mere. It refreshes and cleanses, taking the shape of whatever vessel is used to contain it. Honouring this Element is of great importance in Norfolk because, although we have so much sea around us, the rainfall of the county is quite low, and fields and gardens dry out easily, especially where the soils are light and drain freely.

A large stone, usually a Flint, can be used for Earth. We have used the same one for the entire time we have lived here. It is cold and heavy and shaped just like a skull, reminding us of the chthonic realms beyond. It is the only elemental representation which is never brought indoors, but always sits in the North of the Circle, keeping watch on all that unfolds. Earth is our home, our health, our wealth and our firm foundation. It is the nurturing soil, the source of our food and our comfort, and the place to which we will return in due course.

Calling the Lord and Lady of Norfolk

Whatever the purpose of our rite, we always call the Lord and Lady of Norfolk because they are everywhere around us, and the basis for all that grows and flourishes here, so it would be rude indeed to leave them out. As with all the deities with whom we work, we ask them to come to the rite as a polite invitation. Thus, it is not an invocation, in the sense that the deity is called into oneself, as is common in a number of traditions. Such a technique is only used for very specific purposes and employed relatively infrequently. Depending on how many people are present, one person may call both deities, or two people may invite one each. In doing so, we usually speak of their attributes and our respect for them. It is easy to feel their presence as they draw closer and join us in the Circle.

The Purpose

The Purpose of the ritual is agreed amongst those who will be part of it, then written out clearly on a piece of card, from which one practitioner will then read. It is normally just a couple of sentences, which encapsulates the direction of the work. Stating it clearly keeps everybody focused on the matter in hand and prevents anyone pulling in a different direction, which can be magically disastrous. It is also a way of clarifying what we are doing, to the Elements and to the Lord and Lady, as if we are saying, "We have invited you here, now this is what we are going to do."

Offerings

"Nothing comes from nothing", as the old story says, "so, bring me the heart of the thing you love the best". Magical work demands considerable sacrifices from its serious practitioners, and the offerings we make during our rituals reflect this. Especially in seasonal work, presenting one's offering is a moment in which each individual can speak of the magical and practical effort which have brought them to this particular point in their progress or their

293

understanding. Offerings may take many different forms. Some people like to write poetry, produce craft items, paint pictures, make ritual attire, sing a song, play a tune or dance. The important thing is not the technical expertise of what has been produced but the passion, effort and love which have gone into it. Sometimes people use their existing talents to create an amazing piece of work. Under other circumstances, it may be appropriate to bring something far less skilfully executed, but which emerges from an attempt to learn a new skill, or to struggle with what we find challenging.

The more creative endeavour we invest in our ritual offerings, the more we receive as a result of them, on so many levels. This could be in terms of knowledge, improved skills, insights as to our next magical steps, or a glimpse of something which is beyond words. We do not make the offerings to gain from them: they are an expression of something much deeper and more profound. Yet magic has a mysterious kind of mutuality, so that we learn, in order to do more, and the more we do, the greater our store of knowledge and skill becomes. So, the spiral turns, as the Snail upon the leaf constantly reminds us.

The Core of the Ritual
Within the main body of the ritual, there is the safety and potential to enact a sacred drama, to bless, to heal, to transform or to create, as the occasion demands. There could be a pathworking as part of the ritual, or a colloquy, which involves everyone in the ritual sitting and waiting for inspiration to speak on a particular topic. This can be an excellent way to solve problems and develop ideas. Sometimes an elaborately decorated altar will be created on which to place talismans, statues, lights, extra incense or magical tools. Sometimes we may elect to have a central fire, where we burn the sweetest smelling woods we have available, such as Apple, Bay or Balsam Poplar, and this may be the focus of "Treading the Mill", in

which we all dance, process or stomp round and around, building the power we need to drive the magical work to a successful conclusion, or to lift our wishes upwards and outwards and make them real. On other occasions, a garlanded stang or pitchfork will be the only physical point of concentration of the ritual.

It may at times be appropriate to call upon other deities, in addition to the Lord and Lady of Norfolk. One example was in a well-attended ritual in 2001, when we called upon the Lady Hathor to protect the creatures of the county from foot and mouth disease. The ritual, created by Chris Wood, was carried out in the context of a "composition of place", which allowed us to travel within the Circle to meet Hathor in her native land, before offering her milk and asking her to assist us in our magical work in Norfolk. The gods of the Northern Traditions are frequently invited to join us, as they are already so much at home here, but over the years, we have also asked Brigid, Arthurian heroes, local heroes and numerous other Fair Ones, Ancestors, Spirits of Place or totem plants and animals to be with us. We avoid mixing heroes or deities from different pantheons who would be incompatible in the Circle at the same time, but the Lord and Lady of Norfolk are always there, as they are the very essence of the land on which we work.

Oracles are also a significant part of the work, because they can furnish us with such good advice and guidance, in personal matters and for the good of our work as a whole. Anyone may be chosen (usually by lottery) to be the oracle and, at the correct moment during the rite, they will set aside their own human personality and, through a meditative opening up to the oracular forces, take on that of the oracle. This is often aided by putting on a veil, which we have used on numerous occasions for this purpose, to the extent that it has built up a kind of oracular energy within itself. A veil also has the advantage of separating the oracle somewhat from the physical reality within the

Circle, making it easier to connect with the source of wisdom. It also means that those receiving the wisdom do not clearly see who it is dispensing it. A remarkable aspect of doing oracular work is that although everybody else remembers what the oracle said, it is unusual for the oracle themselves to recall much of it all.

The effect of the veil is not dissimilar to the feeling of putting on a mask, which is another magical technique we sometimes use. One memorable rite from many years ago involved everybody making an animal mask and costume, studying the natural history and the mythology of their chosen animal and, in the ritual, taking on the characteristics of that creature in order to learn more about them, and expand their understanding of the natural and the eldritch worlds. This rite produced a huge amount of artwork, poetry and new ideas, both in its preparation and as a result of the inspiration from the ritual itself.

Of the hundreds of rituals we must have carried out here over the years, some have been recorded by individuals in their magical diaries, and some had "running orders", which just set out the bare bones of the ritual, so that we know the direction the work is to take. Others were so startling or dramatic that we will never forget them, but many have been allowed to disperse, carried away on the astral currents, to continue their work in whatever form is appropriate.

One of the most memorable for me was a Samhain ritual, in which we sought the wisdom of the Spirits of Witchcraft from the Past, the Present and the Future. These were powerfully channelled by three witches from different generations, who stood in elaborate, woven Willow domes, and spoke words which surprised all of us who were present, and which had lasting effects.

Sometimes it can be good to acknowledge that there are things in our lives which we can control, and others which, due to our Wyrd, our Karma, Fate, or other factors, we must learn to accept and make the best of. On one Summer evening, we sought to act this out ritually. We had built, especially for the purpose, an Anglo-Saxon/Norse-style weaving loom, with large Flint hag stones weighting down the warp, which represented what could not be changed. Beside it was a basket of yarns of all imaginable colours, textures and materials. At the right moment in the ritual, each person went to the loom in turn and wove a piece for themselves, using whichever combination of yarns felt right for them at the time. This represented us taking power over our own current incarnation and building on what we have, to create a wonderful work of art of our own lives. This was a slow, meditative ritual, but by the time we had all finished, the original warp threads were completely covered by our own designs.

Another way in which one can ritually take authority over one's own life is through the magical use of the crown. A Midsummer ritual once involved the making of a huge and beautiful crown out of Willow withies and other leaves. The first person put the crown onto their own head to symbolise their own sovereignty. After spending a while appreciating the feel of the crown and its meaning, they then passed it to the next person, saying that they did not seek to control anyone else and therefore shared the crown with another. This beautiful piece of symbolism was introduced to us by Nigel Pennick, who wrote that particular ritual, but we have subsequently adapted it and used it in other contexts. We have, on other occasions, added the use of a throne, as well as the idea that everybody crafts their own personal crown, which then becomes a physical symbol for them to keep as a reminder of their own power and responsibility.

If we are to find sovereignty over our own lives, we need to discover who we really are, in the spirit of the ancient magical instruction to "know thyself". This is challenging indeed, and we have performed rituals to work on the process, based on the story of Sir Gawain and the Green Knight. One tall person dressed as the Green Knight, covered in a green tatters cloak, leaves, twigs and full green face paint, to look as menacing as possible, burst into the ritual Circle brandishing an axe. He also carried with him a special magical mirror, and dared each person in turn to look into it and really see themselves and who they were. It sounds simple, but in a ritual context it can be both alarming and enlightening.

The Communion

Once the main action of the ritual is completed, we normally share a communion of food and drink. This is sometimes bread and wine, mead or beer, but it may also be cake, fruit or nuts, depending on the feel of the ritual. The drink need not be alcoholic either. Sometimes, plain water or juice is more suitable. The food and drink are blessed, with words which reflect what is needed at that moment, then shared, not just amongst the human participants of the ritual, but with the Earth and her creatures, and with those of the spiritual realms who have honoured us with their presence.

Closing the Ritual

It is important to unwind slowly what has been set up, so that we gradually return ourselves and our working space to the mundane world. We do not banish or dismiss those we have called; rather we thank them for their presence and bid them farewell. Often, we ask that a little of their blessing and power remain with us, even as we bid them hail and farewell. As these farewells are spoken, we become increasingly aware of extraneous noises, of the fact that our feet are absolutely freezing or that it is raining. As an act of grounding, once whoever cast the Circle has unwound it again, is to clap. This brings us thoroughly back to our everyday senses, and also applauds the work of all who have taken part in the rite. Sometimes a ritual may have been too deep and too solemn for applause to be appropriate, in which case we leave silently and return the house for a time of silent contemplation before clapping and partaking of the post ritual feast.

References

Bradley, S.A.J. (1982) *Anglo-Saxon Poetry*, Dent.

Cunningham, Scott, (1995) *Cunningham's Encyclopedia of Magical Herbs*, Llewellyn.

Gaddella, Hella (2016) Speaking at the Quest Conference, Bristol, 12th March 2016.

Gary, Gemma (2008) *Traditional Witchcraft: A Cornish Book of Ways*, Troy Books.

Glyde, John (1872) *The Norfolk Garland: A Collection of the Superstitious Beliefs and Practices, Proverbs, Curious Customs, Ballads and Songs of the People of Norfolk, as well as Anecdotes Illustrative of the Genius or Peculiarities of Norfolk Celebrities*, Jarrold.

Huson, Paul (1970) *Mastering Witchcraft: A Practical Guide for Witches, Warlocks & Covens*, Perigee.

Hutton, Ronald (1999) *The Triumph of the Moon: A History of Modern Pagan Witchcraft*, OUP.

Kennett, Tom (2016) *The Lord Treasurer of Botany: Sir James Edward Smith and the Linnean Collections*, Linnean Society of London.

Leland, Charles Godfrey (1899) *Aradia or the Gospel of the Witches*, David Nutt (2018 Edition, Troy Books).

Pearson, Nigel (2015) *The Devil's Plantation: East Anglian Lore, Witchcraft and Folk Magic*, Troy Books.

Pennick, Nigel (2015) *Pagan Magic of the Northern Tradition: Customs, Rites and Ceremonies*, Simon and Schuster, Destiny.

Pettit, Edward (trans. and ed.) (2001) *Anglo-Saxon Remedies, Charms, and Prayers from British Library MS Harley 585, The Lacnunga: Volume 1*, Edwin Mellen.

Rose, Jeanne (2001) *Herbs and Things: Jeanne Rose's Herbal*, Last Gasp.

Wood, Matthew (2008) *The Earthwise Herbal: A Complete Guide to Old World Medicinal Plants*, North Atlantic Books.

A Sense of Community: Covens, Moots and Magical Groups

It is difficult, perhaps impossible, to pin down practitioners of the Nameless Tradition. Many consider themselves Pagan, but not all. Some also practise other forms of religion such as Buddhism or Christianity, and many have wide occult experience, having trained in other magical systems, from Wicca or the Golden Dawn to Chaos Magic. I therefore make no apology for the inevitable blurring of the lines between those people and activities which could be considered "Traditional" and those which might be regarded as part of the modern Pagan movement. While many old-style witches remain secretive and elusive, there are plenty who reap the benefits of greater openness and enjoy the sociable exchange of knowledge which has become possible. We are not set apart in some special magical bubble, nor should we be. I would argue that there is no clear line of division between the Traditional and the modern approaches and that the hazy distinction between them is yet another liminal space with enormous magical and creative potential.

Traditional Craft has always been pragmatic and uses whatever is to hand, physically, mentally and astrally. This could be a new, fancy grimoire, ordered at great expense, or the secret charm whispered in our ear by an illiterate grandmother. Personally, I have adapted practices from a wide range of sources, both oral and literary, and from the living and the dead alike. Experienced Traditional practitioners from Norfolk and beyond have kindly shared their knowledge with me, but I have also picked up gems of information from modern Pagans in a pub. One of the best little magical tricks I have ever heard came to me quite unexpectedly from a small child in North Norfolk. So, we are receptive to what is on offer around us, but we also give something back to the community, for without that mutuality, our magic would be limited.

It is said that people in Norfolk like to "do different" and this is certainly true of those who follow our magical way of doing things. We have the greatest respect for magical teachers, for people who have greater knowledge or experience than we do, but a hierarchical system just does not suit our way of working. We completely understand and accept that many people like the idea of covens with a set structure, a specific number of members, with high priests or high priestesses, or maybe a magister, a maid and a summoner. There are a lot of folk who appreciate some clear route for progression through grades to reach adepthood and a position of authority. Such regulation may give a sense of security and direction, but it plays no part in the Nameless Tradition. Nobody has authority over anyone and we seek no authority over others. Each one of us answers only to our own conscience and to the spirits and deities with whom we work. We are free to develop as we please, to work with others or to be alone, as and when we feel the need. A group may convene as a one-off to perform a specific magical task; sometimes a number of us may pledge to work together for a year on a particular project; often just two or three people will work together over an extended period of time, but invite others to join them for celebrations and festival times. This flexibility allows us a multitude of different combinations, to do what is needful at the time.

There are training possibilities available within the Nameless Tradition, but the purpose of our course is to show people the building blocks of magical work, the skills of mind and eye, of hand and of breath, the beauty of simple ritual and the power of the land. We teach people techniques which they do not already have, but we recognise that in other respects our "students" know as much, if not more, than we do. We are not trying to mould anyone or tie them to a particular magical way of doing things. Rather, we attempt to open for them the magical cabinet of curiosities from which, with a solid grounding, they are able to select the things which will nurture their own growth and understanding. A basic course normally lasts just a year and a day and involves a mixture of general magical techniques and seasonal land-based work. There is reading to be done, practical exercises, things to make, to write and to try out, in an effort to engage all the magical and mundane senses. Once the year is over, people usually feel confident to continue practising with friends, to experience working with other groups or to continue as a lone practitioner, although they know that they are only at the very beginning of their journey and that, realistically, we are all still trainees with a lot to learn.

All of us within the Nameless Tradition are curious, have an immense thirst for knowledge and are always seeking that which will enhance our magical practice, our relationship with deities and spirits, our understanding of Norfolk, of the world and our place within the great Web of Wyrd. We attend academic lectures; we go to workshops to learn new magical techniques; we share ideas with one another and, perhaps most importantly, we grow magically through regular meditation, observation, "sitting out", making things, walking, ritual and spell work, and through the contacts we make on many levels.

Perhaps it is because practitioners of Norfolk magic have a strong sense of individuality that the magical community of the area is so strong. We are not dependent on anyone, so working together is an active and life-affirming choice. Within the magical world in general, which is far more open and outgoing now than ever it was able to be in the past, there are powerful networks of friends and colleagues, most of whom are willing to advise and assist other seekers. If you have a question about any tradition, it should not be too difficult to find someone in the area who can answer it. Generally speaking, most local practitioners are generous with their time and knowledge and keen to reach out to genuine seekers. Of course, there are occasional spats and disagreements, clashes of personality or horrible misunderstandings, but these are an inevitable part of all human interaction, in whatever sphere we choose to move.

The thriving, dynamic community here is very much a part of the magic of the county. Ideas are exchanged and developed, information is shared, groups are formed. Those in need of support or encouragement know that they have somewhere to turn, while those who have benefited from the blessings of the Lord and Lady of Norfolk, and from being part of their magical world, are able to give something back in practical or spiritual ways.

This, to me, is an expression of the gifu, or gebo rune of our Anglo-Saxon and Viking ancestors, still used today to symbolize a kiss. They knew the importance of the reciprocity of giving and receiving, and the rune is as relevant to us now as ever it was, and fundamental to our magical lives. The gifu concept is so much more profound than the potentially destructive cycle of, "I have done so much for you, now you owe me something." When we step onto our spiritual path we learn, we are given gifts, we absorb concepts, and a treasury of wonders is offered to us. At the same time, a huge amount is required of us in processing and coming to terms with our experiences and, before very long at all, we find ourselves required to draw on our new-found skills and understanding to help others or our environment. Sometimes those demands will be just a little beyond our current level of ability or understanding, forcing us to accept a challenge which will push us that little further along the path. As with most things in life, the more we invest in terms of energy, study effort or creativity, the greater will be the rewards. It is the same with the offerings we make for our rituals: the more magic that goes into them, the better they are in both mundane and magical terms; our ability increases; more and better things are then demanded of us and so the cycle of mutuality continues. We benefit, the gods benefit and our community also reaps the harvest. Equally, our work will assist those who are to follow us, as they will inherit the Wyrd we have left them.

I remember when I began my own magical training, I was told of the importance of the work of those who had gone before, clearing the way of the tangled growth, opening up new possibilities, leaving signposts and making the treading of the path easier for those who would follow. It was an exciting and inspiring image and, in the Nameless Tradition, we are ever mindful of our magical ancestors, known to us and unknown. We are also intensely aware that whatever we do, for good or ill, will have an impact on the magical lives of those who will follow us, and we try to nurture, as best we can, the magical current of our land. This may involve the creation of gardens and sacred spaces on both mundane and astral planes, making or collecting beautiful craft objects for future use or enjoyment, the writing of prayers or charms, the discovery of ancient wisdom, bringing the right people together, performing powerful rituals, sharing food and offering help or the hand of friendship. Sometimes it is the simplest of things which can have the most lasting magical effects.

It can be the easiest thing for a community to give a genuine seeker, new to the ways of magic, an opportunity to find people with whom they can connect and from whom they are able learn what they need, yet for that individual it can be a life-changing gift. Norfolk has long had what we often term the "outer courts", which are groups set up to bring people together, to provide information and maybe some basic magical training. Ideally, it allows the right people to meet, those whose magical energies are compatible, and whose magical work would benefit from combining their efforts. Outer courts open the right doors to beginners who are seeking serious training in the magical arts and wish to work with, or be inspired by, others locally.

However, while new arrivals are, hopefully, always welcomed with hospitality and kindness, this does not necessarily mean that they will immediately find suitable training or a group to join. Many are those who have felt frustrated when they are not showered with invitations to temples or covens or groves. Some folk have a tendency to try to hurry this process, not realising that acceptance into a community of any kind does not normally happen overnight and that, even more so in the world of magic, a certain level of familiarity and trust is required before further doors are opened and secrets revealed. Even in these days of greater openness, the people who become part of any group still need to have the right "chemistry" or the delicate magical balance will be upset.

It is sometimes also the case that newcomers fail to notice, at first, that a magical community even exists in Norfolk. Even recently, I have heard many claim that nothing magical is going on here and some people have even moved away in disappointment to places where opportunities are more obvious. This is typical of the magical current of the lands of Chalk and Flint. It is a vibrant, potent force with a long tradition through which Earth and Sky and Sea flow strongly, but it will sometimes show a blank face to those it does not yet know. To earn acceptance, it is necessary to follow the seasons, to touch the Earth, to sing the song of the North Sea and the East Wind. The seeker must forge their own special relationship with the area and its spirits and, as they come to a greater understanding of and love for the land, they will find that its human inhabitants also draw them closer to the heart of the community.

Norwich Pagan Moot
There are those who would argue that a public moot has little place in the practice of Traditional Craft and some would

question the use of the word "Pagan". Nevertheless, in Norfolk it is certainly the case that many Traditional Witches and practitioners of the Nameless Tradition not only make use of what the Moot here has to offer, but also support it actively and work hard to put on social and educational events. We also enjoy the opportunity, not only to meet new people, but to keep in contact with other Craft practitioners, with whom we are friends, but do not necessarily work with magically on a regular basis, if at all.

There are many here who have been regular moot-goers for over twenty years, including myself, my husband and many with whom I have had close magical associations. Over this time there have been plenty of magical folk within the moot community with whom we are good friends but who would not consider themselves part of the Nameless Tradition.

For at least thirty years, and probably more, Norwich Pagan Moot has been a place for people from all over the county, and of all manner of magical persuasions, to meet and to share their knowledge and experience. It has formed a doorway through which many have passed on their quest for magical or spiritual enlightenment. For most of that time, there was a pub moot on the first Wednesday of every month, as a purely social get together, but a source of continuity. The need for something more became clear, and there have been monthly talks or workshops, on a Sunday night, and walks during the Summer months, for two decades. More recently, a monthly coffee moot has run on a Saturday morning, and seems to have replaced the pub moot as the place newcomers can meet the community.

As far as anyone here can remember, the Moot was started in the late 1970s by Eric Winch, a Wiccan High Priest and Priest Hierophant within the Fellowship of Isis. He was also a member of a national network known as the Green Circle, which was an important way for people to make connections and share magical experiences during the 1980s and 90s, when there were far fewer open events for people to attend, and magical practice had to be kept more secret than it does nowadays. Norwich Moot was initially under the Green Circle umbrella, but later became a Pagan Federation moot, although nobody was ever required to be formally a member of anything.

In 1996, having been ill for some time, Eric asked Chris and myself if we would take care of the Moot until he was better. We were of course honoured to do so. When Eric recovered, he decided that he would prefer to focus all his energy on his own magical practice and his work within the Fellowship of Isis, so we continued to run the Moot, gradually finding our feet and putting on more regular events as a demand was clearly growing. On 3rd August 1997, we started the tradition of monthly talks, on a Sunday, with a presentation, by Eric, on the subject of Ancient Egyptian Religion. The talks initially took place at the Woburn Centre, in Norwich.

By 1998, we had quite a little collection of talks on diverse Pagan or magical topics and these were published in a booklet wryly entitled At the Cutting Edge of Tradition, which had on its cover a beautiful line-drawing of a witch on a dragon by Chaos magician, Anton Channing. The talks have been held in many different venues over the years but still happen, monthly to this very day. There is much to be said for consistency in magical working.

We also ran various short-term or one-off events. There were weekend workshops and more widely advertised talks by such eminent writers and magical practitioners as Marian Green and Nigel Pennick, a torch-lit Earth Day Procession on 20th April 1997, following the success, on Earth Day the previous year, of a day of sustainable crafts. In 2001, on the 50th anniversary of the Repeal of the Witchcraft Act, we ran a full day's conference about different types of witchcraft, at the Assembly Rooms in Norwich. It was widely advertised and proved so popular that people were turned away at the door because we were exceeding the numbers allowed by fire regulations.

Magical successes usually open further doors and the success of Fifty Years out of the Broom Closet, led to an invitation for the Moot to become part of Norwich InterFaith Link. This is not to everyone's taste of course, but the work of those who have been involved with it ever since, particularly Chris, who served as chair over a period of many years, has certainly contributed to the greater respectability of most Pagan paths in the area. Gone are the days, which many of us still remember, where an interest in Paganism and particularly witchcraft could easily lead to dismissal from a job, and numerous other forms of discrimination. It is still wise to be discrete, I feel, particularly in the matter of our witchcraft practice, but the more relaxed attitude of the general public to such matters makes some things easier.

Flushed with the success of the moment, on 14th July 2001, after much soul searching, the Moot took part in the city's annual Lord Mayor's Procession (see Chapter Three). The theme of the procession for 2001 was "Myth and Legend", which given the magical feel at that time, seemed too good an opportunity to miss. We decided to dress up as characters from Arthurian Legend and to walk the route rather than hire a float. A frenzy of costume-making ensued and the talented artist, Julie Mytton created a set of banners to represent each of the royal houses of the Grail legends and one which had "Norwich Pagan Moot" written in gold lettering on a green background. These banners are still in use, magically, both in private and at some more public events. Nev, who played the part of Merlin, made a "sword in the stone" which could be pulled along on wheels.

It was through the connection with Inter-faith that Norwich Moot was given the chance to send four representatives to the Queen's Golden Jubilee garden party at Sandringham. It was a perfect Norfolk July day: clear, fresh skies, sunshine, a light breeze carrying the faint scent of the sea. And there we stood on the lawn in front of the grand house, four Norfolk witches in our finery (straw hats from a beach shop at Wells-next-Sea, price £1.99 each), drinking the Queen's champagne and eating canapés. It was a golden moment, bathed in the light of magical success after much hard work: a fleeting feeling to savour.

That glow was transitory because the work is never done. The witch can always learn something new, improve their skills, push the magical and mundane boundaries that little bit further. We continued to run events for the Moot, but by 2006, the time required for other, massive magical projects was considerable. Members of what we termed "the Fruit Bowl" (no top banana involved), who had for some time been helping us cope with the ever-increasing amount of Moot work, had personal and magical commitments of their own. Chris and I therefore decided that, having run the Moot for ten years, it was now time to pass the wand to someone else.

Rod and Rue Chapman then kindly agreed to take over and ran it by themselves for a number of years before setting up a committee initially to help them, but later to take over the responsibility. Since then, the make-up of the committee has changed but the Moot continues, sometimes busy, sometimes less so, but with its guiding light there for those whose eyes are open enough to notice it. Currently, it has a lovely home in the Silver Road Community Centre in the North of the city, and is run by Nettles, whose dynamic approach and determination to provide a varied and interactive programme, including workshops and beautifully crafted, and very popular, open rituals, is exactly what is required at this time. I even run an annual herb walk, early in the Summer, which at the time of writing, has been going for a magical nine years.

Inanna's Magical Gifts
It is often the case, in both magical fact and fiction, that a shop, be that a bookshop or a specifically occult emporium, provides seekers with an essential key to the next step in their quest. Many such shops come and go, but Inanna's Magical Gifts, has been an important part of Norwich's

magical life since 1988. The owner, Naomi, has, over three decades, not only sold books, jewellery, statuary, cards, incenses, oils and magical equipment, but also dispensed sound advice to her customers and pointed many in the right direction. For people searching for a "way in" to the magical community, this is often the first place they look and they often discover the existence of the Moot there. The shop has an atmosphere which people love and many are those who have fond memories of their first magical meetings taking place there. It has moved a number of times over the years, but has always been at the heart of the city and is currently in an amazing 15th-century weaver's house on St. Andrew's Hill, in the Lanes.

In 1990, Naomi, along with hand-reader and yoga teacher, Johnny Fincham, started Norwich's first Mind Body and Spirit Fair. It began in a historic church building, St. Gregory's, but now takes place, annually in the Spring, in the main library, known as the Forum. As well as providing information, magical shopping opportunities and the chance to try out all sorts of different forms of healing and alternative therapies, this event has given esoterically-minded people in the city and beyond the chance to meet well-known writers, artists and musicians. Each year that the fair took place in St. Gregory's, a well-known person was invited to give talks and sign copies of their work. Guests have included Brian and Wendy Froud, Rae Beth, Emma Restall-Or, Chesca Potter and many more.

Silver Dawn

This was a Moot set up by astrology expert and Wiccan, Mark Shepherd, in Great Yarmouth in the 1990s. I asked Mark for the exact year but he was unable to remember. It was remarkable in that it grew to be so large and so successful in a very short time, demonstrating the enthusiasm for an opening up of magical possibilities to a wider audience. It attracted Wiccans, generic Pagans, Earth Mysteries enthusiasts and Heathens, as well as those whose practices were of a more Traditional nature. There was a talk each month and opportunities to take part in seasonal rituals. These were often held on the beach at Hopton, the most Easterly point in Britain, particularly at solar festivals, and were dramatic events with the sunrise being welcomed by many colourfully robed characters, often with a large bonfire.

Mark was (and still is) a particularly charismatic figure and was able to achieve an enormous amount for the community in a relatively short time. In the late 1990s, Mark and his fellow organisers managed to hire gallery space in the Town Hall in Great Yarmouth for an entire week to put on an exhibition of Pagan Arts and Crafts. Amongst the many exhibitors, Pagan Federation District Manager, Barry Bartholomew showed some of his photography and I had some of my felt hats and other magical items there, as well as a handspun and woven ritual cloak. The event was a great success and remarkable for its openness at that particular time. Although far from specifically Traditional, the exhibition nevertheless tapped into that current within Norfolk magic which fosters and celebrates the creativity and the arts and crafts skills of those who feel its influence, and encourages collaboration between people of different spiritual paths.

Although the Silver Dawn Moot no longer exists, those who were members of it are still active, and have gone on to form smaller groups, such as the Stone Circle Pagan Moot, in Gorleston, and the Lowestoft Sunrise Moot, both of which make a huge contribution to their communities and regularly interact with other groups across East Anglia.

NNOWW

This was a working group which developed directly from friendships made at the Norwich Pagan Moot around 1997-8. Seven people came together for a short but intense period of time and worked closely in magical and mundane ways for self-development, for one another, for the community and the land. The bedrock of our magic was our connection to the Lord and Lady of Norfolk, whose presence was requested at all our rites, but the work was always experimental, since the group included those of Wiccan inclinations, Traditional Craft practitioners, an initiate of an Orphic tradition and a Chaos Magician. The mix was powerful and explosive, but some of the rituals we did were amongst the best I have ever been privileged to attend, and the results of our spells were indisputable. Certainly, some of the magical foundations laid down at that time have proven secure and durable and some of the spells worked then are still having an impact even now.

Nobody was in charge of the group and we all had an equal say in what was to be done and how. Since the work was normally carried out in my garden, I retained the right of veto over anything which was to be called upon or any operations to be performed there. I never exercised this right and never felt that I needed to.

We met specifically for rituals once a month and each group member took their turn in writing something which they wished to perform with us. It was not uncommon for us, at seasonal festivals, to invite large numbers of people from the local Pagan community to join us. We would put days, if not weeks of effort into such events, making garlands and costumes, writing poetry and creating wonderful feasts. Those who were invited brought some lovely contributions and there was a sense in which things made real and rapid progress at that time.

We were able to invite senior magical teachers, not just from Norfolk, but from further afield too, to come to Norwich to lecture and to teach. Some of us travelled to other parts of the country to take advantage of the growing numbers of conferences and courses which were being held at that time, gathering nuggets of magical information which would feed in to our work here. We all expanded our knowledge as much as we could, and in keeping with our way of Norfolk Magic, put it into practice as soon as we could, in a manner which suited the county at that moment.

Of course, there were outbursts and tears and there was drama a-plenty, but always of the kind that made us feel alive and together. The group, in its original form, was never going to be long-lived though, as a number of the members were young and planning to go away to study and work. Nevertheless, in the short time that we were together, we wrote and set in motion the training course which forms the basis of the one we still use today.

The Norfolk Circle of Witches

For while, after the end of NNOWW, various groupings of people worked together in our magical space, celebrating the seasons and continuing with some of our magical experiments. Although we had a solid core group, it became clear that there were a lot of people with considerable magical talent who really wanted, and indeed needed, a safe and supportive group in which to work.

We therefore set up the Norfolk Circle of Witches (NCW) to answer this need. The idea behind it was that people would work magically, either alone or in small groups, but come back at festival times to the main group, to share their findings and celebrate the harvests of the seasons. The dates for each year's rituals were decided well in advance to allow as many people as possible to attend, but there was no requirement to be present, and a number of people were very supportive members but never able to come to a ritual.

A lot of goodwill and much powerful magic and learning was generated by this group over a number of years. Any member who felt inspired to do so could offer to write the seasonal ritual, deciding who should take which parts or allowing the Gods to decide, through means of the lottery. Sometimes the students currently doing our one-year magical training course were encouraged to write the rituals and benefited hugely from doing so, from developing their understanding of the real meaning of ritual, engaging with the magical stories and their symbolism, working out the "choreography" of the rituals, which can be challenging, and gaining the incredible satisfaction from seeing their vision unfold in the reality of the Circle. It also meant that people felt empowered to go away and design rituals for themselves, without feeling that they always had to follow the lead of those with longer experience, although help and advice was always available for those who required it. There was plenty of variety and an enormous amount of creativity in terms of the rituals themselves, and the poetry, music, costumes and paraphernalia which were needed for them. It was fairly unusual for rituals to be strictly scripted. Normally there was a theme, with a running order of specific characters who should speak or carry out an action or symbolic gesture of some kind, and perhaps some particular words to be said, but people usually spoke freely according to the inspiration within the Circle.

At the very first NCW ritual, we had a long length of thick rope, purchased from a boating shop. Each person present tied a knot in the rope to represent themselves within the group and when everyone had done this, the rope was made into a circle. That Circle really did become something of an extended family, with close ties between the members and other friends of the group. Members always had a place to come to and people to turn to if they needed help, not just at festival times, but throughout the seasons. We ate together, laughed and cried together and went out on walks on the countryside, which was always an essential part of our magical inspiration.

Copies of some of the rituals are still in existence and there were group members who filed the ritual running orders diligently, along with notes about the experience itself and any results. Not all rituals needed a written structure though, and sometimes we just agreed a rough outline.

The presentation of offerings was a particularly important aspect of this group. This meant that a huge amount of poetry was written and numerous verse charms. People also

315

sang, wrote chants, told stories, grew things, painted beautiful pictures or made lovely craft objects. All the charms and poems were collected by one group member who used her calligraphy skills to copy them all out, by hand, into a special book. Sometimes though, ritual offerings would be burned in honour of the Gods or to power the magical operations which were being carried out.

A great advantage of having a large group is that if people wish to learn a specific skill, there is usually at least one group member who is able to teach them. The NCW drew on the knowledge of many of its members over the years to run workshops and increase our learning. When we wanted to try something which none of us could do, we discovered that we could easily pay a teacher to put on a day's workshop for us. As a result, we were able to learn a little archery and try some mask making, with John Seabrook. More and more people joined us, and most of the students who finished the course elected to stay with us rather than go to other groups. Things began to feel unwieldy, especially as the house and ritual space in the garden are limited in size. People were also travelling considerable distances to get here. Fewer members were having the opportunity to write rituals and I suspect that there was less magical work going on in between the festival times. Something of the group's vibrancy had declined and it lost its magical shine. We continued for a while, feeling that vague sense of magical dissatisfaction that so often heralds the need for a change.

Then, at Midsummer 2005, one of our founder members and greatest stalwarts died. Without her stabilising influence, it became clear that a change was imminent. Appropriately, just after Lammas that year, a suggestion was put out that we should divide the NCW into much smaller, more localised groups. At first, some members were rather dismayed and resistant to the idea, but eventually saw the sense of the proposal and, over the ensuing months, we attended a large number of rituals to inaugurate new groups all over the county: a bountiful magical harvest indeed.

The rope and all the stones from the cairn were buried deep under the path which leads to our ritual Circle, forming just one of the many magical layers which inform our present and future work.

Hollystick College

During the time of the NCW, I was inspired to run a number of one-day and weekend workshops, which were advertised beyond the immediate community and for which a small fee was charged. Initially, I ran the courses from home, but when numbers increased, I was fortunate enough to be able to hire a lovely 15th-century building, known as the Great Hall, on Oak Street. Courses covered practical and magical crafts, and their titles over the years included First Steps in Witchcraft, Magical Herb Lore, Lotions and Potions, Spellcraft, Divination, Ritual Techniques, Spinning and Feltmaking and Magical Crafts.

Some of the people who attended were already experienced practitioners of various traditions, seeking specific skills or information, but the courses also provided another route into the community and into the Nameless Tradition. Indeed, quite a number of people who attended the courses later joined our one-year training programme and some of those went on to become teachers within the Tradition.

Nameless

For a number of years following the division of the NCW, Chris and I worked only with a very small number of people. We had no named group but continued an intense period of magical work, study and experimentation. Certain things had to be learned and the magical instructions we received proved to be challenging for all concerned.

In my own case, I had always been interested in herbs and used them both magically and medicinally, learning much from an old Swedish cunning man during the seven years I spent in the lands of East Anglia's Wuffing ancestors. I had always liked the idea of training to become a professional herbalist, but never really thought that I would have the money or the scientific capacity for such a huge undertaking. Then, during the weekend of the Full Moon in June 2003, everything changed suddenly. It was one of those mad weekends of magical overload in which we sometimes get embroiled. I was running a two-day, Hollystick College course on Magical Herb Lore; I had a Full Moon ritual to perform with some magical colleagues; and I had agreed to give a talk on herbs for Norwich Moot on Sunday evening.

I was so full of magical energy that everything went perfectly, and I really enjoyed every minute of it. The grand finale was a Plant Oracle, using fresh plants to do a divination. I had said I wasn't going to do it for real, just as an example to show people how to do it, but things started to happen and I ended up doing readings for everybody in the room. As everyone said their "thank yous" and left, I began to get that strange magical tingling feeling which is both exciting and alarming simultaneously. By the time I'd cleared up, I knew, with terrifying certainty, that I had to do the herbal medicine training no matter what the cost in time, money and effort.

It took a year to save the money, so by the time the NCW was divided, I was about to start on my second of four years. It is interesting that such a magical task can actually remove someone from the magical community for some time, but such was the case for me and for a couple of my close associates who were also "given" onerous tasks by one of our major contacts. Even once I had completed the course, it was a number of years before I returned to take an active part in the community outside our tiny magical group. Others too were similarly affected. Such are the labyrinthine patterns traced out by seekers on the magical quest.

Harvest Moon
The Harvest Moon Festival was the dream of some of the younger members of the Norwich Pagan community,

in particular Cat Ward, whose determination and drive transformed a lovely idea floating on the astral into a fabulous first conference, held at the 4Women Resource Centre on Colegate, in the city, on the 29th September 2012. Nigel Pennick kindly agreed to be the keynote speaker. There were numerous other talks, stalls, chanting workshops and dancing. The venue was packed and the atmosphere full of excitement. The oldies amongst us were delighted to witness and support this new, youthful development, which heralded an ever more vibrant feeling of community which is still developing today. The event ended with a beautiful closing ritual by the Coven of the Horned Hare. Not surprisingly, we left the building that evening under a magnificent Full Moon, which looked as if it had been polished for the occasion.

The following year Harvest Moon moved to the delightfully atmospheric Puppet Theatre, which could accommodate far more people, and since then it has gone from strength to strength, with an impressive list of illustrious speakers from Norfolk and from all over the country, including Marian Green, Gemma Gary, Pete Jennings, Peter Gray, Nikki Wyrd and many more. The venue lent itself to having an evening gig. Touch the Earth played in 2014 and Inkubus Sukkubus in 2015, both wonderful, memorable occasions. 2016 was the last for now, but we hope to see it return in the future.

Twelfth Night: Adapting Traditions
On the Sunday after Harvest Moon 2015, a number of us were spending a relaxing afternoon together at the home of Matthew Fox, one of the main organisers of the event. Gemma Gary had been a speaker that year, giving an excellent presentation about the use of bones in magic, and was there with her partner, Jane Cox. They decided to show us a video of their Montol celebration in Penzance, in which an oss' parades through the streets at Yuletide, followed by dancers and musicians and many people wearing elaborate costumes, masks or animal skulls. The oss' itself is a Horse's

skull mounted on two poles, one of which is used to snap its jaws. A cloth hangs down from it to form the body and hide the person inside.

It looked fantastic and, fired with the enthusiasm of the moment, and the success of the previous day, the now invincible Mr. Fox suggested that we should create our own, Norfolk version. It was jokingly pointed out that saying 'oss in a Norfolk accent would make it sound something like "arse". This term was rejected in favour of the title "The Ickeny One". Ickeny is an old Norfolk word for something which is stroppy and difficult to handle, particularly a troublesome Horse, but also has a connection with Boudicca's tribe, the Iceni. We selected the all-important Twelfth Night as the best time for a Norwich event and decided that there should be a procession across Mousehold Heath, a magical place overlooking the city, with a long history of being on the edge and a venue for the meetings of witches.

The spell was spoken, the magic bubbled and the community came together to make it happen. In no time at all, a massively heavy Horse's skull had arrived; the route was chosen and permission granted from the police and the Mousehold Conservators. The only thing we wanted to do, but could not, was to have real lanterns and flaming torches. Thank goodness for battery-operated lights!

The creation of roles for the procession reflected a dynamic mix between Craft practices and some of Norwich's civic tradition. So, just as in the Lord Mayor's Procession in the Summer, the person at the very front was to be a Whiffler, whose job it was to clear the path of evil spirits or anything else which might block the path. A Sword Bearer and a Master of Ceremonies was then followed by the Ickeny himself and two "Teasers". Behind them were to be representatives of all four Elements, the Wild Hunt, musicians, lantern bearers and animals.

There was a frenzy of costume making and experimentation, not least in the construction of the Ickeny itself, which was brilliantly accomplished by Matt Fox and Kev Ward, who created the snapping jaw mechanism according to Gemma and Jane's instructions. On a drizzly January day it all came together. During the course of the day, the main officers prepared, ritually, for the event and, just prior to joining with the public, the Ickeny was invoked into Chris (chosen for the role on grounds of height) and he put on the costume. Claire was covered in stars; Nettles had an amazing costume of feathers, skulls and bones; Emily, the Sword Bearer, wore a tatters coat and a top hat; and Vicki had on an elaborately decorated, fringed tunic and fur wraps. As Whiffler, I wore a purple robe with a gold coat (the colours of Twelfth Night) along with a massively pointed white witch's hat trimmed with purple. I carried a huge besom whose bristles were decorated with little starry lights.

From where we were standing, we could not see whether anyone had come to join us on the procession. We thought a handful of people might have turned out, but it was cold and rainy and, although we wanted to do this partly for the community, it was really for the Gods, for the Spirits of the Place and the magical benefit of the area. As it turned out, more than 90 people were there to take part in the procession. I could not see a great deal from the front, concentrating on what I was doing, but at one point, at a curve in the road, I was able to glance back. It was a magical sight indeed. Lamps and lanterns glittered in the darkness and revealed the long line of costumed characters snaking back into the distance. Music filled damp air and the notes from drums and flutes mingled with the night as the water droplets slipped from the overhanging boughs to bless all in attendance.

The procession passed beneath two special Oak trees which formed a gateway to a large circular area of grass, where the ritual would take place. I had never before stood in a magical Circle with so many people. It evoked an amazing feeling of connection and belonging. Everybody was fully focused on that magical moment, even those who had never taken part in any ritual work before. The Ickeny, who was a truly terrifying embodiment of Dark Forces, even to those who knew with their everyday minds who was inside it, broke into the Circle, menacing and snapping at everyone. Finally, he selected his unsuspecting victim, whose task it was to become the Champion, take up the Golden Bough, accept the blessings of all the signs of the zodiac and drive the Ickeny from the Circle, away from the community until the next year's dark times. The crowd cheered their Champion; the fight criss-crossed the magical space until, eventually, the Ickeny was defeated and fled from the Circle along with the teasers. Light triumphed over Dark and, for a short time, a large number of people were given a taste of the very best that dramatic ritual can achieve.

Thus are traditions born. The Champion became the Guardian of the Golden Bough (which was not Mistletoe, but a large branch of Bay, cut from a tree in our garden and sprayed gold) and charged with the task of keeping it until the next year, when it would be handed to the next person who is chosen to fight the Ickeny, in an annual event which has now become part of the city's magical life, and hopefully will remain so for long into the future.

Although there is consistency in the theme of the ritual, it always has its unique aspects. In the second year, for example, the new Champion was invested with the powers of the seven classical planets, and the emphasis was on community and that together we are a "Circle of Stars". Most recently, the Ickeny's chosen adversary was given the gifts of the herbs of the Anglo-Saxon Nine Herbs Charm. Each herb was represented by one of the participants in the ritual, who had volunteered in advance to play this part. The Champion was anointed with a salve, beautifully made by Sam Frosdick, in accordance with the instructions in the 11th-century manuscript. At the end of the ritual, everyone in attendance received a wooden disc, with the nine-stroke glyph, which represents the herbs, Odin's "glory twigs", and Yggdrasil, the World Tree of Norse mythology. Each disc had been ritually anointed with some of the salve, so these were powerful gifts indeed.

Boudica's Brocante

A new Moot venture, Boudica's Brocante, started in the Autumn of 2017, and shows every sign of developing into a successful tradition.

We didn't know what a brocante was until a couple of years ago, when we were staying with the amazing Dave and Barbara, on their magical farm, in Cornwall. They took us this wonderful event in a nearby village, which was a mixed market of crafts and second-hand items, where we picked up some rather magically useful agricultural tools. There was music too, and a very lively atmosphere. We enjoyed it so much, we thought it would be a good thing to do in Norfolk, and name after one of our local heroes.

We were not sure initially whether or not it was going to be possible to go ahead with the brocante, as we were having venue problems for Moot events. However, just at the right moment, the Moot found its new home. We had to act very quickly to ensure that we had enough stallholders, and that there was adequate interest generated to make it worthwhile. This meant a huge amount of both magical and mundane work to make it happen. We knew that we needed to have a really special Boudica altar, so set about trying to find a suitable statue of her. We thought that would be easy, as we were sure there would be plenty of London tourist market replicas of Thornycroft's famous statue of her. We searched but found nothing. There was a company offering to produce a replica of it using 3D printing, but the cost was astronomical (well into four figures). However, right at the last minute, Nettles came across an eBay seller offering a beautiful brass statue of the Iceni Queen in a chariot, brandishing a spear. It was mounted on a wooden plinth, with a sword on the front, with Boudica engraved on it. It was perfect, and duly ordered, arriving just in time, as we knew it would.

It is always gratifying to receive confirmation that we are doing the right thing. Having gone to the venue to set up the tables and the altar, the night before the event, we were walking back to the car when we saw a little horse-drawn chariot coming down the road. Several more followed, as if Boudica's army was really on the move again.

We had decided that the event should be opened by the Ickeny, because of his obvious connections with Boudica, and because he enjoys a good ritual, and indeed any excuse to "come forth". So, prior to letting in the general public, we called for silence and the Ickeny was led clockwise around the hall, stopping at every stall, to bow to the stallholders, who were also offered a wooden disc with an Iceni-style horse on them in pyrography. On the other side of the discs, was written simply BB and the date, which could be interpreted in a number of ways. These discs were a little like giant Iceni coins, and had been blessed to bring the stallholders good fortune and good profits for the day.

We decided that over the lunchtime period we would have various mini-talks. This gave various people, who were not used to speaking in public, the opportunity to have a go, without the pressure of having to hold forth for a whole hour. It worked really well. All the talks were very well received and became full-length talks for the Moot's next programme. Particularly spectacular was 's talk about pierre stones, which are also known as eoliths. These are basically natural stones which are shaped like deities. had never given a talk before but spoke with the authority and confidence of seasoned lecturer. The Brocante also meant firsts for some of the stallholders. Pherlin the Fair's Litha's Cauldron, selling handmade as well as second-hand magical items and books, had previous only been an on-line venture, as had Vicki's art business, Feoh. They all did very well and were encouraged to venture out on future occasions.

It is always nerve-wracking putting on an event, especially one which is completely different from anything we have done before, but everything turned out very well and the day just flew passed. We closed the event with the Ickeny processing anti-clockwise around the hall, effectively unwinding the Circle which had been created earlier.

Fluffy Bunny?

It has been argued by some that the opening up of the community has enhanced the lighter, nature-honouring aspects of the Craft at the expense of the real, deeper work, the search for arcane wisdom and what might be seen by some as the darker side of things. There is indeed a lot on offer now in Norfolk to seekers who are looking for something which honours the land and is gently and safely magical. Many within the Nameless Tradition have been very happy to encourage and support people to work in ways which they find comfortable and life-affirming. It does take time, but it is also very rewarding to help people find their feet upon the path. It is a wonderful thing to watch people discover that they do have the confidence to face some of their fears, that they can learn things which they had not realised they had the capacity to understand, that not only can they see the Hikey Sprites in the trees and sea spirits dancing across the water, but they can trust their own experience. Souls are nourished by connection with the physical and spiritual beings of the landscape and those who benefit are enabled to reciprocate in their own ways so that the flame of the old magical mutuality between humans, the landscape and the Eldritch World is kept alive. The Nameless Tradition loses nothing from this; it has everything to gain. Those who wish to push the boundaries of magical experimentation still do so, alone, in pairs or in small groups and perhaps do so more safely and more successfully in the context of the firm magical foundation provided by the wider community.

Congregational Paganism?

There is of course a risk that greater openness and more people within Paganism may ultimately lead to the emergence of a kind of orthodoxy to which people are then expected to conform. Thus, an energetic and meaningful spiritual and magical practice based on individual experience and direct contact with spiritual forces could potentially become rule-bound and controlled by an "official" priesthood. This is exactly what happened to Christianity of course, turning it into an oppressive and dangerous Churchianity. Chris Wood wrote of the potential dangers of this as long ago as 2002, in his Pagan Dawn article, "Congregational Paganism?" Should this threaten to be the case, most of us within the Nameless Tradition would probably just fade away into the landscape, returning to a much smaller community and continuing with our work in a quieter and more secretive fashion, scuttling along beside the hedgerows with the souls of our ancestors.

Communities can be valuable for support, friendship, magical co-operation and training the next generation of practitioners to pick up where we leave off. But in the end, no one person can tell another how to do magic. You can be given tips and techniques, study the books on suggested reading lists, be shown magical sites (and sights), learn craft skills and follow meditations and pathworkings. In the end, though, it is the relationship of the individual to the land which is important. Our kind of magic wells up from the very Earth itself and pours down from the heavens and from the Shining Ones. There can be no magical tests or assessments either. We all have our successful magical moments and a few less satisfactory ones too as we contribute to and draw from the community. We all have different strengths which we can use, and weaknesses for which we may seek human or divine support. Nobody can tell us how good we are at magic. That is for us to know and to continue working on, as there is always room for improvement and those who become complacent and think that they now know enough often find themselves removed from the path in strange and sometimes disturbing ways. While consistency is good, change and transformation are essential. Over the quarter of a century I have been involved with the Pagan and witchcraft community of Norfolk, I have appreciated the consistency of the warp threads of our magical tapestry, but delighted in the vibrancy of its ever-changing weft, full of colour, texture, light and shade. The significance of the contribution of so many talented practitioners cannot be underestimated. The strength of the community is based on the magical and creative powers of the individuals who are part of it.

Times are changing and the Nameless Tradition adapts and flows with the currents, although, at its heart, it remains ever true to its principles and to the Grey Lord and the White Lady who are its bedrock.

A Treasury of Talent

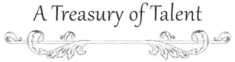

Athriving community relies on the dedication of its members, and within Norfolk's Nameless Tradition, there are a great many magical folk who contribute to the work in a wide variety of ways. After all, as Forby pointed out back in 1830:

> *Indeed the soil [of Norfolk and Suffolk] appears to have been always peculiarly favourable to the production of witches.*

(pp. 388-9)

This was the clearly the case in the times he describes and is most certainly true today. Thus, our overall strength is mixed in the heady cauldron brew of the combined magical talents of many individuals, each bringing their innate abilities, their experience and learning and, of course, their quirkiness. Each person shines out with their own colour and vibration, and the bonds between us shimmer and crackle (or cackle) across the county and out towards those with whom we have links elsewhere in the world.

Threads of connection do run back in time, too, to our magical ancestors of blood or of place. Our relationship with the many witches of the past is complex. We certainly admire their power and audacity, especially those of low social status, whose magic enabled them to carve out a living for themselves and improve their lot. Whilst we appreciate the huge differences between our modern lives and the lives of those who worked their magic here before us, we still recognise their significance and seek out their stories, even if we would not wish to emulate some of their activities. A number of authors, including Nigel Pennick (2004; 2011) and Nigel Pearson (2015) have already researched and discussed, in some detail, many of the great, and in some cases, notorious, characters of the magical past of the region, but it is only right to acknowledge a few of them here, as the traces of their magic are still to be found in the Earth, along the paths they walked and in the memories of the ancient trees whose shade they once enjoyed.

We all have our personal favourites and relish the tales of some of their escapades, even if we would not necessarily wish to emulate them. One such is the 19th-century, Tilly Baldrey, who soured the milk of a farmer who annoyed her. When Tilly's husband ran off with a woman from another village, she said charms to make him return to her, walking backwards all the way and bringing with him a lock of his lover's hair, which Tilly then used to kill her, magically. Her story is told in full by Nigel Pearson (2015).

Another, more amusing, cautionary tale of a witch's revenge is that of the Norfolk farmer's wife who consulted the famous Nan Barrett about how to retrieve some feathers which she had lost. Having been assured that they would be returned, the woman refused to pay Nan's fee. Nan then told her that the feathers would indeed come back, but that their owner would be no better for them. At milking time, the feathers duly came flying back "like a swarm of bees", but flew into the full milk churn and were ruined (Glyde, 1872).

We also respect the memories of all those "witches" in Norfolk, and beyond, who have been persecuted and killed over the centuries, whether or not they were genuinely practitioners of magic. One of the few witches to be burned at the stake in England (as opposed to being hanged) was Margaret Read, who, in 1590, was executed at the Tuesday Market Place in King's Lynn. At the moment of her death, her heart burst out of her chest and smashed into the wall of a house on the North side of the square, before bouncing off and heading for the River Ouse. As the heart entered the river, the water is said to have fizzed and bubbled and then appeared to boil before the heart disappeared beneath the surface. Today the spot where Margaret's heart struck the red brick wall is marked with a black outline of a heart set within a diamond. This story has been told and retold in various forms, but I first heard it from Matthew Hannam (previously) of North Wootton, near King's Lynn. A recent version was written in the local press by Stacia Briggs (2017).

One of my personal favourite wise woman characters from the past is Mrs. Lubbock of Irstead. The following information is based on an 1849 report, in Norfolk Archaeology, by the Reverend John Gunn, Rector of Irstead, who talked to her about her knowledge and practices. In 1813, Mrs. Lubbock was left a widow with several children, so made her living as a washerwoman, managing to remain independent and to support her family. She continued to work in this capacity until well into her eighties. She had no education but was an avid observer of the natural world and human interactions with it. She had a prodigious knowledge of weather lore, of the significances of occurrences on saints' days and of the prophesies of Mother Shipton of Yorkshire. Her memory must have been phenomenal and she had many stories to tell.

One of her tales was of a Jack o' Lantern who, prior to the 1810 Irstead Enclosure, could be seen on roky (foggy) nights at Heard's Hold, in Alder Carr Fen Broad, on the Neatishead side. Mrs. Lubbock connected the troublesome spirit with a man by the name of Heard, who had been drowned at that place for "unmentionable crimes". She herself had seen the spirit rise and fall and twist about many times and appear as a candle in a lantern. If a traveller passed the spot and failed to put out his own lantern, this Jack would come and smash it to pieces. He even once knocked from his horse a gentleman who had mockingly referred to him as a Will o' the Wisp.

The people of Neatishead became so troubled by Heard's spirit that they wished to lay it, and had three gentlemen read scripture at it. However, the spirit always kept a verse ahead of them, and the attempt was unsuccessful. Finally, two Pigeons were put in front of Heard's spirit, at which point, it lost its place and they were able to bind it. This old story is a good indication that the Pigeon totem of the Lord and Lady of Norfolk, or even just Pigeon feathers, can be very helpful in dealing with ghosts or bothersome spirit beings, and recent experience does bear this out.

Not only was Mrs. Lubbock a compelling story-teller, with a colourful turn of phrase, but also skilled in the practical application of useful techniques for sensible, everyday magic. In her work, she used salt to "keep the thunder out" of the laundry and to stop it being interfered with by evil spirits. Barking dogs seemed to annoy her, and she could quiet them by taking of one of her shoes, turning it around three times then putting it back on. When asked what she did if she was in bed when she heard barking, she said that she always kept a shoe on the floor nearby and would simply reach out and turn it over, which always worked. Her predictions were usually accurate. She noted that if the Ash keys failed that would portend a change of government, and that it was possible to tell who would die and who would be married during the year by watching the church porch on St. Mark's Eve. People who were to die entered the church alone and didn't come out, but those who were to be married went in in twos and came out together. This information she had received from Robert Staff, one-time landlord of the Maid's Head Inn in Stalham. Mrs. Lubbock was particularly skilled at foretelling the coming of storms, which led to some harassment by local lads who would come by her house and rattle the windows.

One of the reasons that Mrs. Lubbock was targeted in this way was because of the suspicion that she might be a witch rather than a cunning woman, a clear distinction being made between the two. Witches tended to curse people, while cunning folk would be helpful and for a fee, remove curses and heal people. Many who now work within the Nameless Tradition, and consider themselves witches, would probably have preferred the term cunning man or woman had they lived in the 19th or early 20th century. Thus, our use of the term witch, in a modern context, differs somewhat from its earlier usage, since it now covers a much wider range of practices, not specifying whether the person is conducting beneficial or harmful magic. Besides, in a long magical career, a witch may well carry out both kinds, although it is not always easy to decide what is "good" or "bad", as this can prove to be a somewhat artificial dichotomy.

Even a past practitioner who veered more towards the cunning folk end of the scale, could be a scary character and far from totally benign. Such was certainly true of the Great Yarmouth cunning woman, Mrs. Mortimer. Her help was sought by a young man, Charles, who had been bewitched as a result of eating some sausages he had won in a raffle. He visited the cunning woman, accompanied by his mother. Initially, Mrs. Mortimer refused them entry as she would have no man in her house. However, once she realised that they would probably be good customers, she let them in. The young man's mother was terrified of Mrs. Mortimer, and later reported that she had "trembled from head to foot" on entering Mrs. Mortimer's house, and dared not look into the divining cup, as directed. Having been paid a sovereign, Mrs. Mortimer gave Charles a copy of the Lord's Prayer, to wear next to his heart, and a potion to take. She also kept some of his hair, finger nails and urine, which she said she needed to work on to complete the cure. Mrs. Mortimer demanded a further ten shillings in payment once Charles had recovered. He foolishly refused to pay her anything extra and his health soon began to decline once more, so he gave her the required sum, recovered and continued in good health until Mrs. Mortimer died. (I assume that the hair, nails and urine were kept as insurance against non-payment of the second part of the fee.) Charles later consulted a cunning man in Norwich because the copy of the Lord's Prayer given to him by Mrs. Mortimer had worn out. Clearly, he felt that he needed to keep using the charm indefinitely in order to maintain his health (Glyde, 1872).

Some of these past magical characters did not confine themselves to local matters either. Ray Loveday has kindly told me the story of a brother and sister who were both magical practitioners and lived together in the village of Worstead. They were personally known to him in the 1980s, although they were very elderly by then. The woman had a great dislike of Mrs. Thatcher and told Ray that if she carried on as she was, she would "set the dolls on her". Sadly, Ray does not know who else she had set her dolls onto and exactly what form this magic took. We have scant information about these dolls and are unsure as to whether they had physical as well as astral form. Nevertheless, this snippet of information is certainly one to fire the imagination.

These characters are certainly our magical ancestors in many respects, but any discussion of lineage or of centuries of unbroken tradition must be approached with caution. A few current practitioners have a traceable bloodline, and some are in possession of notes and papers going back at least three generations, but many of us have no verifiable, connections to the witches of the past. What is important to most of us now, is that the magic wrought by our forebears is still present in the warp and weft of the county's fabric, for every act of enchantment is remembered somewhere, and no magic is ever truly forgotten. In my own garden, I feel the power of its magical past, although I have no documentation, no "evidence", no names, as yet (although I have asked), which I could present to a magical historian. Yet the power and memory of these past practitioners is most definitely a constant presence and a strong influence on the work we do here. They leave us the clues we need, even if they do not wish to tell us the whole story.

Various of the 20th-century characters of the witchcraft and occult communities have had interests in, or connections with, Norfolk magic, and have each added their unique contributions to the county's magical granary. The artist, Monica English, who lived in Gayton, near King's Lynn, between 1953 and 1970, has been a source of fascination for magical historians, including Nigel Pearson and Michael Howard, and Lois Bourne came to Norfolk and was initiated into the coven. Monica appears to have been fairly secretive, and only those with direct contact with her coven have much knowledge of her magical work and methods, although they would appear to have involved dancing and silent working, rather than wordy or elaborate rituals. She still gives little away to outsiders, even at Samhain rites, which is not surprising, given the value her group placed upon silence (Bourne, 1998; Howard, 2004; Pearson, 2015). Numerous documents related to Monica's life have been listed on the website, www.deadfamilies.com. However, one way in which those of us with no direct connections to her coven can approach her magic is through her artwork. Her paintings are fabulously atmospheric, often depicting Horses, of which Monica had practical as well as esoteric knowledge, having been Master of the Hunt while living in Gayton. The work is full of wild energy and seems to express a connection to Horse deities, possibly Epona, or maybe some unnamed Iceni god or goddess.

Doreen Valiente is also known to have connections with Norfolk, having been initiated into the Coven of Atho, in 1963, by Ray Howard. Howard had been an associate of the notorious Charles Cardell in Surrey, but had moved to Field Dalling in Norfolk, having broken off relations with him (Heselton, 2016). The coven had a carved Head of Atho, which Howard claimed to have inherited from Alicia Franch, a Romany who used to park her caravan on the farm near Swaffham, where Howard stayed as a child. A small bowl of water was placed at the back of the Head, creating an awe-inspiring effect, with glowing red eyes and steam emanating from the tips of the Cow horns (Eastern Daily Press, 1967). Doreen describes the Head of Atho as:

> *...having a crude strength and power, which make it a remarkable work of primitive art. ... It is covered in mystic symbols, representing the beliefs of the followers of Atho.*

(Valiente, 1973, p.24)

Doreen drew a picture of the Head, which is reproduced in her ABC of Witchcraft and also in Heselton's biography of her. Photos of the Head itself appeared in local newspapers on at least two separate occasion (Eastern Evening News, 1961; Eastern Daily Press, 1967). In the manuscript given to Doreen to copy on her initiation, linguistic similarities are noted between "Atho" and the names "Hathor" and "Thor", as well as "Arthur" (Heselton. 2016). Of course, all of these names do have their relevance to Norfolk magic.

Howard was not averse to seeking publicity. In 1961, he held a Halloween party at the George the Fourth pub on Ber Street Norwich, where he openly revealed details of the coven and displayed various artefacts, including the Head. Howard also maintained that the pub was on the 400-year-old site of a witch's hut, but no traces remain as it was compulsorily purchased in 1962 and demolished for road improvements (www.norfolkpubs.co.uk). Sadly, the Head of Atho was stolen from Howard's antique shop, in April 1967, soon after it had been displayed publicly and photographed for the press. No money or other artefacts were taken, so it appears that it was specifically the head which was targeted (Valiente, 1973).

Despite the fact that, in July 2008, Howard's son claimed the Head to be a fake (Seims, 2008), there are many Norfolk practitioners now who would very much like to see it. Various suggestions have been mooted as to where it might be, with meaningful glances and grins occasionally being exchanged when the subject is brought up. Probably only the person who now has it knows if and when it will be revealed once again (and that person is not me, honest). Another luminary of the wider magical world, Marian Green, who often visits Norfolk, and has over the years contributed greatly to our magical work, believes that the Head of Atho may have been claimed by the River Wensum as an offering. Marian also believes this to be the case for another, rather grotesque head, which was stolen, in 1998, from an exhibition of sculpture at the King of Hearts arts centre in Norwich, while she was giving a hugely well-attended lecture on witchcraft as part of a weekend witchcraft course. As organisers of the event, we were mortified that someone associated with us (even loosely) would be involved in a theft which risked putting the community in such a bad light. Magical work was done to try to retrieve the piece, but although there were certainly results from this work, it did not produce the desired effect and the piece remains missing to this day.

Normally, the individuals who make up our large and vibrant community nowadays are rather more magically successful than we were on that occasion. I am delighted that so many of these devoted practitioners of Norfolk Magic, have given me permission to mention them by name and to give a little flavour of the work they do.

Rod and Rue

I first met Rod and Rue in the mid nineties and was struck by how much they looked the part of traditional cunning folk. We were talking about spells and Rod took a sprouted potato from his pocket and explained how helpful it was in preventing and easing the pain of arthritis and rheumatism. The starch of the potato absorbs the disease which is sent out into the shoots. Once it gets too tangly, it is best replaced by a new one. I was initially surprised to discover that Rod and Rue had for a while been members of the Orthodox Church, but exploration and the widening of experience is such an important part of the magical Quest, and it often takes a while to find a spiritual structure which complements our feelings and inclinations, or to realise that we do not need anything formal or rule bound. I asked Rod to write something about his own path and connection with Norfolk:

About the Pagan community, where do we start? Well it started rather late in life for Rue and me. I had always been into trees, plants, grasses and nature. As I write this on Candlemas day (Imbolc) I remember that my Mother always used to give us snowdrops on this day, and it is our daughter, Sarah's, birthday, February 2nd. When going to the Orthodox church, the Priest used to talk about the old English festivals, Lammas, Beltane, etc. I had never heard of these before. One day I found a second-hand book in Norwich about witchcraft and the occult, and found out all about the festivals. A few weeks later we saw a small poster in Head in The Clouds occult shop in Norwich, about the pub moot and a talk about Beltane. There we met Chris and Val. Val is such a good teacher, we were soon under her wing as it were! Soon we were going to work shops on how to call the quarters, etc.

The pagan community, it can't be stressed enough the importance of the community. You can be a solitary but you do need to feel a sense of community. We have Pagan friends in the USA, Germany, Cyprus, the Isle-of-Man, & all-over the UK. We celebrate most of the festivals, and some of the Heathen ones as well.

We have started a new tradition, celebrating Mistletoe Day, Dec 1st (well new to Norfolk that is), with a Mistletoe walk, and a toast to the Mistletoe Gods. Also we have revived the Anglo-Saxon Charming of the Plough. We have an old horse-drawn plough in the garden, and we both come from farming back grounds. My passion is Mistletoe. I give talks, workshops, etc., I've helped with the Mistletoe festival in Tenbury-Wells, and a survey of Mistletoe in Norfolk with the Norfolk Wild Life Trust. Mistletoe can give you an indication where you can find The Lord and Lady of Norfolk, and the spirit of the place. For us we also see The Lord and Lady of Norfolk in the Norfolk Flag. This is why we fly it a lot!

Rod and Rue are now generally acknowledged to be the Mistletoe King and Queen of East Anglia and no one can encourage Mistletoe to grow the way they do. I have even seen it growing on a Cotoneaster bush in their garden.

Although Rod kindly praises my teaching, the teaching and learning dynamic between us has been mutual over the years. He and Rue know so much about the county, where so many of the magical spots are to be found, particularly the stones and the barrows. Without their help, I would have far less knowledge about our ancient and magical sites. They are also experts on heraldry, runes, trees and many other magically-related topics, and have run their own groups, supporting and encouraging many seekers on the path.

A few years ago, Rod and Rue became guardians of a wonderful area of land in Mid-Norfolk, with a meadow, woodland and a delightful stream. Initially it was rather troubled with an over-abundance of Blackthorn, but through months of hard graft they have been able to bring this under control and plant a wonderful selection of rare and interesting trees. Not only that, but they have also created a really magical space which they have generously shared with the Pagan community, often inviting groups of people there for rituals, parties and other events.

Rod and Rue's surname is Chapman, the same as the well-known Pedlar of Swaffham who, by following the instruction of his dreams went all the way to London only to discover that the treasure he needed was in his own garden all along. Long may Rod and Rue follow their dreams and continue to develop their magic.

Witches of Costessey
Costessey, to the West of Norwich, is something of a hot spot for witches, many of whom are completely secretive and, as I understand it, work within the safety of the hedgerows and only share their magic within their own families. However, the witches of what is now known as Crow Corner are an exception, and are outgoing and community-oriented.

The first member of this family with whom I came into contact was Jean, who started to come to the Moot at about the same time as Rod and Rue. Born in 1929, she came from an unconventional family in South London, where her Irish grandmother had been herbalist, treating the cab horses. Jean's Uncle Frank had been a well-known medium and the whole family were Spiritualists, so seances were all part of Jean's upbringing. At the age of six, Jean went to live for a time in Devon. Her carer, Miss Goss, walked the lanes of that lovely county with a trug over her arm, taught her and encouraged her interest in the natural world, and her love of Nature, which was to be her lifelong passion. Even after her death, Miss Goss stayed with Jean as a spirit guide, who was often present in her dreams. In London, Jean trained as a hairdresser, at which she really excelled, and she was at one time hairdresser to Princess Margaret. When she moved to Norwich in the early 1960s, she became hairdresser to the great and the good of Norfolk.

Jean loved Natural Magic, the Tarot and working with Egyptian deities, but until the 1990s had kept her occult studies completely private. It was through her eldest daughter, Sharon, a powerful force in the London occult scene, that she was encouraged to join the Pagan Federation and seek out like-minded folk in Norwich. Sharon writes of her mother:

> *The thing that strikes me about my Mum, Jean, was her truly genuine belief and the strength of her spirit. Her power was very pure and her connection to the Natural World and its Magic very real... I think my Mum's true beliefs and purity of spirit shone through her and inspired others. The one thing that can be said about her was that she was the genuine article!!*

Jean became part of our immediate group and brought to it a gentle but powerful energy whose full extent we did not truly recognise until after her death. One of her great talents was that of keeping people together and maintaining the peace when disagreements threatened. She loved the group and what we were doing, and was fiercely protective of us and what we stood for. I only ever saw her lose her temper on two occasions, but when she decided that enough was enough, she could be terrifyingly unstoppable.

Jean was incredibly hardworking and determined. If she volunteered to take charge of a particular ritual (and she was excellent at designing rituals), she would put in days of effort, writing the right words, making garlands and other items and preparing offerings. On one well-remembered occasion, we had planned a Samhain fancy dress party. For a long time prior to the event, we kept asking Jean if she wanted to come out and do various things but she kept telling us that she was too busy with a certain project. We were mystified until the day of the party when she appeared dressed in the most amazing pair of runic pyjamas, which she had created by writing the runes of the Elder Futhark over and over again until it completely covered all the fabric. It was, of course, the winning costume.

Jean was always doing magical work for people, for her friends and family, and particularly for her grandchildren, and her house was full of spells and magical items. However, she rarely spoke much about what she did in her solo practice and maintained an aura of mystery and fierce independence about her. On one occasion, we were on a walk from Sheringham to Cromer, along the beach. As we got nearer to Cromer, Jean began to look pale and tired, and we all became rather concerned, which irritated her. She struggled back to the station, refusing even to let anyone carry her bag for her. However, somebody did pick it up when the train arrived and was shocked by the weight of it. It turned out to be so full of big hag stones that she had nearly done herself a mischief trying drag them so far, but she wouldn't let any of them go or ask one us to carry some for her.

I don't think Jean liked asking for help, but she was forced to do so when the bus service from her house to ours became so appalling that it was difficult for her to get to our Sunday meetings. Many are the times she would phone to say that she had waited for a couple of hours with no sign of a bus, and I would drive over and fetch her. Eventually, we gave up on the buses and I would collect her in the morning and she would help us with the setting up. After her death in 2005, when we came to scatter her ashes, in the places she had loved, we did leave a little sprinkle of them at the bus stop where she had spent so much time.

Jean was a huge influence on my magical life and attitudes and those of many others within the Tradition. I think of the years I was privileged to be associated with her as a Summer of Swifts, Swallows and Martins, for she loved the migratory birds. It's easy to take these Summer visitors for granted, but once they have gone, we recognise how important they were to us and how much they enriched the skies. Fortunately, Jean still sends us messages, via the Crows or in the shriek of the Swifts, or in the visitations of the Deer, which was an important totem to her.

It was remarkable how Nettles, following her mother's death, seemed to take on the mantle of her power, as well moving back into Jean's cottage, in Costessey, where she had been brought up. Prior to that she had only a fleeting interest in matters magical, indeed had not had time for it given the pressures of working and bringing up her family as a single mum. As might be expected, Nettles is both like and unlike her mother, and has adapted her home and magical practice accordingly. Her garden, which had perfectly reflected Jean's magical personality, has been developed by the considerable physical and magical strength of its new guardian. It now has its very own stone circle, each stone having been a birthday gift from a family member, and sunk deep into the Earth by Nettles herself. During the day, this Circle is patrolled by a flock of Hens, whose first leader was a magnificent, huge and clever Black Orpington called Morgana. Over the last year, this magical space has developed yet further to become a refuge for injured Crows who are not able to be return to the wild. They live in a huge and luxurious aviary, and she often spends time sitting in the enclosure with them, listening to their concerns and concocting spells with their assistance.

As the current facilitator for Norwich Pagan Moot, Nettles has shown great dedication to the work and the community. She will regularly turn up to organise an evening event, having worked a ten-hour shift as a nurse. She will always be the very last to leave, making sure that everything is cleared up, and finally locking the iron grill across the community centre door, long after most people have gone home to relax. And she will often be back for another long shift from 6am the following morning. Nettles is a Virgo too, so everything she does has to be perfect and beautifully presented, for she knows that the ideas and visions which are given to us by the Lord and Lady of Norfolk have to be manifested in the most magical and artistic way possible.

Recently, Nettles organised a very impressive and popular Corvid ritual, which was attended by a Raven and a Crow from the charity, Wild Touch, in Bacton. Jean must be thrilled with the way events have unfolded, even more so now that the next generation of this remarkable family is showing early signs of magical talent and interest in the Craft. One of Nettles' nieces, on her visits to Crow Corner, demands an explanation of every picture and ornament, which led to her asking how she would get her own power. As a result, the child, just short of her third birthday, her mother and Nettles performed a full ritual in the garden and created a charm bag for the very young witch, whose favourite time of the year has always been Halloween. Nettles writes of her own magical journey:

> *My Mother Jean was always a strong influence in my life, especially her advice. She never told me what to do or what path to take but she would always say, "I can only advise, then it is up to you what you do." While growing up there were always books about magic and nature, also a lot of historical novels which,*

*in my younger days, I would pick up and read or look through.
Nothing was ever said about magic or witchcraft while I was
growing up. I attended church as a child and sang in the choir
at the local church, St Edmund's. I went to a Catholic infant
school run by nuns, but this was for convenience as it was the
nearest local school and Mum had to get us there before heading
off to work.*

*As a child I can remember having an affinity with the seasons
and loved each of them, always seeing a beauty in the landscape
as it changed. I spent most of my childhood in the woods, the
corn fields, or swimming in the river Wensum. Costessey has
always been home to me and we lived in two different houses,
one just off Folgate Lane and the one where I have come back
to, where all my teenage years were spent up until I got married.*

*One of my favourite pastimes as a child was picking the wild
flowers in the meadows. There were lots in the area, but sadly
many have been built on now. I would pick bluebells by the
armful and take them round the houses, knocking on people's
doors and giving them a bunch of bluebells or wild flowers. Sadly
now most of these are in decline due to the habitat lost for
building. The wood is still there and I have given it another
name. I call it Dragon Wood as it has a huge tree at its entrance
and each year when the leaves come back its shape is of a dragon
who, I believe, guards the wood. The Dragon I discovered on
returning to live in my mother's house after her death.*

*I left Costessey and lived the other side of Norwich when I
got married, had my children and was kept busy bringing them
up and working as a hairdresser. I used to watch Mum as a
child doing people's hair and found it fascinating, transforming
their appearance.*

*Later I changed my career and started in the nursing profession,
which I still do and have been doing now for over 20 years.*

*My Magical training did not really start until after Mum's
death. I had looked after her, staying with her in hospital. I can
remember the chaplain coming round and she would politely say
she was Pagan and was happy with her own faith. When she
died, I knew I had to give her a Pagan funeral, so approached her*

coven to help with what I and my family needed to do. The whole coven made her gifts and a beautiful coffin cloth was made by one of the members, with a fantastic Green Man on, which I know Mum would have loved. Her house had many green deities in it.

I was coming back to the house on my own and started to look at some of the things around the house, picking up items and just thinking of her. I was in her bedroom when I got a strong smell of lavender. It was so strong that I started to look for where the scent must be coming from, walking out of the room and back, then it just faded away. It was then that I knew Mum had come to visit. I picked up a pack of her Tarot cards, The Green Man Tree Oracle, and drew 3 cards, laying them on one of her coats which I spread out. My first cards were Gorse, Beech and then Hawthorn. Mum had written her own interpretations along with the card meanings as part of her study. It was like she was showing me what direction to take. Some of the things she had written were about going to nature to give me strength, enjoying get-togethers, enjoying a goal, collecting treasures, but making sure things were also shared, what lies beyond ancient knowledge, guidance from the past. For Beech she had written, "Don't be scared of what lies beyond; if you hold back you remain in a stagnant position." Beech can signify the death and end of something, but also stands for the changes that arise from realisation.

It was like this was written for me to find. There was so much more, but that was the start of my Journey.

I would confide in my sister, telling her what cards I had pulled, when she just said, "I have been waiting for you." I knew Mum and Sharon held a magical bond and they would correspond with each other about their own magical workings. As time went on Sharon revealed a little bit more about our history, telling me we were hereditary witches and it went back generations, something I was completely unaware of. You will see me referred to as Nettles. This name was given to me by my Nanny who we visited in London regularly. All my childhood and part of my adult life I was known as Nettles. Hardly anyone used my Christian name, even some of the teachers at school. It wasn't until my later years, after Mum died, that Nettles was not used so much, but now all my close magical friends call me Nettles.

Sharon said she would ask if Mum's friend, Val the book author, would take me under her wing, as Sharon lived outside of London and could not help me like she wished.

After Mum's passing over ceremony was completed on October 30th 2005, I started my magical training with Val and committed to my course. I was paired up with someone to work with and we worked together magically for over 10 years.

I had joined Norwich Pagan Moot and attended off and on for many years. Then the opportunity came for someone to help on the committee. I had been doing that a couple of years when the other committee members, for health and other reasons, said they could no longer commit to running the Moot. Myself, Val and a few others had been looking for a place to hold a Yule ritual for the Moot and, on coming to Caistor St. Edmund, an old Roman settlement site near the river Tas, it seemed the perfect place. We were looking for confirmation and we turned round to see a double rainbow which we took as a sign, not forgetting the bit of bibliomancy we had done about the running of the Moot where I was given a clear sign of how things should go.

I am still facilitating the Moot now: all part of the sharing and giving back to the community that Mum first showed me in the readings.

Matthew Hannam

Matthew, who was born and brought up just outside King's Lynn, started writing to me when he was only fifteen, having been given my contact details by a respected author to whom he had written, via her publisher. Matthew, a real magical child prodigy, was keen to join a group and the Pagan Federation (PF), but had been prevented from doing so by the strict over-eighteen rule. He turned up on my doorstep one weekend and, in a whirlwind of power and enthusiasm, shook our magical world to its core, profoundly influencing our future direction. Matthew's magic is indescribably wild, powerful and exciting, and the results he gets are often instant, startling and sometimes terrifying. He is the only person I have ever seen to disappear in a ritual, leaving only his dark eyes watching all worlds simultaneously, and probably the only person ever to walk up and down our street in Norwich with a Boa Constrictor (Morticia) wrapped around his arm.

When Matthew's efforts to persuade the PF to lower its age of admission failed, he decided just to set up his own group for under-eighteens. The decision was taken at our dining room table one Sunday, in 1997, while eating vegetable stew. In no time at all, Matthew had set up a contact network, using Norwich Moot's P.O. Box, and letters from young people started pouring in. Such a thing would be difficult nowadays, when safeguarding is a priority. Even then Minor Arcana, as the group was known, ruffled a lot of magical feathers nationally but, true to his Norfolk roots, Matthew would obey only his magical contacts and refused to be thwarted by those who spuriously claimed to have authority over him. So, the group thrived and many young people, who had experienced considerable loneliness on their magical path, now felt secure and supported, in an organisation which was run entirely by young people for young people. The group's magazine, Pagan Teenage Voice, was a place where young writers, artists and illustrators had their first opportunity to publish their work, many of whom are now well-known and well-respected in various branches of the serious magical community, in the UK and beyond. It was a superb achievement of Matthew's to open up for others an opportunity to present their work in this way and to forge friendships which, in some cases, will last a lifetime.

When Matthew turned eighteen, he decided to give up running Minor Arcana because he thought that it should be run by someone younger, but nobody stepped forward, most of the other original members also having come of age at the around the same time. Eventually the organisation was taken over by the PF and run sensibly by a responsible adult.

It never really thrived though, having been very much of its time, and probably dependent on the subtle dynamic of that first and very special group of people it brought together.

Over the years, Matthew has applied his considerable magical and mundane talents to crafting for himself the kind of successful and glamorous lifestyle that his teenage self desired. He obtained a good degree in Psychology (always one of his major passions) and worked as a psychiatric nurse, before going to live in Cyprus, where he joined an international shipping company, grew Grapefruits, Lemons and Pomegranates in his garden and wrote three detective novels, which were published by Hale. Recently he moved to the Philippines, and now has an apartment in Manila, where he still works in shipping, and a weekend cottage in an island paradise, where he researches the traditional magic of the area. Being at the cottage also enables him to spend much of his time diving, which has been important to him ever since he first tried it as a young teenager on holiday in Australia, and he is now a highly qualified diving instructor, introducing others to the magic of the ocean's depths.

Matthew slips seamlessly back into his Norfolk magic whenever he visits us, for he has never lost his Norfolk connection despite all his travels. On his most recent visit this Summer, we spent time at Old Hunstanton, his favourite beach, admiring the cliffs and drawing inspiration from the play of sunlight on sand and sea.

These were the thoughts that Matthew himself provided:

Norfolk and Magical Connections to Land and Season –
Having grown up in North West Norfolk, heir to generations of my family that were born and lived in East Anglia, and having been involved in the local magical community since a young age, I have perhaps a somewhat unique understanding of the intimate relationship between the local land of the area and the Gods and Goddesses whose presence can be felt across the region. These are beings of particular importance locally, and the land is as much a part of them as we, as local inhabitants, are. This reaches into

seasonal festivals and none of these elements can essentially be considered without the other.

When I was very young, I realized this connection and it spoke to me in dreams and in spirit, through ancestors and clairvoyance. This is a constant that has never left me. Even though I left Norfolk - and the UK - a number of years ago, I have come to realize that, despite geographical distances, the essence of this connection never actually leaves us.

Even from afar, there is much that I can accomplish in regards to these connections. It all forms part of a much broader picture, and fits seamlessly together whenever I am blessed to return to Norfolk and the beaches and forests of my childhood. For, in these destinations, is really where you come to understand the essence of the spiritual and magical landscape that is abundant in this region of England.

Having been privileged to spend over a decade in Cyprus learning the Greek language, and the past couple of years in the Philippines, I've really been able to understand much more the intimate connection between land and deity. The energy and deities of foreign lands make us welcome as magical travellers and have much knowledge to impart, but due to language and regional differences, there really is, in the most magical sense, 'no place like home'.

I am extremely grateful for the opportunities that have come my way and which have led to my lifestyle, wherein I can experience magic in an international context. This sense of activism and internationalism came early to me during my involvement with 1990s Pagan community politics whilst I (and many others who supported me more than can be mentioned here) struggled to setup the UK's first Pagan teen network, 'Minor Arcana'.

It was a personal commitment I made to my own Gods and Goddesses who have blessed me since. That privilege however comes with a sense of loss. A loss of being physically present with dear friends and loved ones. Like all in life, everything comes to us in balance. I wrote many years ago about magic as the gift we come to understand that gives and takes in equal balance. There is no night without day, no moon without the sun, and no light without the dark. It is our job and privilege as magical beings to honour this life-affirming principal. For, as I have been reminded often by some of the greatest magical mentors, there is truly a blessing on all who serve.

Michael Clarke

Michael is the kind of magician who endows upon a situation, a sense of gravitas, as he is a true intellectual and a tireless researcher into a variety of magical topics, including Hekate, the folklore of East Anglia, Hermetic Magic and much more besides. He regularly speaks on these subjects for local groups, and is often asked to give presentations further afield, as his academic rigour is appreciated in many circles. It was a running joke at Norwich Moot some years ago, that whenever there was a party, my husband, Chris, who is also an intellectual, would write a really difficult quiz which only Michael could tackle with any success. Chris took it as something of a challenge to come up with at least one question which Michael couldn't answer, although it proved a tricky task.

Michael does have a sense of humour, though. I recall one Beltane ritual he attended, when he began his offering by saying that he wanted to talk to us about family values. Some eyebrows were raised, but he proceeded to tell a charming tale about a mother Stoat and her kits, who had taken up residence in his garden.

Michael has been a great friend and magical companion over the years, and I am particularly grateful to him for introducing me to the works of W.A. Dutt, some of which I have quoted in this book. This is what Michael chose to write about himself:

Michael Clarke: A Partial Esoteric Biography –
He is at first sight an unlikely folk magician.
For many years he was interested in and sought out details of esoteric and magical systems, Western and Eastern, as well as collecting an extensive library and personal museum to aid him.

By the later nineteen nineties he had collected together details, rituals and some implements of all the main Hermetic and Gnostic versions of modern magic, as well as the then newly evolving Chaos Magick.

In the late nineteen nineties he decided to contact the then emerging Pagans of the Norwich and Great Yarmouth area, in order to see magical systems in action. He was curious about Wicca but did not find that it was easy to access the right teachers locally. Although, at first, his chosen role was more of a wish to observe than to do, he adapted to participation.

In the late nineteen nineties several groups locally were practising broadly in the Western Magical Tradition in the Norwich area. Although these groups did not agree in their objectives and were sometimes openly dismissive of each other's existence, taken together they made up a culture of operative and initiatory magic in which much could be observed and practised.

As the years passed much of this experimental impulse died away and groups either went out of existence or became Pagan groups celebrating the Wheel of the Year and similar festivities, of a more religious than magical kind. Having been involved with Natural Magic, Hermeticism and Chaos Magick, he gravitated to occasionally attending a group which was and is broadly Heathen, run by a friend of his.

At the same time as this progress through magical systems, he was evolving his own system of esoteric thought based in the folk magic and witchcraft of the East Anglian Region. In 2012 he was requested to speak on the subject by the Pagan Federation Devon and Cornwall at their Annual Witchcraft Seminar.

After several months of research, he presented his findings to the seminar. He was impressed by the interest shown in what was at first sight a purely operative, low magical system. Being more confident about how the system worked, he self-initiated himself into the East Anglian Toad Ritual. Over the years he continued to evolve his own system of magic with a foundation of East Anglian Folk Magic but going well beyond it in practice.

Broadly speaking his system is one that is not as reliant on ritual as it is on trance and oneiric states, reflecting the changing view of modern scholars of the nature of folk and traditional witchcraft. The subliminal and borderland states are actively sought out. Although his system itself has not been taught, features of it lend themselves to the talks which he gives occasionally on request to interested groups.

Above all he is convinced that the magical universe of pre-Modern Europe has a value above and beyond its objective truth or falsehood and that embedded within it are universal themes which may be used for empowerment and self-development. He likes the raw experiential aspect of folk magic. In a Post-Modern World he believes that the choice of background system is of less importance than the means employed to approach its mysteries.

Mel

Mel was born into a farming family in South Norfolk, but has sought a different way of interacting with the land. She has a deep, intuitive connection with the worlds of plants and animals and is a skilful and compassionate healer. We first met in the mid-90s, on a course in holistic horticulture, at Otley College, in Suffolk, and have maintained a magical connection ever since, despite Mel's years in Southern France where, with her then partner and two sons, she bought a farm, grew herbs, fruit and vegetables, rescued animals and passed on her extensive knowledge to the many seekers who came to work with her.

Mel is also a talented artist and, during her formal training in Manchester, her teachers included artists who had themselves been taught by Charles Rennie Mackintosh: a proud lineage indeed. Unsurprisingly, much of Mel's artwork features animals, most recently Pigeons, which fascinate her, particularly the feral Pigeons, whose iridescence she captures perfectly in her work.

Recently, while spending time in Norfolk, Mel found a baby Squirrel lying in the road. Initially she thought the little creature was dead and stopped only to move it onto the verge so that it wouldn't be squashed by passing cars. It turned out to be alive, although abandoned by its parents. Mel was able to care for it, despite having no prior knowledge of Squirrels' needs, and Kefir, as he became known, lived in her barn for some months until he was ready to return to the wild. Sometimes we find ourselves in situations where we have to rise to a magical or practical challenge of this kind and learn as we go along, producing a successful outcome and an increase in both knowledge and confidence.

Julie Mytton

A nurse, a potter, a textile artist, a single mother and much more besides, Julie lavishes love, hard work and tremendous focus on all the magic she undertakes and keeps, on her stang, a small hand-stitched memento of all the rites in which she has been involved. When Jean died, it was Julie who created the most exquisite pall for the coffin, which depicted a gold foliate head on a rich green background.

Julie is striking-looking and very witchy, with blonde hair and eyes that fix you with a dark intensity, even though they are blue. She is a great ritualist and writer of rituals and, over the years, has done much experimental magic. She and Andy, her magical partner of the time, investigated the efficacy of Steam Punk Magic, long before it became popular and fashionable. They produced fabulous artwork and costumes and some striking magical results too, in addition to drinking a lot of absinthe, in the correct manner, using special absinthe spoons, perhaps in the way that our Romano-British ancestors used their Faunus spoons. New fashions may fire our imaginations, but basic magical principles remain constant.

Like many women in the Tradition, Julie started her magical work at a young age but stepped back from serious involvement in magical group work when her children were small, although she did reappear sometimes for special occasions. Now her children are a little older, she is moving back to being more active in groups once again, and her contributions will be of great value to all the magical work which we undertake. She writes:

I've been a practising Pagan and witch for nearly 30 years but have always been drawn to the magical world. My practice has evolved from the more ritualistic to one grounded in the day to day and the wheel of the year. As a mother the mundane informs and roots my practice and I enjoy sprinkling the mundane with as much magic as I can, whether it's blessing the bath water for healing, growing herbs for magical and culinary purposes, or creating offerings with paint, pottery, paper and textiles. I'm particularly drawn to the earthy practicality of Kitchen and Hedge witchcraft, the work of Dr Dee, and the Northern and Celtic traditions of East Anglia.

A Witch of Hethersett

Everything that Denise did as Witch of Hethersett exemplified the virtues of temperance. She was slim, elegant, quietly spoken and frugal in her approach to most things. Her home was tiny but immaculately clean, neat and well-organised, with beautifully created spells in cabinets, on top of the dresser, around the pictures on the wall and hanging from the ceiling. Likewise, her garden was small but perfect year-round, without a leaf out of place. At the bottom of the garden, furthest from the house and guarded by the Fae, was the Tarot Shed, where she saw clients for divination and for hand reading, a skill which she learned from local expert, Johnny Fincham. She painted lovely water colour pictures, sang and played the recorder, quite often using her musical skills in rituals. Everything she made, her gifts or ritual offerings, were small but exquisite. She had a dark side to her magic, unsurprisingly, given that her work, as a nurse specialising in palliative care, brought her into daily contact with the dying.

I remember fondly a series of Full Moon rituals with Denise, my husband, Chris, and another magical colleague, Andy, around the Vinegar Pond on Mousehold Heath. We always spread out around the edge of the pond and all our work was conducted in silence, by means of gesture and psychic connection, as the moonlight filled the depths of the dark pool.

Denise left Norfolk some years ago now, drawn West along the Michael and Mary Line to continue her work in a completely different way, in the place where the Sun sets into the Water. Not long after leaving, she wrote the following:

Memories of the Norwich magical groups —
Marked by the seasonal round within the sacred space of our workings, the passing of the years has witnessed students on our magical path come and go. Some have left early following a change of heart or direction, while others have gone on to form covens of their own; people have sooner or later drifted off or moved away; a few of our members have shaken off this mortal coil, leaving us behind in grief and sorrow, but yet in the joy of a life well-lived and fondly remembered. Our numbers have been as high as thirty-three and as low as three, and yet we endure, across the flatlands of Norfolk and deep into the rugged landscape of Cornwall.

As for myself, I joined the group in the mid to late 1990s, having sought admission to the coven via a year and a day of magical training. My father, my original magical teacher, had died a few years previously, his final words exhorting me to 'find my own way now'; but frankly, I was lost. My father was Christian of course, not Pagan, but I knew that distinction would be of little significance to him, something that my mother was later able to confirm, adding family tales of her own to our stories of Didicoys and magical seers in the vein of that body of knowledge we would now call cunning craft.

In my early days with the Norwich group we numbered eight, I think, the Inner Court making up four of that number and the remainder of us being students in varying stages of the training. Occasionally, someone previously unknown to me but obviously well-known to the Inner Court would turn up to join in our rites. I found this curious, but not unsettling. Generally, the training was relatively easy and fun, although not without its challenges, and the whole group was friendly and supportive.

The seasons passed and with them the years. Early on, we opened up the group in spectacular fashion to include some of the more vulnerable in our community. This in turn led to bigger picnics and day trips and parties and, of course, rituals. Our numbers swelled and receded as the moon and tides, and all along the Inner Court remained steadfast and strong, sometimes amid a maelstrom of emotions and difficulties as people's lives were challenged and changed by events both inside and outside the circle.

We came 'Out of the Broom Closet' quite magnificently in 2001, with a series of talks held at a prestigious Norwich venue. We took over the greater part of the multi-roomed conference centre and yet were still so oversubscribed that we were obliged to turn people away. It had been fifty years since the repeal of the Witchcraft Act and exactly the right place and time: and we were there, making our mark.

Sometimes, later, there were 'fallings out', bitter words and friendships lost; but overall we remained cohesive, burying our hatchets in the sacrificial loaf rather than in one another.

I left the coven myself for a couple of years during my mother's protracted final illness and death, spending much of my time travelling between Norfolk and her home in Kent, but then the wheel turned again and I returned to the group to find only we five remained. Our work became more insular as we undertook the Grail Quest and sought the Green Chapel more in contemplation than boisterous celebration. Then, almost taking us by surprise, five became three, leaving all of us licking our respective wounds in the grudging acceptance of further loss and change.

At last, however, we branched out again; new students were admitted for training and the sacred space rang out with unfamiliar voices, growing in strength and confidence in the clear night air.

Finally, however, it was my time to go. I moved away from Norfolk, leaving the Chalk and Flint behind for a new life amid granite hills and ruined engine houses some 450 miles away to the West. My life and magic have inevitably changed, but my allegiances still reach out to me across the web and call me eastwards to an ancient open-cast mine hidden in the City of Norwich where I received my Craft initiation nearly 20 years ago.

Pherlin the Fair

Pherlin is so named because he has such a strong connection to the Fair Ones. They seem to follow him everywhere as he wanders around with his fortune basket over his arm, forever collecting flowers or thorns or pretty stones for his spell work, which he does all the time. Although he loves the countryside, and particularly the beach, he is very much the city witch. While living in a small flat beside one of Norwich's busiest roads, he grew numerous plants on the windowsills and the kitchen table, even Jack-by-the Hedge, which is one of his favourites. Home and the concept of the witch's cottage are very important to him, and he can always make space for several altars or shrines, even in a small room.

Pherlin is another artist, craftsperson and singer, but does little to promote his own work, despite its high quality. He has produced some wonderful oracle cards, and maybe it is the magical process rather than the finished product which is important to him. He writes beautifully too, and no doubt in the future will produce a book of magical words and pictures. I am lucky enough to have a beautiful painting, by Pherlin, of a pale-blue Hikey Sprite, which fell out of a Cherry tree in my garden while we were doing a ritual at blossom time. I think the Sprite may have been drunk on the perfume and leaned out just a little too far to watch what we were up to, and although it scuttled away pretty quickly, Pherlin was able to capture the perfect image of its tumble.

For some years, Pherlin was adamant that, although he wanted to be part of our magical learning and exploration, he did not want to do ritual work with us as he was an exclusively solo practitioner. Things changed, however, as they often do, and Pherlin is now as keen as anyone to contribute and to draw on the power and inspiration of a group working, and he now even takes major roles in public rituals. When asked to write a little about himself and his magic, Pherlin was characteristically coy and wrote only:

Ooh that's a tough question. I don't really think about it lol. I would say I'm quite instinctive with my craft though, and definitely put the craft into crafty.

Szara and David

I first met Szara and her partner, David, just three or four years ago, but they had been practising for many years prior to that, and Szara was already a good friend of Nettles. Since becoming more involved in the work of the community, they have been stalwarts of Norwich Moot, and a great asset, as neither of them is afraid of hard work and they are full of magical ideas and enthusiasm. At the first Boudica's Brocante, they cooked and washed up all day, at the same time as looking after their own stall and one for a friend who was not able to be there on the day. It was their idea to have a "guess the number of hag stones in the jar" competition and to ask all the stallholders to provide a cake for sale in aid of Moot funds. As soon as the event was over, they were putting together ideas to make it bigger and better the following year. At regular moot events throughout the year they are there, quietly collecting the money, dispensing cups of tea, decorating the hall with handmade items and putting heart and soul into ensuring that everything runs smoothly, and that people have a good time.

Szara and David are both great crafters and makers of costumes and magical items, and it was they who made the regalia for the first outing of the Summer Ickeny, in 2017. It is a fabulous white and green creation with long green strips of fabric for the mane and tail. They are also great ritualists and played the part of the King and Queen of Summer at that ritual, on Mousehold Heath. They looked wonderful in their costumes, which matched that of the Ickeny. They were so beautiful and regal, crowned with garlands of freshly picked leaves and flowers, as they sat on their fur-covered thrones under a lavishly-decorated gazebo, and dispensed the blessings and gifts of Summer to the forty or so people

357

who had come to take part. When asked to write a little about her magic, Szara produced the following account:

> *I am an urban-based witch that adapts according to my environment, taking full advantage of what surrounds me and by visiting areas of interest.*
>
> *I honour the moon cycle within the seasons and also honour my own cycle within the moon cycle. I celebrate every ¼ at the minimum by creating an altar; sometimes it will include a grand ritual or a smaller ritual with my partner David. I love to take part in community events raising awareness of the Pagan community and what being a Pagan means to many people, destigmatising many myths along the way. I use my beliefs within my working day as well as my personal day, setting intentions and honouring moments whilst educating. My family have supported my journey since I was in my teens but, since meeting Val, I have been able to be proud and not afraid of who I am.*

Alice Kerridge-Crick

Alice has a gentle nature mixed with remarkable determination, an impressive intellect and a wealth of knowledge which is both wide-ranging and thorough. If anybody has a question about a goddess from any part of the world, is the person to ask. She will have read a book about them, probably done some magical work to contact them, and most likely has a statue of them too, for she is a great collector of magical objects. Alice loves to make beautiful things, and has created some of the loveliest goddess dolls I have ever seen. I am privileged to have had one for many years. She is Iris of the Rainbow, which made especially for me, stitching the body from Iris-patterned fabric, as she knows that this colourful goddess is a particular favourite of mine.

Alice has a charming humility despite her great talents, and has in the past been reluctant to put herself forward. However, over the last year or so, she has played a major role in creating and performing open rituals, as well as giving talks and running workshops. Her first ever, full-length talk was about the figure commonly known as the Venus of Willendorf. Not only was the talk itself brilliant, and imaginatively illustrated with picture boards set out on easels, but there were other activities for people to enjoy. had buried a lot of tiny goddess figures in a dish of sand, and people were given brushes with which to uncover one which they could then take home as a memento. It sounds simple but was very effective and indeed magical. Everyone treasured the figures they received, which were, of course, just what they needed at the time.

Alice is also a devotee of Mary Magdalen and in 2018, on the Sunday closest to Mary Magdalen's Day (22nd July), she ran a Magdalen Garland workshop for the Moot. One of the activities involved tearing up fabric, which represented our frustrations, problems and things we wished to be transformed. All the resulting strips of cloth were tied to a metal ring and, by the end of the session, a fabulously colourful wreath had been created, in a communal act of physical and spiritual recycling overseen by the mysterious Lady of the Garden.

Alice has recently moved from a town in South Norfolk to a remote and intensely magical area of Mid-Norfolk. I am sure that this will enhance and develop her magic. She is already a leading light amongst those who are openly part of the Nameless Tradition, but she is as yet young and will certainly accomplish great things in the future. She writes:

My magical practice has evolved over time and as I have got older it has made more sense, as my matrilinear line is from Malta, a country rich in history and ideas. In Sunday school I knew there was more, and I asked 'those' questions until it was decided it was not for me. Then one day I picked up a book at a carboot and my soul was set.

As a female my practice has always been more leaning to the Goddess and Her many images: a continued fascination which I love to share. But I am very conscious of the need for balance and the place of the masculine. I personally practise a mix of Celtic, Northern and Egyptian, so a harmony of the three streams. The Virgin Mary and Mary Magdalene also hold a strong presence in my practice and at times of trouble have been the pillars I stand on. A mix of Christianity I do feel has its place, as being sacred and part of the rich tapestry of the world, and it does not take away from my reverence to beloved Anubis or my first Lady Neith, the Egyptian 'green' Goddess.

I now live in a remote village in Norfolk, home to my Great Grandparents and overlooking the land they worked. I am reminded of the soul of the land and the blood of my ancestors in it, and the memory of my Grandfather who, unknowingly, helped me on my path. I now follow the Deer tracks and trace the Goose wings across the sky.

May Holda grace and bless you.

There are so many other folk who have been influential in the Tradition during the time that we have been working here. There is Simon, who taught me to read the Tarot and encouraged me to expand my Natural Magic practice by undertaking formal magical training, with Marian Green. He was with us when we first began our work here, although after many relocations, he now lives on a narrowboat in Ely. Also, during the early days, Helen and Bob, whom we met on a course at Runnings Park, in the Malvern Hills, played a significant role in our work and were part of our initial experiments with the evocation of the county's heroes. They have never lived in Norfolk and, at the time, they were living in South London. Nevertheless, they felt that strong pull of Norfolk Magic, and regularly undertook the three-hour journey to Norwich to take part in rituals. Nowadays, though, they live and work in the West Country. With the well-known Chaos Magician, Anton Channing, I learned to catch falling stars and to be much more daring with spells and rituals, sometimes with crazy consequences. Andy was another influential character, who appeared at a course we were running about Sir Gawain and the Green Knight, received, from the lottery, the major role in the ritual, and performed it with considerable aplomb, although it was the first piece of formal magical work he had ever done. He joined our group and, having completed the training course became one of its tutors. He was part of the group for over a decade and taught us how to do choreographed sword-fighting: a useful skill when creating dramatic rituals.

I feel honoured to have met so many gifted and dedicated individuals, not only those I have mentioned here, but also the many others who have made their contributions to the magical life of the county and helped to produce and garner such a rich harvest.

References

Briggs (2017) Weird Norfolk: The Witch's Heart of King's Lynn, *Eastern Daily Press*, 21 April 2017 (available at: https://www.edp24.co.uk/news/weird-norfolk-the-witchs-heart-of-kings-lynn-1-4984567, accessed 12th January 2019).

Bourne, Lois (1998) *Dancing With Witches*, Robert Hale.

Eastern Evening News (1961) 'Clean Sweep' by Broomstick Brigade, EEN November 1st, 1961.

Eastern Daily Press (1967) Room where witch would feel at home, EDP 6th March 1967.

Forby, Rev. Robert (1830) On the popular superstitions of East Anglia, Appendix to *The Vocabulary of East Anglia; An Attempt to Record the Vulgar Tongue of the Twin Sister Counties, Norfolk and Suffolk, As It Existed In the last Twenty Years of the Eighteenth Century, and Still Exists; With Proof of Its Antiquity from Etymology and Authority, Volume II*, J.B. Nichols, pp. 385-435.

Glyde, John (1872) *The Norfolk Garland: A Collection of the Superstitious Beliefs and Practices, Proverbs, Curious Customs, Ballads and Songs of the People of Norfolk, as well as Anecdotes Illustrative of the Genius or Peculiarities of Norfolk Celebrities*, Jarrold.

Gunn, The Reverend John (1849) Proverbs, adages, and popular superstitions still preserved in the parish of Irstead, *Norfolk Archaeology* II, pp. 291-308.

Heselton, Philip (2016) *Doreen Valiente Witch*, The Doreen Valiente Foundation in association with the Centre for Pagan Studies.

Howard, Michael (2004) A Very English Witch, *The Cauldron* 111 (February 2004), pp. 31-2.

Pearson, Nigel (2015) *The Devil's Plantation: East Anglian Lore, Witchcraft and Folk Magic*, Troy Books.

Pennick, Nigel (2004) *Secrets of East Anglian Magic*, Second Edition, Capall Bann.

Pennick, Nigel (2011) *Operative Witchcraft*, Lear Books.

Seims, Melissa (2008) *The Coven of Atho*, updated article published in The Cauldron 126 (November 2007), available at www.thewica.co.uk (accessed 13th January 2019).

Valiente, Doreen (1973) *An ABC of Witchcraft Past and Present*, Robert Hale.

A Harvest of Norfolk

Twenty-five years sounds, in some respects, like a long time for a magical project. Indeed, Michael Howard, Editor of The Cauldron, said to us, not long before his death in 2015, that he thought we really had been working a strong Tradition because most don't last more than three years. However, Marian Green's Quest Conference has now been running for over twice that length of time, and quite a number of people from Norfolk's Nameless Tradition were there to help her celebrate her Golden Anniversary in March 2017. Our time here doesn't really feel very long. There is still such a wealth of knowledge to pursue, so many rituals as yet barely dreamed of, so many harvests to gather, so many stories waiting to delight our ears, our minds and our emotions. So, we acknowledge, with gratitude, all that we have done and experienced and learned, and all that we have been able to share with others. Sometimes we have just passed on a flicker, the spark of an idea, sometimes we have worked with people for years, building together a rich hoard of Thought and Memory, under the watchful eyes of Odin's Ravens.

At the same time, we know that we have barely scratched the surface of the magic of this land, even of our own sacred space, which is filled with ancient memories and spirits which flit constantly at the edge of our vision. Some of them we know to have been Guardians of the Nameless Tradition in the past, but we need so much more time to encourage them to offer us yet more which can be used for the benefit of Norfolk Magic in the 21st century. As I write this, our twenty-fifth Samhain here fast approaches. People are already treading the rain-washed leaves underfoot; skies are stormy and good harvests have been gathered and stored. Plummeting temperatures after a fantastically long, hot Summer are awakening the ghosts and memories, calling them to re-join the living for a short spell, to celebrate the unfolding of incarnations and the magical community which spans the centuries. So perhaps we will receive a special Silver Secret, a charm to help us continue our studies and our magic through another quarter of a century.

When I first came to live and begin the work here, my hair was thick and dark, but the Moon has poured her blessings upon me and turned it to wisps of silver. At this moment of surveying the harvests, I am looking back through a crone's eyes on what has been done, and trying to assess things wisely. It is all very well to keep going and get older, but much more difficult to develop wisdom and act accordingly! The important thing though is that our harvests now should be garnered and stored carefully to ensure that things are in place when they are required. For there is a bright future for Norfolk's Nameless Tradition, whose work and skills will be all the more necessary when times are hard. More talented people will step onto the Path: strong, magically active individuals, who are confident in their own abilities, and centred in their own beings, while always open to learning more and trying new approaches. But they will also be cooperative and flexible enough to work with their fellow practitioners and appreciate the importance of being part of a community.

The Norfolk Harvest Ritual, performed at the close of the Harvest Moon Conference at the Puppet Theatre, in Norwich on 26th September 2015, exemplifies what can be achieved when a group of strong characters come together for a specific magical purpose. It was performed by a group of practitioners, from all over the country and beyond, some of whom had never worked magically together before, yet who were all focused on the success of the conference and bringing it to a close in a moving and meaningful way.

The ritual was designed to be very clear and comprehensible even to someone who had never attended a magical event of any kind before, and yet to encapsulate and express something of the true spirit of Norfolk Magic. It was also important that those taking part represented people who had long been involved in the Nameless Tradition, those who were quite new to the work, those who had been an integral part of the Tradition but moved on, and some of the speakers from the conference, who were friends of the Nameless Tradition but not necessarily a part of it. Gemma Gary, who had travelled from Cornwall to speak at the conference took part, so the rite brought East and West together. At the last minute, the strong magical connections along the Mary and Michael line also drew Denise Hunt back to her old magical hunting grounds, and with Matthew Hannam coming all the way from Cyprus for the conference, the rite spanned not only a large geographical area, but also friendships and magical connections going back across two decades and more. It also showed how much things have changed, as even a few years ago we would not have felt comfortable conducting a ritual of this kind in such a public arena, with some 200 people.

It felt right to include within the ritual Circle everyone who was in the "audience", for we were on the stage, and all those not taking an active role were seated in the auditorium. Certain modifications therefore had to be made. For example, those calling the four directions stood in the appropriate places but faced the audience so that they could easily be heard. It is really difficult to administer a communion to large numbers of people, so it seemed most sensible to bless and distribute gifts instead, something which would be a physical and magical souvenir of the day. It seemed particularly appropriate for Brenda and Robert to distribute the gifts as they had prepared all the food for the conference and spent most of the day serving it. They sat

in the front row with Alix and John, who had kindly agreed
to assist, so that they would be ready to pick up the baskets
and offer people the charms in a perfectly choreographed
way. Most of the people there cannot have imagined how
much preparation went into those few minutes. It took a
whole group of us the best part of a day just to make all the
charms. The Marlpit Cunning Man cut out circles of linen
fabric with pinking shears, while some of us spooned in the
ingredients and others tied the bags up. This often unseen
and frequently forgotten work is all part of the building of
the magic.

We had hoped to walk through the ritual before the
event, just to make sure that everybody knew where they
needed to be at each point and to avoid any unseemly
confusion, because we feel very strongly that if rituals are
to be performed publicly, they should be well-crafted, slick,
truly honour the gods and do credit to all those involved.
Yet it proved impractical to get everyone together at the
same time. The night before the conference not everyone
had arrived, although some of us did work out the logistics
of it between the sound check for Inkubus Sukkubus
and the wild pre-conference party, the very one at which
the magical ferret, Birch Pyewacket, had his greatest
moment of glory when he kissed Candia. Throughout the
conference itself, the stage was in constant use, except
for a brief moment at lunchtime, but then not everybody
was available. So, we had to leave it to the Will of the
Gods and trust the magical professionalism of all those
taking part. Everything had gone well, the talks had
been brilliant, the atmosphere was perfect. Author, Pete
Jennings, who was also speaking at the conference and
whose birthday it was, blew out all the candles on his cake
in one breath. Then, with a deep breath and a banishing
of nerves, the ritual began. Everyone was hushed and
focused, the audience spellbound, the officers of the rite
all completely on their contacts. Immediately, you could
feel the magic building all around us.

A Norfolk Harvest: Ritual for Harvest Moon Festival September 2015

Welcome

Val T
Welcome to our closing ritual, in which we celebrate another wonderful day's conference, as well as a rich and varied harvest from this beautiful, magical county of Norfolk. Share with us the gifts of the harvest. Share with us this harvest from Norfolk.

Casting the Circle, to include the whole auditorium

Denise H
I cast the circle between the worlds, the sacred space of meeting and of mystery, of protection, inspiration and of magic.

Calling the Elements

André H
Behold, the airy sieve: riddle of soil and riddle of words, sifter of flour and sorter of souls.
By Circle and mesh I call upon Air, Spirit of the East and blessings of Spring. You who are our breath of life and inspiration grant us your presence and protection at this our Harvest Rite. Element of Air, we bid you hail and welcome.

Matt F
Behold the fiery pitchfork, horns of the God, Lord of the ripening fields. By the flame of your brow, we call upon Fire, spirit of the South and the blessings of Summer. You who are our warmth and light, our energy and passion, the divine spark within, grant us your presence and protection

at this our Harvest Rite. Element of Fire, we bid you hail and welcome.

Marian G
Behold the silvery sickle, crescent Moon and full-blown flower, ancient one and harvester. By the gleam of your reflected light, we call upon Water, spirit of the West and the blessings of Autumn. You who are the raging sea, the still, calm pool and the gentle rain, grant us your presence and protection at this our Harvest Rite. Element of Water, we bid you hail and welcome.

Amanda H
Behold the shears which clip the wool and gather the wealth yet sever the thread when life is done. By the power of your blades we call the Earth, the cold dark North and the blessings of Winter's rest. You who are our firm foundation, hearth and home, our food and our security, grant us your presence at this our harvest rite. Element of Earth, we bid you hail and welcome.

Lord and Lady of Norfolk

Chris W
Lord of Norfolk, grey Lord of the Flint, we ask for your presence and protection at this our Harvest Rite. Sharp arrow and felling axe, building block and bringer of fire, we bid you hail and welcome.

Annette D
Lady of Norfolk, white Lady of the Chalk, we ask for your presence and protection at this our harvest rite. Nourisher and nurturer, giver of life, of comfort and of love, we bid you hail and welcome.

All say: Share with us the gifts of the Harvest, share with us this harvest from Norfolk.

Enter Grain – Pete J

I bring the grain, the king of the fields, the bread on your plate, the drink in your cup, the foundation of life.

Share with me this gift of the harvest. Share with me this harvest from Norfolk.

The grain offering is poured into the cauldron.

Enter Apple – Vicki D

I come from the orchards and hedgerows, with apples, crisp and sweet. Flesh to nourish, cider to refresh, vinegar to preserve and secret pentacle of hidden power.

Share with me this gift of the harvest. Share with me this harvest from Norfolk.

The Apple offering is poured into the cauldron.

Enter Wool – Gemma G

I bring the wool to keep you warm when Winter's chill whips through our land. The gentle Sheep sends her soft comforts: spin well her yarns and treasure her wealth.

Share with me this gift of the harvest. Share with me this harvest from Norfolk

The wool offering is placed in the cauldron.

Enter Sugar – Matthew H

I bring the sugar, sweet from the dark earth: cakes for your feasts, preserves for your stores, power for your spells. I bring pleasure, wealth and danger. Use my gifts with wisdom.

Share with me this gift of the harvest. Share with me this harvest from Norfolk.

The offering of sugar is placed in the cauldron.

Enter Lavender – Gareth L

From city gardens and seaside fields, I bring the fragrant Lavender. These dusky flowers to cleanse and heal, to ease your pain, to gladden hearts and scent the air.

Share with me this gift of the harvest. Share with me this harvest from Norfolk.

The Lavender offering is placed in the cauldron.

Enter Flax – Michael C

I bring the Flax, the Goddess' flower, the heavenly blue across Midsummer fields. I bring the fibre and the seed: fine cloth, rich food and sacred oil.

Share with me this gift of the harvest. Share with me this harvest from Norfolk.

The Flax offering is placed into the cauldron.

Enter the Seventh Harvest – Kevin W

I bring the mystery of harvest's bounty, the seed grown tall, the ripening fruit, the thought made manifest within the mundane world.

Share with me this gift of the harvest. Share with me this harvest from Norfolk.

The seventh harvest is poured into the cauldron.

Mixing the Charms

Val T
We mix our harvest charms with love and blessings and with the magic of this perfect time.

All say together as the charms are mixed:

Share with us the gifts of the Harvest. Share with us this harvest from Norfolk.

The charms are ladled out into baskets.

We ask you to accept these harvest charms. May they bring you abundance and good fortune during the seasons to come.

The charms are distributed to everyone in the audience.

Farewells

Lady of Norfolk, we give thanks for your presence here and for the gifts you have bestowed upon us. As our rite draws to a close, we bid you hail and farewell.

Lord of Norfolk, we give thanks....

Earth
Air
Water
Fire

So, a good harvest has been gathered, and with it the seeds of what is to come. Long may the Magic continue.

Endword

Anyone can be part of the Nameless Tradition, here in Norfolk, elsewhere in Britain or in some far-flung land across the world. No certificates are required, no proof of lineage. It is the simplest of paths but will demand a lifetime's commitment. All you need to do is be present in the landscape, seek your place within the great Web of Wyrd and work your magic.

How? Put your hands into the Earth. Pick up a piece of Flint. Feel its history and its origin as the son of the Chalk. Know its sharp edge and its enlivening spark. Place it in a dish beside the soft White Lady. If your land is not one of Flint and Chalk, find what it is you have beneath your feet and sink your roots in deeply.

Paint or draw the treasures of the landscape, sing and dance for the sunrise. Spin a thread from the wool of local Sheep and hear their eldritch bleating as the wheel turns. Carve a spoon from the prunings in your garden or twist dry Iris leaves into a herb basket.

Honour the gods; learn from the heroes; pray with the saints; commune with your familiars and with the Fair Folk. Talk to friends and neighbours. Listen, read and remember, and let your curiosity lead you along the sacred pathways.

Watch the flight of birds across the sea, across the woods and farmland and across the city, as our ancestors have always done. Know that others will do this after you are gone. Find Summer in the shriek of a Swift and the scent of the Bird Cherry, but embrace the wintery message of the North East wind.

Shed a tear for the brevity of life, for this incarnation is too short to learn and love all the riches this beautiful land spreads out before us.

CPSIA information can be obtained
at www.ICGtesting.com
Printed in the USA
BVHW030508201221
624412BV00003B/93